Creative English, Creative Curriculum

New perspectives for Key Stage 2

Paul Gardner

Routledge
Taylor & Francis Group

LONDON AND NEW YORK

First published 2010
by Routledge
2 Park Square, Milton Park, Abingdon, Oxon OX14 4RN

Simultaneously published in the USA and Canada
by Routledge
270 Madison Avenue, New York, NY 10016

Routledge is an imprint of the Taylor & Francis Group, an informa business

© 2010 Paul Gardner

Typeset in Garamond by
GreenGate Publishing, Tonbridge, Kent
Printed and bound in Great Britain by
TJ International Ltd, Padstow, Cornwall

British Library Cataloguing in Publication Data
A catalogue record for this book is available from the British Library

Library of Congress Cataloging-in-Publication Data
Gardner, Paul, 1954–
Creative English, creative curriculum practical, new perspectives for key stage 2 / Paul Gardner.
p. cm.
1. Language arts (Elementary) – Great Britain. 2. Creative teaching – Great Britain. I. Title.
LB1576.G34 2009
372.60941–dc22

2009001986

ISBN 10: 0-415-48522-3 (hbk)
ISBN 10: 0-415-46685-7 (pbk)

ISBN 13: 978-0-415-48522-7 (hbk)
ISBN 13: 978-0-415-46685-1 (pbk)

I wish to dedicate this book to:

My children: Ashrup, Nanaki and Kiran

Maz for giving me back myself

And my students, past, present and future

Contents

Illustrations

Acknowledgements

I wish to thank Maureen Desouza and Krystle Fenn for allowing me to use their research findings from their B.Ed dissertations.

Abbreviations

BFI   British Film Institute

BICS   Basic Interpersonal Communication Skills

CALP   Cognitive Academic Language Proficiency

CPD   continuing professional development

DART   directed activity related to text

EAL   English as an Additional Language

ITE   Initial Teacher Education

KAL   knowledge about language

LINC   Language in the National Curriculum Project

NARA   Neal Analysis of Reading Ability

NATE   National Association for the Teaching of English

NLS   National Literacy Strategy

PNS   Primary National Strategy

SATS   Standard Assessment Tests

ZPD   Zone of Proximal Development

Introduction

Q8 rules, OK?

THIS CHAPTER PROVIDES the reader with the following:

- a brief discussion of different modes of curriculum organisation and delivery, including the relationship of curriculum, pedagogy and learning;

- a brief discussion of the nature of creativity and what it means to be a creative teacher;

- a synopsis of the content of each chapter of the book.

After a protracted period in education policy, during which primary teachers have been told what to teach, how to teach and when to teach it, there is finally the glimmer of a recognition that teachers are people able to exercise professional judgement. That glimmer is encapsulated in standard Q8 of the third revision of the standards for qualified teacher status. It states that teachers and student teachers need to have 'a creative and constructively critical approach towards innovation, being prepared to adapt their practice where benefits and improvements are identified' (TDA 2007: 8). This view of the teacher, as an autonomous thinking professional who is able to not only modify existing practice in the light of new found pedagogic knowledge, but who is also able to critique innovative ideas and, presumably, on finding them wanting, is free to reject them, marks a significant change in the political discourse that has surrounded teachers since the implementation of the National Curriculum (DfEE 1988). This discourse began with the political debates surrounding education that resulted in the launching of the Great Debate by James Callaghan in 1978. However, the world of education is never simple and teachers are often subject to contradictory pressures when making pedagogic decisions. The kind of professional judgements enabled by Q8 may be countered by statute or non-statutory guidance that is elevated to the status of quasi-statute, by inspection regimes that are influenced by political diktat.

One topical issue is that of synthetic phonics, which has been privileged above, not only analytic phonics but, more holistic perspectives on the teaching of early reading. A teacher may be critical of the theoretical underpinning of synthetic phonics, particularly since the major study cited as exemplifying its value, the so-called Clackmannanshire Study, of Johnston and Watson (1998, 2008), was found to have flaws (Washtell 2008: 28). However, the teacher's professional judgement in this matter is constrained by the prerequisite statutory requirement to teach synthetic phonics as the main method of teaching early reading. To some extent the final report of the independent review of the teaching of early reading, which advocated the privileged status of synthetic phonics, countered the possibility of an overly narrow perspective by also placing the teaching of synthetic phonics in the context of classrooms that are language 'rich', creative and where purposeful talk is the basis of learning (Rose 2006). However, contradictory discourses cause professional tension and teachers can find themselves caught in the middle of opposing demands, like Truffaldino, the protagonist in, *A Servant to Two Masters* (Goldoni 1970). On the issue of synthetic phonics, I propose to utter not another word and allow that particular debate to flow elsewhere.

Accepting the point that teachers will always have to struggle with competing discourses, standard Q8, along with the demise of the National Literacy Strategy and its prescriptive daily literacy hour, offer greater scope for the creative application of theory and practice in teaching. The time is perhaps ripe, therefore, for a moment of reflection, for a fresh look at how creative teachers might view the future, based on the privilege of hindsight.

In the first chapter of the book, I take a backward glance at past perspectives on the teaching of English and suggest that some of them provide clues as to where to go next. It is my intention in this book to review the nature of English as a subject and to provide some practical examples of creative approaches to the teaching of English. Many of the changes that have taken place in English in the last twenty years have been founded upon flimsy research evidence and a paucity of sound theory (Wyse and Jones 2008), or else they have been founded upon theoretical perspectives from cognitive psychology that have lead to a 'reductionist transmission' mode of teaching (Larson and Marsh 2005). There is no question of the important function theory has in informing practice and I make no apology, therefore, for referring to theoretical perspectives, or for creating theoretical models in order to underpin innovative approaches with reasoned thought. What has been missing from the theory underpinning the teaching of English in recent years has been plurality. Recent constructions of the English curriculum have tended to be informed by research in cognitive psychology to the almost total exclusion of other disciplines. However, there is a wealth of evidence from other fields to broaden our perspectives on the teaching of English. The fusion of practice and theory that runs through the text is an essential attribute of what it means to be a critical, reflective and creative teacher in the twenty first century. Indeed, having a critical eye on theory is an essential prerequisite of meeting the standard Q8.

The curriculum

In order to identify what a creative curriculum might entail, it is necessary to consider what it is not. This requires a brief exploration of various curriculum models.

At a very basic level, a curriculum may be defined as a set of subjects to be taught. A more elaborate version would require each subject to have a defined syllabus and learning objectives. The English National Curriculum (1988), with its Programmes of Study and Attainment Targets in each subject, is typical of this model, as are successive Literacy Frameworks (1998, 2006). A much broader view is one that takes an holist view of education, regarding everything that happens in school to be part of the curriculum. A school's daily practices and procedures; the values and attitudes of its staff and their relationship to one another; the school's relationship to parents and carers and to its constituent community; are all aspects of its implicit or hidden curriculum. A broader view not only encompasses subject content but pedagogy also, since the positioning of the pupil and teacher in relation to one another and the process of teaching and learning are integral to what is learned in classrooms. This process includes how meanings are arrived at in the classroom and how knowledge is constructed. Whereas in the first two models, it is possible to view the curriculum as the transmission of knowledge, this last model places the curriculum in a sociocultural perspective. That is, it considers the social practices and the patterns of behaviour adopted by the school to be an integral part of learning.

To further illustrate this point, in their discussion of the curriculum in general and the English curriculum in particular, Larson and Marsh (2005) draw upon the work of Bernstein (1974). They cite his concepts of 'classification', 'frame', 'visible' and 'invisible' pedagogy in order to analyse official curricular models. Classification refers to the extent to which boundaries are set between subjects, thereby establishing specific subject content. Strong boundary maintenance is evident in models that have dominated the English primary curriculum since 1988. Frame refers to the pedagogical context in which knowledge is exchanged. This amounts to the degree of choice both teachers and pupils have over the way learning occurs. Allied to these perspectives are the kinds of pedagogy possible. A visible pedagogy refers to a didactic model in which the teacher is in explicit control of a transmission mode of learning. In contrast, an invisible pedagogy is one in which the teacher has implicit control of the negotiation of meanings and knowledge construction.

In Chapter three, on talk, we shall consider Barnes' (1976) view of the teacher's role in constructing patterns of communication in the classroom and find some accord with Bernstein's perspectives. Models of curriculum that are strongly classified and framed tend to result in a visible pedagogy and are associated with objectives based teaching and the assessment of discrete skills, or aspects of knowledge. Conversely, a loosely classified curriculum with weak framing can lead to a more invisible form of pedagogy. In this case, not only is subject content integrated but methods of teaching and learning are more varied and account can be taken of the experiential knowledge pupils bring to school. Hence, the 'cultural capital' (Bourdieu and Passeron 1977) of pupils and the local community is included as a valid part of the curriculum. It is under these circumstances that more creative teaching and learning can operate because both teachers and pupils have greater control of curriculum content and the modes in which learning takes place. In Bernstein's terms, a loosely classified curriculum with weak framing and invisible teaching is likely to lead to the most creative forms of learning.

The nature of creativity and the curriculum

The term creativity evokes multiple interpretations, the most traditional of which is perhaps associated with individual genius within artistic endeavour. However, wider definitions, associated with imagination and problem-solving, are applicable to broader spheres of human activity, including Science and Mathematics. In the field of education, Craft (2005) has identified three 'waves' of creativity, the last of which differs significantly from the traditional view. She locates the first 'wave' around thinking that emanated from the 'Plowden Report' (Central Advisory Council in Education 1967). From the late 1960s creativity in education was associated with child-centred discovery learning methods within an integrated curriculum. However, Craft cites four problems with this early conception of creativity. First, there was an assumption that creativity could operate without the child having any prior knowledge. Second, there was an assumption that creativity existed outside a moral or ethical framework. Craft points out that one can be creative in negative ways as well as positive ones. Third, creativity was restricted to the Arts and neglected the wider curriculum. Finally, play was seen as the main mode of creativity. However, play need not necessarily be creative; it can be purely imitative (Craft 2005: 10). Three curriculum initiatives in the 1990s are cited by Craft as initiating the second 'wave' of creativity.

In the first of these reports, encouraging individual pupil's creativity was associated with the cultural development of society. The National Advisory Committee on Creative and Cultural Education (NACCCE) referred to the notion of 'democratic creativity', which sought to recognise that everyone can be creative in some aspect of life, providing the right conditions exist and that individuals have prerequisite skills and knowledge (NACCCE 1999: 28). The NACCCE report identifies four characteristics of creativity that are essential to a definition that is both workable and democratic. These characteristics are: imagination, purposes, originality and value. Imagination is described as a form of mental play in which something is viewed and interpreted from a fresh perspective, producing unique associations of existing ideas or unconventional applications. Creativity implies a dynamic process leading to the production of something. Inherent to this process is a purpose for pursuing the development of the product, or outcome. The effect of both imagination and purpose is a product or outcome that is original. However, originality, according to NACCCE may be viewed from three perspectives. First, an individual's work may be original in relation to their own previous work. Second, there is the notion of relativity. In this sense the work may be original in relation to work produced by the peer group. Third, originality might be viewed historically in the context of all previous work in a particular field (NACCCE 1999: 29–30). The fourth characteristic is value. As well as creativity being about producing something, the product has to be evaluated. That is, a judgement is made about the value of the product in relation to its purpose. In short, creative also involves critical thinking.

The second curriculum initiative referred to by Craft (DfEE 2000a) located creativity in children's play and the artistic subjects, but it raised the profile of the imagination, problem-solving and the development of a range of means of communicating feelings and ideas (Craft 2005: 9). Craft identifies a succession of reports from the Department for Education and Employment/Qualifications and Curriculum Authority (DfEE/QCA), which view creativity as a key skill across the curriculum. They also provided the impetus for taking discussion of creativity further than previous initiatives (1999a, 1999b). Arising out of thinking in the second wave, creative activity was located around activities that involved pupils in:

- Questioning and challenging;

- Making connections and seeing relationships;

- Envisaging what might be;

- Exploring ideas and keeping options open;

- Reflecting critically on ideas, actions and outcomes.

(QCA, 2005, cited in Craft 2005: 11).

Craft notes that a significant difference between first and second wave creativity is the emphasis on creative endeavour situated in sociocultural contexts with practical, social, intellectual and values-based practices coming to the fore. Furthermore, she suggests that the pedagogic model implied in this perspective is that of apprenticeship, with the 'expert adult offering induction to the relative novice' (Craft 2005: 11). Such a perspective places creativity in education firmly in social constructivist theory and practice, as advocated by Vygotsky (1962). The adult, who may or may not be the teacher, initiates pupils in creative and artistic practice by modelling and engaging pupils in that practice. By locating learning in authentic creative practice, pupils acquire personal relevance and meaning. There are certain parallels in this approach with existing good practice in the National Curriculum. The pedagogical approaches advocated in the teaching of History, Design Technology and the investigative aspect of Science are very much in line with the authentic methodologies of experts in those fields. In other words, pupils undertake historical investigation by scrutinising various sources of evidence in order to create a meaningful interpretation of a significant past event, or the way people in the past lived. In Design Technology, they construct a product after undertaking research into existing similar products to identify how they are constructed; they then design their product; make it, use it and finally evaluate its effectiveness. Science involves pupils as 'scientists' engaged in authentic experimentation by designing fair tests, conducting those tests, recording findings and applying scientific knowledge to explain outcomes. However, similar processes have not always applied to how pupils learn through English. The English curriculum has been characterised by pedagogic models of instruction, rather than by, for example, encouraging pupils to develop their writing by behaving like real writers.

Although in the apprenticeship model the adult is the expert, the pupil is seen to be exercising control over decision making and is allowed to take genuine risks (Craft 2005: 12). Having initiated the learner in authentic creative practice, and having modelled that practice with the learner the 'expert' must then judge when and how to dismantle the scaffolding (Bruner 1986). Craft notes a tension in this approach in terms of balancing negotiation between the creative needs of the individual and the creative needs of the group, since the apprenticeship model is essentially learner-centred (Craft 2005: 12). The third wave of creativity builds on the thrust of the second by conceptualising it in the context of everyday social and cultural values and practice (Craft 2005: 15). There are resonances here in the field of multimodal literacy in which creativity is seen as an aspect of general human activity that does not reside in the specialist domains of artists, poets and musicians (Kress 2003: 40). The second and third waves make for an altogether more egalitarian view of creativity than the traditional perspective of creativity as a an attribute of artistic genius.

However, Craft identifies a potential problem in this view. If creativity is culturally situated, how do we develop it in the context of multicultural classrooms

(Craft 2000: 15). In a way this is a redundant argument. It assumes cultures in a multicultural context are separate and discrete entities with exclusive value systems. In fact, cultures are far from static and people across all cultures share values that are essential features of human beings as social animals. Cultural practices emerge out of human need and common experience. In addition, there is significant evidence to show that in multicultural societies cultural fusion occurs. One only has to look at the field of popular music to discern the cross fertilisation of rhythms and beats within a single piece. Bhangra, reggae, hip-hop and latin American music move comfortably within creative arrangements that give rise to new forms of popular music.

Creative teachers

In creative-oriented classrooms, teachers draw upon a repertoire of methods and strategies to engage and interest pupils, rather than adhere to pedagogic diktat. They recognise that pupils bring into the classroom their own repertoire of skills, knowledge and interests, and know that everything we have learned about learning teaches us to begin with the experiential knowledge of the learner. Creative teachers are not afraid to experiment, nor are they fearful of self-reflection and self-criticism.

In their investigation of the nature of creative teaching, Woods and Jeffrey (1997) identified four generic components of creative teaching: innovation, ownership, control and relevance. Innovation may be initiated by an individual teacher or collaboratively with colleagues and involves either the creation of a new idea or the adaptation of existing ones. However, Woods and Jeffrey caution that innovation must be applicable to pupils' interests and cultures otherwise it becomes irrelevant and self-indulgent. Nevertheless, the teacher derives professional satisfaction from the fact they have a degree of control over pedagogy because they have ownership of the direction and implementation of change.

In addition, Woods and Jeffrey identified a range of characteristics that typified the creative teachers they observed. Based on their empirical data they state that creative teachers:

- are able to see alternatives;

- are able to achieve analytical distance from their professional role;

- continuously evaluate their own performance;

- are able to apply their talents to change or modify circumstance;

- are able to increase the range of possibilities open to them;

- have a theory of pedagogy that is pluralistic;

- have holistic perceptions of pupils, of learning and of the curriculum;

- are concerned with affective as well as cognitive aspects of learning;

- consider the whole child;

- are knowledgeable of subject matter, of pedagogy and of their pupils;

- experiment in order to achieve their aims;

- act upon hunches and play with ideas in disciplined ways;

- are adaptable and able to cope with change.

Woods and Jeffrey (1997: 67)

The identification of these characteristics is useful because it helps to give greater substance and clarity to the meaning of the professional standard Q8, quoted above.

The structure of the book

In addition to the reference above to Chapter one of the book, let me now outline the book's remaining structure. In Chapter two a brief critique is made of 'official' literacy frameworks and an alternative model is proposed in which the four language modes of speaking, listening, reading and writing are integrated in an holistic process. It is suggested that development in English should begin with, and continually take account of, pupils' linguistic repertoires. Talk is central to empowering pupils as constructors of meaning and is integral to their development as both readers and writers. This perspective is further developed in Chapter three where I revisit the work of Douglas Barnes and look at the classroom as a social arena in which the teacher establishes modes of communication. There are resonances here with Bernstein's curriculum dichotomy discussed above. In classrooms where teachers hold a 'tight rein' on pupils' contributions to communication there is little opportunity for their cultural resources and linguistic competence, gained outside the classroom, to be included. However, in classrooms where teachers adopt an 'invisible pedagogy' and where there is 'weak' framing, to use Bernstein's terms, there is the potential to create collaborative talk in which pupils are able to reach collective understanding and negotiate meaning. In these circumstances pupils' knowledge, experience and skills, acquired outside the classroom, are valued as contributory factors in the child's ongoing learning. The theme of speaking and listening is then located in the function of drama in education in Chapter four. A brief history of drama in the curriculum is given, followed by an exploration of the uses of drama as a tool for the development of language and thinking. The essential function of drama for learning resides in its pivotal use as a means for bringing the world outside the classroom into the classroom. In doing so, it makes it possible for teachers and pupils to observe interpretations of the human condition and to evaluate language, behaviour and thinking.

Chapter five introduces the use of film as a resource for learning. In some primary classrooms across the country pupils are using their implicit knowledge of film narratives, to make their own films. In Peterborough, for example, this work has been given value by the annual film competition which primary age pupils can enter (see www.peterborough.gov.uk). In addition to the speaking and listening collaborative work of this nature stimulates, film making contributes to pupils' learning of conventional forms of literacy. If film is the means by which some children are introduced to narrative, Chapter six takes this knowledge and explores story in all its dimensions. Considerable thought is given to the versatility of story for learning, as a cross-curricular resource. Pupils as story writers is also given attention through discussion of a practical example in epic narrative writing.

One of the most neglected areas of the English curriculum, poetry, is the subject of Chapter seven. Along with the preceding chapter on story, this is one of the longest chapters in the book. My experience of working with students over many years has led me to the view that poetry is an aspect of English they feel least confident about teaching. I deal with this issue and try to get inside the process of writing and reading poetry by discussing original examples. This discussion foreshadows an explanation of readers as creative meaning makers, which is taken up in Chapter eight. Strategies for encouraging poetry writing are also provided. Chapter eight looks at children's fiction but considers it in the context of texts that take children beyond their field of familiarity by dealing with issues they might find sensitive. Encouraging children to read beyond their 'comfort zone' may require preparatory or supportive work, on the part of the teacher. A model is proposed to identify the possible positions of various readers in relation to sensitive texts. This is considered as an essential element in teachers' preparation of enabling pupils to utilise their prior knowledge of the world in order to construct meanings, when engaging with texts that challenge their reading and understanding. The final chapter considers a range of non-fiction texts. In part, this involves a brief discussion of the difference between the linguistic and textual features of fiction and non-fiction, followed by an exploration of ways of helping pupils to access, use and construct information-bearing texts.

In order to discuss the different elements of what constitutes the subject of English, it has been necessary to separate those elements into chapters. However, this separation is a false construct and the reader will notice how discussion of creativity in English seeps from one chapter into another. For example, when dealing with non-fiction, I use an example of a session in which role play was the medium of learning. In another chapter I combine film work with improvisation as a way of helping pupils to write playscripts. It is necessary, therefore, to state from the outset that a creative approach to English involves the integration of the four language modes of speaking and listening, reading and writing. It also requires a curriculum in which connections are made between text types and between subjects. Creative English in a creative curriculum requires a pedagogy in which pupils' existing knowledge, skills and understanding is located within the sphere of learning rather than outside it, as is the case in transmission models of teaching and learning that have dominated English teaching under the literacy frameworks. Such an approach involves an exploration of the meanings that already exist in pupils' minds. It requires pupils to be central to the process of further meaning making, as active participants rather than as passive recipients of skills-based learning. The meanings that pupils bring to school derive from home and community, and creativity involves the dissolution of the boundary that can exist at the school gates. It requires teachers, many of whom may not live in the communities of the children they teach, to acquaint themselves with the social and cultural experience of those communities and utilise that experience in the curriculum, as a real resource for learning. In so doing, the knowledge and meanings that pupils have about their world, which may be implicit, can be made material, can be observed, discussed and made explicit, thereby making pupils conscious of the knowledge they have rather than leaving it as latent knowledge. Creative approaches to teaching English involve active learning in which pupils engage with knowledge, making purposeful choices, and use their emerging linguistic competence to challenge, justify and support thinking, through collaborative meaning making.

Before looking forward, towards a future in which teachers can develop creative approaches to pupil involvement in learning, and one in which they have greater control over curriculum delivery, teaching and learning strategies, and curriculum content, it might be wise to take a look at the past: to review how English has been viewed over the years and consider whether aspects of the past can tell us anything about the future of the subject in an integrated, creative curriculum. On then to Chapter one and the retrospective of English.

1

Janus

Looking at English past and future

> I know tomorrow for I have seen yesterday.
> (Heathcote 1978)

THIS CHAPTER DEALS WITH the following:

- the way in which the possible future direction of English mirrors aspects of the past;

- changing views of English from the early twentieth century up to the Primary National Strategy (PNS);

- the politicisation of English as subject.

For those of us who have more than twenty years experience as educational practitioners, there is something of a recursive feel about the way the primary curriculum is changing. Continual change in English, brought about by amendments to the National Curriculum and successive literacy frameworks, along with parallel, albeit often contradictory, discourses around what constitutes good practice, has taken its toll on some, leading to the denting of self-confidence and loss of direction. In the main though, teachers are highly creative people who either adapt to external pressures by accommodating change, or else subvert them by applying a deeply held philosophy and vision of teaching and learning. Changes to the way the curriculum was organised following the publication of the Primary National Framework (DfES 2006) may have made some colleagues feel a little like Janus, the Roman God of doors and gateways who, with his two heads, was able to see in opposite directions simultaneously. This distinctive characteristic enabled him to reflect on the past and see into the future. Senior teachers will reflect on the time when, prior to the National Curriculum, they set about the collegial process of medium and long term curriculum planning, using specific themes rather than subjects as their starting points. A brief survey of schools in the University of Bedfordshire Schools Partnership, conducted in July 2008, showed that 60 per cent of schools either had or were returning to this mode of curriculum delivery for whole or part of the curriculum. As Heathcote says above, 'I know tomorrow for I have seen yesterday'. Except the future is never quite an exact mirror image of the past; it is always modified in some way by the ideas through which it has passed.

As stated above, before the introduction of the National Curriculum (DES 1988), many primary schools taught through a thematic approach. Wherever possible subjects were integrated, but care was taken not to contrive integration. The National Curriculum tended to bring to an end such an approach in favour of a subject based model of curriculum delivery, more commonly found in secondary, or upper, schools. It was not that cross-curricular integration was negated by the National Curriculum. Indeed, advice was available to suggest that integration and cross-curricular links continued to be a strong possibility (DES 1989: 4.1; SCAA 1995: 27; QCA 1998: 6). However, educational change is often accompanied by dominant discourses that tend to overshadow alternatives and the documentation often contained contradictory messages. The corollary is that many teachers felt their creativity stifled by a subject-based curriculum, accompanied, as it was, by testing arrangements at the end of each key stage (Woods and Jeffrey 1997: 66). In some quarters, the introduction of the National Literacy Strategy (NLS) (DfEE 1998), which was seen as definitive guidance on the teaching of reading and writing, could be said to have further reduced opportunities for innovation and creative teaching. This is a point noted by Marshall (2000) who recognised that teachers of English were constantly required to redefine the subject to meet changing policy demands.

It may be argued that the NLS (DfEE 1998) was viewed from two opposing points of view. Those who advocated it may have seen it as a clearly defined and tightly structured 'life-belt' for the non-English specialist. It was a means of ensuring full and detailed coverage of the Programmes of Study, established in the revised National Curriculum (DES 1995). It established termly literacy objectives and gave teachers a framework for conducting individual lessons that included whole class, group and individual work; and the term plenary became part of teachers' everyday lexicon. Although the strategy was not statutory, a significant number of schools felt that their provision for literacy was best suited to the model proposed by the framework's literacy hour because it appeared to be part of a dominant discourse that was subject to scrutiny by Ofsted. The counter-view was of a didactic pedagogy that 'straitjacketed' the teaching of English, making it aridly formulaic, dry and uninteresting. Indeed, in the dominant discourse, the term English was superseded by the more fashionable term literacy. Not surprisingly, therefore, critics noted the absence of objectives for speaking and listening and the lack of time for extended reading and writing. For some, the English curriculum in primary schools became fragments of discrete word, sentence and text level work, without children being guided through a full exploration of whole texts, as either readers or writers. To avoid this approach some schools applied the literacy hour four days a week and devoted the fifth to extended writing. However, some took a more balanced view and acknowledged the possibility of creativity within the structure provided (Martin *et al.* 2007: 1). Others observed teachers being creative by resisting what they saw as a technicist approach that endangered their professional autonomy (Woods and Jeffrey 1997). Alongside dominant models of curriculum delivery in schools, it may be argued that for at least a decade, student teachers have been trained in how to teach literacy in accordance with the hegemonic perspective of what English was. Although, many English tutors in Schools of Education have shown the same forms of resistance noted by Woods and Jeffrey, thus perpetuating bipolar perspectives in the teaching of English.

In the period of my career to date, which spans some thirty years, education has been in a state of almost permanent transition; change has been the order of the day. It is perhaps not surprising, therefore, to see concurrent with the publication of Excellence and Enjoyment (DfES 2003) and the new Primary National Strategy for Literacy (DfES 2006) a move away from the subject oriented curriculum to a more thematic mode of delivery. One might be tempted to say we have gone full circle, but that would be to negate positive attributes acquired in the process of change. New ways of working with language have emerged in the intervening years. These innovations have added to the pedagogic repertoire available to teachers. However, the discourse of official curriculum guidance has tended to privilege certain pedagogic approaches over others. Approaches to the teaching of writing have been heavily influenced by the pedagogy of the genre theorists. While close analysis of textual genre, as recommended by both the NLS and PNS, provide pupils and teachers with a useful means of deconstructing texts, in order to identify textual structures, word choices and syntactic conventions associated with different genre, if overused as a strategy, could lead to formulaic and stultifying teaching and learning, which is ultimately demotivating for teachers and pupils and is, therefore, likely to prove counterproductive. Shared and guided reading sessions have also been seen as useful supportive mechanisms for developing young readers and writers by helping them to develop strategies for understanding texts. These approaches to reading move us beyond simple decoding skills and comprehension exercises and offer opportunities for readers to engage affective and critical responses to texts.

If continual change characterises education in general, and English in particular, teachers need a strong vision of their pedagogy and philosophy in order to make critical judgements about top-down innovation, and they need the confidence to adapt and modify curricular guidance. Having an historical perspective of the development of the subject, combined with a knowledge of different approaches to the teaching of English, provide a platform from which to critically view innovation. Let us now turn briefly to a review of the changing nature of English in the curriculum.

A brief overview of thinking about English

In their concise and informative overview of the history of English as a subject in the primary curriculum, Wyse and Jones (2008) reflect on the progressive nature of the Hadow Reports of the 1920s and 1930s. With reference to the second report, covering the 7–11 age group, (Board of Education 1931), they note that it made a number of recommendations which influenced the teaching of English through-out most of the Twentieth Century. The reports signalled the beginning of what came to be known as 'child-centred' education and replaced more mechanistic approaches to teaching, based on rote learning methods. The Hadow Reports consolidated the work begun in the Newbolt Report (Board of Education 1921), which had created the subject of English by synthesising under one heading a disparate set of skills, previously taught in an isolated manner across the curriculum. Furthermore, as Protherough and Atkinson (1994: 7 cited in Wyse and Jones 2008: 8) point out, Newbolt initiated a vision of English that was much broader than the teaching of grammar. English was to be a 'fine art' combining literacy, children's self-expression, the study of literature and the development of 'mind and character'. This broader view of English resonates strongly with official reports towards the end of the century, notably the Cox Report (1989) discussed more fully below. The Hadow Reports gave further substance to English as a subject. The following recommendations from the reports, extrapolated by Wyse and Jones, are indicative of thinking at the time:

- The privileging of practical activity and experience over the acquisition of knowledge and facts;

- Oral work around subjects of interest to the child;

- Class libraries;

- Silent reading and an emphasis on reading for pleasure and information;

- Oracy as the basis for writing, again based on topics of interest to the child;

- The learning of spellings related to the reading and writing of the child;

- A rejection of formal, decontextualised grammar teaching.

In addition, the final report (Board of Education 1933), which focused on 'infant education', stated that young children should be free to develop reading and writing when they felt ready to do so. The report went on to advocate that writing should be on subjects that interested children and that early writing involved the child communicating by imitating the environmental print they saw around them. This sounds strikingly like a precursor to the concept of 'emergent writing' in which children's initial writing appears as random marks on paper. As they progress, the marks adhere more closely to conventional forms of print, culminating in more fluent grapho-phonic representations and syntax, capable of being read in the absence of the writer. At the heart of this approach to children's early writing is the theory of the child as an active agent in their own learning. The child is seen as a sentient and creative being who is primarily driven to express meaning through mark marking because they recognise that language can be represented visually, as well as aurally. The conventions of writing are socially situated; that is, they are agreed or accepted at a social level, rather than being random hieroglyphs. In the act of writing, therefore, the child, although engaged in individual pursuit of communicating what is in their head, is enculturating him or herself into a society where literature and literacy are valued. The 'voice' of the final Hadow Report resonates in early years practice even to the present day. Current non-statutory guidance for early years practitioners sets out indicative stages of children's mark marking from birth to the age of five and provides advice on practical strategies that adults can make to facilitate children's early writing (DfES 2007: 57–58).

The final Hadow Report also emphasised the importance of play and of children's language developing out of practical experience. Not surprisingly, therefore, it recognised the role of drama as a means of language development. In addition, its recommendation for the teaching of reading appear remarkably similar to the 'searchlights' model (DfEE 1998: 4), which has since been replaced by the 'simple model of reading' (DfES 2006: 8) and the systematic teaching of synthetic phonics. The report advocated that reading should be based on three methods: a look and say approach (word recognition and graphic knowledge); phonics; and contextual cues located in an understanding of syntax and meaning (knowledge of context and grammatical knowledge). Finally, the report highlighted the importance of children being read to and of them hearing stories (Wyse and Jones 2008: 9–10). This was a practice that was once so common in primary classrooms, but tended to wane under the constraints of the National Literacy Strategy. I return to the importance of story in the chapter that deals exclusively with the subject later in the book.

The consensus falls apart

The recommendations of the Hadow Reports had resounding influences on primary education, to the extent that both the Plowden Report (DES 1967) and the Bullock Report (DES 1975) echoed much of what their predecessor had advocated (Wyse and Jones 2008: 10–11). The centrality of the child's interests and the embedding of language development in contexts that are meaningful to the child characterised official views of good practice in English. However, this consensus began to fragment in the latter part of the twentieth century, when opposing views of good practice created pedagogic and philosophical tensions. The fault lines of dissent were drawn between, on the one hand, politically driven imperatives to raise standards and, on the other, evidence based practice founded upon research and scholarly thought. During the late 1980s two reports published recommendations on the teaching of English (The Kingman Report 1988; The Cox Report 1989). Neither report was in accord with the highly politicised educational doctrine of the Conservative Government, which favoured a return to traditional grammar teaching. The Kingman Report introduced a view of knowledge about language that differed significantly from previous models which focused solely on grammar, whilst The Cox Report proposed five models of English teaching. In his review of the Cox Report, Goodwyn (2009 online) identifies these as:

> Personal growth – this model placed the child at the centre of learning and emphasised the relationship of language and learning for the child. Literature was seen as essential to the development of the child's aesthetic and imaginative attributes.

> Cross-curricular – this model posits that all teachers are teachers of English and that language development is the responsibility of the whole school. It recognises that each subject makes different language demands of the learner and that explicit attention needs to be given to equipping the learner with the necessary linguistic competence to be able to fully access the subject. The distinction between English as a subject and a medium of learning in other subjects is evident in this model.

> Adult needs – this model views English in a wider context beyond school and beyond the immediate needs of the child and the curriculum. It recognises the learner requires a language for life; one that will equip them for the demands of adult life, both as a life skill and as means of earning a living. The child as an effective communicator in both literacy and oracy is an essential outcome. Cox also included media education in his report and we might speculate on the likelihood that if he were writing the report today, critical analysis of media would also be an essential feature of this model.

> Cultural heritage – this model emphasises the importance of the learner having a knowledge and appreciation of literature widely regarded as exemplary.

Cultural analysis – at the heart of this model is the development of the learner's understanding of how meanings are culturally embedded and constructed. It also includes the competences required for individuals to be able to critically analyse the construction and communication of values embedded in language across a variety of media.

If we view these models as strands of what English is and synthesise them into an holistic model, we begin to see the enormity of the subject and how it differs markedly from the curriculum models that dominated the teaching of English in the two decades following the publication of Cox.

Parallel to the Kingman and Cox Reports, two projects, combining the work of academics and teachers, were collating findings in relation to, on the one hand, writing (National Writing Project 1985–1989) and on the other, speaking and listening (National Oracy Project 1987–1991). Wyse and Jones (2008) note how the findings, based on considerable empirical research, had only partial influence in the National Curriculum (DES 1988). Central to the conflict between politicians and English specialists was the nature of what should be taught to pupils on what came to be known as 'knowledge about language' (KAL). Richmond (1990: 23) traces the origin of the term back to the booklet *English from 5–16*, written by Her Majesty's Inspectorate (HMI 1984). Among the HMI recommendations was a return to formal grammar teaching. However, much research had shown that the formal teaching of grammar had little impact on children's use of language or improvement in writing. English specialists were well aware of this research and opposed the suggestion.

Perhaps the indicative symbol of the schism between politicians and English subject specialists came with the findings of the Language in the National Curriculum (LINC) project, which existed between 1989 and 1992 and was, like the two projects referred to above, a collaborative enterprise of academics and teachers. As with the Kingman and Cox reports, the Government directly interfered with LINCs findings by suppressing publication of the project's informative materials, again because it did not agree with the theoretical underpinning and model of language that informed teaching. However, these highly regarded materials are still available through the National Association for the Teaching of English (NATE) A review of the materials, is also available on the NATE website (McIntyre 2008). Discussion of the LINC project's theoretical underpinning and model of language was published (Carter 1990).

We might question the reason why English, as a subject, seems to be so coveted by successive governments who wanted to tightly control its content and the manner of its delivery. The answer perhaps resides in the relationship of a language to its culture and the embeddedness of culture in perceptions of nationality. English is a world language with a strong heritage of economic and political power. In the 'mind' of the Establishment there is a symbiotic relationship between English, the language, concepts of 'Englishness' and Britain's economic standing in the world. During the 1970s and early 1980s Britain's economic status in the world faltered and collapsed. In a symbiosis, one part affects the other. If the economy was on the wane, with the resultant loss of political power, internationally, so the same must be the case of the language or, to see it from the other side, standards of English are perceived to be falling, therefore, the economy is on the slide too. The result is that politicians, rather than educationalists, took the reins of the national language, steering it along the tramlines of tradition to the place of its rightful heritage. Concurrent with the last cry of 'falling standards', with which we are still living the legacy, there was the ascent of the 'cult of the accountant'. One philosophical characteristic introduced by governments in the 1980s was the ethos of the measurement of 'standards'. It seemed nothing had a value unless it was proven by quantifiable indicators. Hence, in the teaching of English, grammar, spelling and handwriting were privileged over more qualitative aspects, such as individual expression, voice or creativity, because the number of verbs a child could identify is quantifiable. This measure of control over English makes it, with perhaps the exception of History and Mathematics, the most politically contentious area of the curriculum. Teachers of English therefore, which includes all primary school teachers, since we all teach the subject, are constantly working in a controversial field of pedagogy and subject content. With this point in mind, in the next chapter, I offer a view of English that attempts to counter the technicist model of English that dominated the teaching of English from the late 1990s through to the latter part of the first decade of the millennium.

2

English as a creative process

THIS CHAPTER BEGINS WITH a critique of the teaching framework suggested in the Primary National Strategy. It then discusses the following:

- the creative nature of reading;

- the importance of teachers as writers;

- a model of English that integrates speaking and listening, reading and writing, thereby creating an holistic perspective of teaching and learning in English.

For at least a decade, from 1998, English teaching was dominated by a literacy framework that required teachers in primary schools to follow prescribed learning objectives within a tightly structured programme of study. This was replaced by a less constricting programme that allowed room for greater teacher initiative. At one level then, the Primary National Strategy's Framework for Literacy (DfES 2006), provided teachers with more opportunities for developing creative approaches to English than its predecessor, the National Literacy Strategy (DfEE 1998). It made clear reference to the interdependence of speaking and listening, reading and writing and the importance of integrating all modes of language in planning for learning, something the old framework omitted. The new strategy offered wider possibilities for structuring sequences of lessons across several weeks, rather than as single units bounded by the formulaic literacy hour, and renewed opportunities to teach 'skills' across the curriculum. At first glance, the Primary National Strategy framework appeared to be a refreshing change from what came before. However, on closer inspection much of the discourse surrounding the 2006 framework encouraged teachers, student teachers and those who teach them to focus their teaching on learning objectives and learning outcomes in relation to technical aspects of literacy. What was largely missing from this approach was recognition of language as a creative process and children as creative meaning makers. Furthermore, the proposed 'technicist' approach to writing negated personal choice and author aims (Wyse and Jones 2008: 129). A technicist approach involves the learner being taught certain skills before they are able to construct texts of their own. This view is contested, partly because it assumes no prior knowledge on the part of the learner, but also because it can lead to a very mechanistic mode of teaching and learning in which language is systematically deconstructed at word and sentence level.

In addition to the emphasis on literacy skills, the dominant approach to teaching remains somewhat formulaic, although the formula is not restricted to single lessons and has greater coherence than was the case with the literacy hour. As Wyse and Jones (2008: 18) point out, the pre-requisite sequence for teaching literacy is likely to become repetitive and, because it appears to be privileged as the dominant mode, is likely to blur teachers views of other pedagogic options, despite the suggestion that teachers can match pedagogy to purpose (DfES 2006: 11). The dominant mode of teaching about texts is represented in Figure 2.1, 'Teaching Framework: Primary National Strategy'.

This pedagogic sequence begins with the teacher working with pupils during shared and then guided reading sessions, dissecting texts in order to identify their

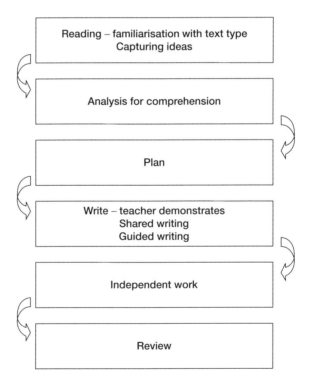

FIGURE 2.1 Teaching Framework: Primary National Strategy

constituent grammatical and textual features. Once these have been identified, pupils plan their writing but, before embarking on their draft, the teacher models the type of writing expected through shared writing and then supports pupils' initial attempts by means of guided writing. The next stage is independent writing, followed by a review of what has been written. The focus for teaching about texts to pupils then, as both readers and writers, is texts themselves. The structure of the framework required teachers to work with children, fine-tuning their analysis of texts at word, sentence and text level and then applying their findings to the construction of their own texts. If this approach required teachers to engage their classes in the reading of whole texts, then this too was a marked improvement on what had come before. However, pedagogic discourses need to incorporate models of teaching that are interactional, that is, ones that engage teachers and pupils, working with language in exploratory ways, rather than in just didactic, transmission models of teaching and learning. Putting pupils at the heart of the process and drawing upon their implicit knowledge of language is as important, if not more important than instructional approaches.

In successive frameworks there were the germs of good ideas but they tended to be obscured by restrictive practice. In addition, there was a tendency for the findings of important research studies and insightful thinking about how best to teach English to be lost by these successive frameworks. What is required of any framework for teaching English is an holistic pedagogy that encompasses a range of methods rather than the privileging of just one. There is a need to take stock of what we have learned about good practice and attempt a synthesis. It is hoped this book contributes to that outcome.

One of the problems with the previous literacy strategy was the prescription of the literacy hour in which time was tightly structured for different purposes. The inherent danger of that approach was that textual analysis was reduced to the study of parts of texts rather than whole texts. Indeed, there has been a tendency in recent years for pupils across all key stages to be given a diet of extracts, with infrequent opportunities to read the complete novel, or to have complete novels read to them. However, aspects of the guidance given to teachers in the 1998 strategy tend to be more detailed than the 2006 framework, which is more open-ended.

The following comparison of aspects of text level work illustrates the point:

Year 4 term 2 (1998 strategy)

Pupils should be taught:

- to understand how writers create imaginary worlds, particularly where this is original or unfamiliar, such as a science fiction setting, and to show how the writer has evoked it through detail;

- to understand how settings influence events and incidents in stories; to evaluate form and justify preferences;
- to compare and contrast settings across a range of stories; to evaluate form and justify preferences;
- to understand how the use of expressive and descriptive language can, e.g. create mood, arouse expectation, build tension, describe attitudes or emotions.

(DfEE 1998: 40)

Core learning in literacy Year 4 (2006 strategy)

- Deduce characters' reasons for behaviour from their actions and explain how ideas are developed in non-fiction texts;

- Explain how writers use figurative and expressive language to create images and atmosphere;

- Read extensively favourite authors or genres and experiment with other types of text;

- Interrogate texts to deepen and clarify understanding and response.

(DfES 2006: 30)

For the purposes of textual study the rubric of the 1998 framework provides non-specialist teachers of literature with more helpful guidance than does the rubric of the 2006 framework. What successive government documents seem to do, is tear up good practice in the teaching of English and replace it, whole-scale, with fresh initiatives and new language. This may be due, in part, to political rather than educational influence. However, it is teachers who, equipped with a knowledge of good practice, based on sound research, are best placed to make professional decisions about the required approaches to meet the specific needs and interests of their pupils. Some schools recognised that the structure of the 1998 strategy was inappropriate and abandoned the literacy hour for parts of the week, to allow for more complete literacy work, such as extended writing. Confident, creative teachers will always extract what is good in new ideas and synthesise it with what is good in existing practice.

However, professional judgements may be compromised by political expediency, particularly where initiatives have strong political backing, combined with an inspection framework with a brief to investigate the teaching of those initiatives. In the battle between professional judgement and political will, the latter tends to have the upper hand. Teachers, especially those educated in Schools of Education over the last ten years, may be forgiven for feeling confused about what constitutes good practice in English. Those who have been teaching much longer will remember when the primary curriculum involved thematic approaches, in which English was taught through other subjects and was itself the medium for learning about other subjects. The 2006 Primary National Strategy reflects the rubric of Excellence and Enjoyment (DfES 2003) which suggested schools should use creative ways of delivering the curriculum. The year 2006 marked a turning point in the teaching of English. It opened up the possibility for more imaginative and more holistic methods of teaching and learning. In moving forward, however, we sometimes have to look to the past for guidance about how to shape the future. What follows below is a consideration of what a holistic model of English teaching might look like. It is preceded by a discussion of the thinking of some respected figures in the field.

Towards an holistic model of English

Drawing upon a wealth of research evidence and his own empirical work, Corden (2000) highlights the value of group discussion as a means of pupils' developing critical awareness of texts and an ability to transfer what they learn from writer's, through their reading, to their own writing. As well as peer discussion, he also identifies the importance of teacher–pupil interaction around texts. With focused teaching this can lead to pupils moving beyond implicit understandings of how writers create effects, to the development of explicit knowledge and metalinguistic awareness; that is, the ability to discuss texts, their own and other people's, using appropriate technical language.

Barrs (2000) points out that the text is a meeting place where readers and writers relate to one another, where the writer's voice is heard by the reader and the reader learns the 'characteristic tunes and patterns' of the text. Through exposure to whole texts, pupils develop an 'ear' for language, which helps tune their own voices, as writers. It is imperative then that pupils have frequent opportunities to read and hear whole texts by a range of authors, in a range of genres. While this is alluded to in the 2006 framework, by extending the time allocated to the study of particular genres, as stated above, there is still a restrictive feel about the units of work. For example, the framework, like its predecessor, takes discrete elements of texts as the focus for study. In the above example from Year 4, the foci are character and figurative language. So, despite its apparent freedom, the curriculum is still centrally driven. When discussing texts, pupils may identify aspects that do not appear in the curriculum schedule for their particular year. Should the teacher truncate discussion and steer pupils back to the specific focus stated in the framework, or would it be more fruitful to encourage the discussion and extend pupils' interests by guiding them to explore further the aspects of texts they have identified? It is at this point the spirit of standard Q8, quoted earlier, should be invoked because, as Barrs suggests, pupils are engaging with the text in a way that is meaningful to them. The meeting of the reader and writer is inherent in this situation; it does not have to be fabricated by the teacher, attempting to meet curriculum objectives.

In their brief summary of the development of English in the primary curriculum, Wyse and Jones (2008: 121) note that the approach to the teaching of English in the respective national frameworks appears to be heavily influenced by the 'genre theorists', a group of Australian academics who advocated the teaching of skills over the development of pupils' self-expression. Implicit in this approach is an assumption that equipping children with sufficient technical know-how will lead them to become good writers and readers. This approach is like telling a footballer that she must practise ball control, passing, and other ball skills without playing regularly in a whole match. Those readers who are familiar with sporting activities will recognise that while there is a place for the development of discrete skills, a player only really develops holistically through frequent and sustained performance. The notion of 'match-fitness' is different from that of being physically fit. Indeed, evidence suggests that teaching the technical aspects of writing in isolation, as advocated by the first literacy strategy, did not lead to vast improvements in pupils' achievements as writers (Wyse and Jones 2008: 127).

In her critique of the former National Literacy Strategy (DfEE 1998) and its supplementary document *Grammar for Writing* (DfEE 2000b), Hilton (2001) reasserts the importance of giving children sufficient time to write independently and to experience whole texts, as both readers and writers. She reminds us of the wealth of research evidence that points to the fact that writers develop by engaging in the process of writing whole texts and of having whole texts read to them, or by reading them independently, rather than by spending vast amounts of time undertaking decontextualised exercises in which discrete skills are learned. In her analysis of Hillocks' work, which was influential in the formulation of the National Literacy Strategy, Hilton carefully identifies the ways in which his position on the teaching of writing was misinterpreted by those who wrote the strategy and its allied documents.

Hillocks' (1995) work is far more detailed and sympathetic to notions of 'free process' for the development of the inexperienced writer than his NLS interpreters. He suggests that unstructured free writing, particularly personal narrative in the form of diaries and journals, is a tap root of further development and should be encouraged alongside more didactic approaches. . . . Hillocks argues that procedural knowledge – that is, knowing the steps of how to go about writing in a particular genre with its main stylistic features – is largely learned through the act of self-expression in writing rather than through the teaching of rules. His 'environmental' approach is in fact a delicate balance between procedures and practice.

(Hilton 2001: 8)

To reiterate this position then, while there is a need for pupils to investigate how different types of texts are constructed and there should be opportunities for them to apply this understanding in their own writing, the current Primary National Strategy Literacy Framework (DfES 2006) offers scant opportunity to explicitly consider reading and writing as holistic creative acts, or to look at textual creation as a cultural or social process. It is my contention that both teachers and pupils need to be aware of both writing and reading as creative social processes, as well as have an understanding of how texts hang together, if pupils are to become informed users of literacy, who not only know how to 'do it', but also enjoy and gain pleasure from reading and writing and understand the purpose and function of literary texts as social and cultural artefacts. What I am advocating is not entirely absent from the framework; in Year 4, when engaging and responding to texts, pupils should 'explore why and how writers write, including through face-to-face and online contact with authors' (DfES 2006: 30), and in Year 6, progression to Year 7, when creating and shaping texts they should 'independently write and present a text with the reader and purpose in mind' (DfES 2006: 37).

It is a little worrying, however, that references to writers and readers appear to be so restrictive when these features should permeate literacy work across the whole age phase.

Teachers as writers

If we are to encourage pupils' writing and develop their expertise as writers, surely teachers and student teachers need, as part of their own subject knowledge, an understanding of the creative processes involved in both writing and reading. My experience of working with student teachers for the past decade indicates that whereas the majority are avid readers, only a minority write for any other reason than to complete assignments. Grainger (2005 cited in Domaille and Edwards 2006) also comments on the lack of experience most teachers have as writers. The writing that students do tends to be purely functional, which may influence their attitude to writing generally. Without an insider view of writing as a creative process, this functional view of writing may be transferred to classrooms and inform the way writing is taught.

What is lacking in many courses of Initial Teacher Education are opportunities to engage student teachers with their own personal, creative and descriptive writing. It is possible for a teacher to teach pupils about say, narrative writing, without ever writing a story themselves, as an adult. It is my view that if we are to really get inside the creative process and to see that process from the perspective of pupils as writers, we need to be inside the process ourselves, by being writers ourselves. This perspective informed the creative writing project described by Domaille and Edwards (2006) in which teachers and PGCE students worked with an established writer in creative writing workshops to develop subject knowledge through practice, and to consider how the teaching of creative writing might be better addressed in schools. The project successfully helped both teachers and students to develop their own writing but it also enabled them to acquire fresh views and attitudes to writing; ones that took them beyond a narrow objectives-orientated curriculum. The first-hand experiences, gained through the writing workshops, encouraged a more creative approach to writing in the classroom; one that enabled pupils to exercise greater choice and autonomy over what they wrote.

Having the creative space to develop one's own writing and the feeling of empowerment that comes with being able to manipulate language in ways that affect others is an important aspect of the English teacher's subject knowledge. The acquisition of subject knowledge in praxis is essential to developing a more informed view not only of how texts are constructed, but also of the emotional and cognitive engagement of the writer. Otherwise, teaching around the objectives of successive literacy frameworks, which are no more than manuals that guide us through the technical aspects of writing, is likely to lead to restrictive practices in which pupils are required to deconstruct texts, under the teacher's guidance, and then replicate identified linguistic and textual features in their own writing. As suggested, technique, though important, is only half of the equation; the other half is creativity. Exploring why and how writers write and where they draw their material from is important knowledge for all children, whatever their age. Knowledge of the creative process and the relationship between writing, the writer, the text, reading and the reader, can be lost in frameworks that subdivide literacy learning into discrete sets of skills for writing on the one hand, and reading on the other.

Perhaps the conventional view of writing is of an individual engaging their imagination in a solitary act in order to produce a text. The text appears to be the creation of a single mind working in isolation. Certainly many professional writers such as Philip Pullman and Alan Ahlberg use their garden sheds as a refuge for writing. While the act of writing itself may be solitary, the process is a social one. Indeed, Pullman (2002) would readily agree that writers are magpies who steal ideas from the world around them. That world includes the work of other writers. Consider Janet and Alan Ahlberg's *Each Peach Pear Plum* (1978) in which the whole text is a montage of the reworking of fairy tales and nursery rhymes, or Pullman's *I Was a Rat* (2000), with its close textual associations to the story of Cinderella. These links with other texts, known as intertextuality, provide an exciting area of investigation for, and with, pupils. Knowledge of the creative process by which texts come into being needs to be a key part of the teacher's repertoire of subject knowledge.

In order to begin addressing the absence of such knowledge, two models are presented here (Figure 2.2 and Figure 2.3) as explanations of how texts may come into being and how the creative process does not end when writers dot the last word on the final copy of their manuscript. Figure 2.2 is a simplified version of the process I am seeking to explain, whereas Figure 2.3 is a more elaborate theoretical construct. The writing process begins even before the writer picks up the pen or sits at the keyboard. In their 'magpie' mode writers are constantly observing the physical and social world around them, constantly collecting and recording brief descriptions of what interests them. These recordings may include snippets of conversation; pen portraits of people they see or meet; ideas that spring to the mind, prompted by some causal event they witness. The notepad or journal is the stock-in-trade of the writer in which they hoard details to be used later. I once wrote a full-length play based on people I met and the conversations they had, whilst on a summer vacation. However, in the various published frameworks there is no mention of pupils being asked to work like real writers

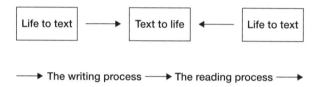

FIGURE 2.2 Writer to reader: a continuum of meaning construction

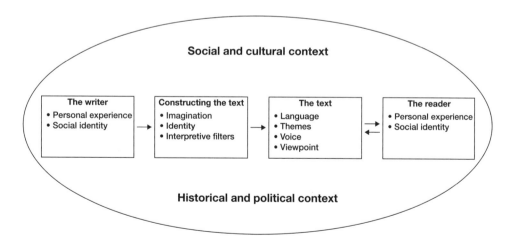

FIGURE 2.3 Writer to reader: the construction of meaning in texts

and keep their own journals. Good teachers of writing have, however, taken account of this aspect of the process and encourage their pupils to keep jottings in a notepad. In some classrooms, time is set aside for children to use these notes as stimuli for writing, in whatever genre they choose.

Reconstructing literacy as a creative process

The first stage of the writing process then is 'Life', the conscious world that surrounds the writer. The writer draws upon 'Life' as the raw material for the text. Once completed, the text stands as a product, but it is an artefact that remains part of the social and cultural world of its construction. Until someone picks up that text and begins reading, it is inert. The moment they do, they breath life back into the text. Far from the creative process and the construction of meaning ending in the text, reading is, itself, part of the creative process and is, therefore, a further stage in the construction of meaning. Reader-response theory has contributed to our understanding of the importance of the reader's biography and sociocultural experience in the construction of meaning. What is meant here is that in the act of reading, readers bring to the text their own experiential knowledge and that texts are imbued with meaning by readers because of this knowledge. This is a far cry from asking, 'what did the writer intend', as is the case in much literary analysis, particularly that required of pupils at GCSE and A Level.

In the continuum of meaning construction then, the reader, as well as the writer, plays an important, creative role. This is a liberating idea for the primary classroom because it shifts the emphasis away from what a text, or an aspect of a text, was intended to mean, to what it might mean for the reader, and how the reader responds to the text. This shift in emphasis can be empowering for both pupils and teachers and can lead to creative and discursive activities, around what texts mean from the reader's perspective. For the teacher the shift in emphasis is not a difficult one to make. Sometimes all that is required is the simple rephrasing of questions. Instead of asking what a phrase, passage or a complete text, might mean, the question, 'what do you think it means?' or, 'what does this mean to you?' repositions the learner as an active creator of meaning, rather than as an interpreter of what the writer might have intended. In the hands of readers, texts can take on a curious vitality of their own and live beyond the mind of the writer. By that I mean, readers can imbue texts with meanings that writers did not consciously realise when writing them. The fact a writer did not intend a particular meaning does not invalidate the viewpoint of the reader because the text is a cultural artefact that is open to interpretation. I have found this particularly to be the case with poetry. There are occasions when I have read a poem I wrote several months earlier and have found in it a meaning that I had not originally intended. When a writer becomes the reader, even if it is their own work, they bring to the text a slightly different set of interpretive lenses.

We often ask pupils to justify their answers with reference to the text. While this is valid, the above example shows it is equally valid to encourage pupils to justify their answers with reference to their own experience. Figure 2.3, 'Writer to reader: the construction of meaning in texts', attempts to explain in greater detail how texts are socially constructed and how reading is a social process. First, the act of writing and the act of reading both take place in a particular social, cultural, historical and political context. The time between the writer producing the text and the reader reading the text may be different, in some cases several centuries, but the fact remains both take place in particular sociocultural and politico-historic contexts. These terms are really a form of shorthand to define the world inhabited by the writer, the reader and the text. In the process of writing, the writer draws upon personal experience and their interpretation of the world around them for the raw material of the text. Characters might be based on people they know or have seen; narratives may be partly constructed on real life narratives or episodes from real life; relationships between characters might reflect real life ones and direct speech may be prompted by snippets of everyday conversation. Certainly themes that emerge in the text derive their place from issues that are very much part of real life. Themes such as love, hatred, jealousy, revenge, the battle between good and evil are universal ones that find a place in all societies, at all points in history. Contemporary themes such as drug abuse, bullying, broken families, racism and sexism, have particular resonance in modern times.

The essential point is that the text is drawn from life and is reconstructed by the writer who weaves a virtual reality through the telling of a story. There is one further dimension to the relationship of life to text and it is the social position of the writer. The world inhabited by the writer is reconstructed through a series of personal experiential lenses. I have called these 'interpretive filters'. They form part of the social identity of the writer and they influence how the individual experiences the world. Writers come from different social classes and different cultural and ethnic backgrounds. They can be male or female and have different physical abilities or disabilities, as well as different sexual orientations. Each of these factors, and their combinations, form the writer's social identity. It is our social identity that shapes, and is shaped by, the way we experience life. I elaborate upon this argument elsewhere (Gardner 2007: 18). Our experience of the social world is also personal and becomes part of our creative being. It therefore enters our imagination in the process of textual creation and resides there once the text is complete. It is there in the language, themes, voice and viewpoint that make up the text.

However, as already explained in Figure 2.3, the text is not the end of the story because the reader enters the equation, bringing with him, or her, a tapestry of personal experience and a social identity, just as the writer does. In the same way that the interpretive filters of the writer, based on his or her social identity, influence the way the narrative is constructed, the interpretive filters of the reader influence the meanings the reader brings to the text and how the text is read. The process of reading then is a transaction of meanings; of those meanings embedded in the text by the writer and the meanings created by the reader. This point is summarised by Rosenblatt (1994), an advocate of reader-response theory:

> The reader can begin to achieve a sound approach to literature only when he (sic) reflects upon his response to it, when he attempts to understand what in the work and in himself produced that reaction, and when he thoughtfully goes on to modify, reject or accept it.

The reader's response could be in relation to any aspect of a text. For example, it could be the way the writer uses a particular word or phrase; describes a scene; creates tension or deals with bigger issues through thematic concerns. In its extreme form, reader-response theory asserts that the intentions of the writer are of no concern; that 'the writer is dead'. However, what the theory does do is position the reader as an active agent in the process of making meaning with texts. The reader's response is, therefore, an important area for study in the classroom. Asking pupils to consider what affect a text, or part of a text, has on them and extending this study by asking them to identify the reason why they respond in the way they do, is likely to encourage pupils' engagement with texts in a much more meaningful way than repetitive sessions of textual analysis. A further dimension of the theory enables the validity of multiple interpretations. If we ask, 'what does the writer mean?', we are possibly narrowing the response to a unitary one, based on the assumption there is only one intended meaning. However, reader-response theory allows us to engage with different interpretations of a single text because the experiences that different readers bring to the text are different.

Armed with the knowledge of writing and reading as a continuum of meaning making within social and cultural contexts and of writers and readers as active interpreters of their social world, teachers can approach literacy development by placing the pupil at the centre of the creative process rather than position him or her as the recipient of technical know-how. Such a position completely changes the pedagogy of English teaching, which I would argue leads to pupils who are empowered, more prepared to take risks and leads to a creative approach to teaching. While there is nothing essentially wrong with the model of teaching in Figure 2.1, in fact, it closely resembles the model advocated in the UKLA/PNS research on raising boys' achievement in writing (UKLA/PNS 2004). However, the UKLA/PNS study highlighted the importance of drama, the visual media and the use of collaborative talk as key supporting strategies for writing. The problem with the PNS model is that insufficient emphasis is given to creative and holistic approaches to English teaching in the framework document. This makes the model problematic because once published, its visual impact can 'burn' itself into the collective memory as orthodoxy. This being so, it is important that the model is as comprehensive as possible, from the outset. In Figure 2.4, I propose an alternative model which attempts to integrate talk, reading and writing, in a phased, creative and holistic approach to English. It is an attempt to place the pupil's emerging experience and interests within a pedagogic process, instead of outside it, as is implied in the PNS model.

Discussion of the integrated approach to English

The model has a central strand, or spine, that connects two sets of evolutionary phases: the left-hand one being concerned with pupils as writers, and the right-hand one with them as readers. The central spine represents what they do as speakers and listeners. Taking Barrs' (2001) point that the text is where readers meet the voice of the writer, I see voice as an important aspect of both sets of evolutionary phases. Allied to the concept of voice in which pupils hear the voice of the writer and develop their own voice as writers, is an ear for language. It seems to me that far more important than the identification of textual features for the developing reader and writer, is this intuitive knowledge and 'feel' for language. If an undue early emphasis is placed on getting pupils to deconstruct texts and pick out the salient technical devices used by a writer, there is a danger that pupils' enjoyment of language may be lost. As we work down the central spine we can see that the 'ear for language', or implicit knowledge, is developed by pupils through talk about books on the one hand, and their own writing on the other. Once pupils have developed an 'ear for language', teachers can then elicit this implicit knowledge and enable pupils to explicitly identify what they are already able to do with language. By refining the 'ear for language', and by making the implicit, explicit, a technical vocabulary can then be applied so that pupils are able to talk about their responses and key textual features, using appropriate metalinguistic terminology, as suggested by Corden (2000).

We already know that many writers make jottings of things they see and hear, as well as spontaneous ideas. They utilise perceptive observational skills to do so. This practice is an important aspect of pupils' development as writers and is present in the model in the initial phase of the writing process. At this stage, pupils need guidance about how to observe, using their senses as the means of identifying and selecting sensations that interest them. They should be encouraged to try to put into words their observations in a way that they feel expresses what their senses detect. Rather than letting these observations fade

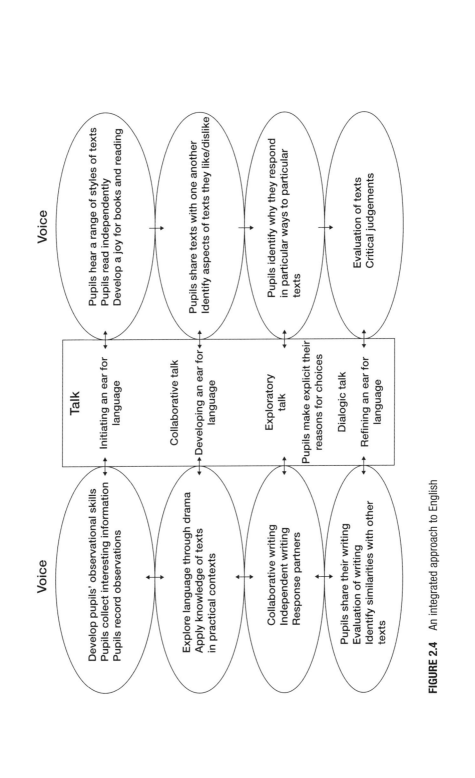

FIGURE 2.4 An integrated approach to English

Voice

Pupils hear a range of styles of texts
Pupils read independently
Develop a joy for books and reading

Pupils share texts with one another
Identify aspects of texts they like/dislike

Pupils identify why they respond
in particular ways to particular
texts

Evaluation of texts
Critical judgements

Talk

Initiating an ear for
language

Collaborative talk

Developing an ear for
language

Exploratory
talk

Pupils make explicit their
reasons for choices

Dialogic talk

Refining an ear for
language

Voice

Develop pupils' observational skills
Pupils collect interesting information
Pupils record observations

Explore language through drama
Apply knowledge of texts
in practical contexts

Collaborative writing
Independent writing
Response partners

Pupils share their writing
Evaluation of writing
Identify similarities with other
texts

from memory, they need to be recorded in a writer's notebook or jotter. Martin and Rothery (Martin 1984; Rothery 1984 cited in Czerniewska 1992: 129) found that writing in the early years of primary education tended to be based on pupils direct observations and involved the labelling of pictures. They suggest this practice is an embryonic form of the genres of report and recount writing. The act of noting observations is an important function of the written mode; the making of a permanent record of ideas, thoughts, feelings etc. for future use. The activity is given purpose by pupils knowing that these jottings, snippets of descriptive language or the germ of an idea, provide them with a store of words, phrases, sentences and even paragraphs that can be used later, in more extended pieces of writing. Such jottings could be the stimulus for writing and thereby help those pupils who find extended writing difficult, to circumvent the awkwardness of staring at the blank page and then resorting to a repertoire of displacement activities such as, sharpening their pencil three times, or spending ten minutes looking for a rubber to erase the non-existent words on the page.

In order to assist pupils to develop an ear for the kind of language required by various forms of the written mode, they need opportunities to hear and read good quality reading material. In terms of literary texts, we are fortunate that in the English language there is a plethora of excellent authors and books to help pupils acquire a good ear for language. The relationship between reading and writing, at all stages of language development is symbiotic. By that I mean that reading informs the pupil's knowledge of how language works in print, and writing helps them appreciate the craft and linguistic 'magic' of the writer, which accentuates their insightfulness as a reader. So, the development of observational skills; opportunities to hear a range of stories and the acquisition of an ear for language are not discrete and separate but integral and mutually supportive practices. Nor do they stop in the initial phase of the model but permeate all phases. The model thereby operates on two dimensions: horizontally and vertically. It also makes possible the organisation of the sequence of learning from the right-hand side as well as from the left. So, the reading of texts could precede writing, but key to whatever sequence, is the fulcrum of talk, represented by the central spine.

Closely allied to the first phase, the next phase places emphasis on speaking and listening and the engagement with texts through drama and collaborative talk. The importance of group talk, as a means of learning, and the function of drama, are discussed later in the book. Talk is fundamental to learning and it was gratifying to see this being acknowledged in the updated framework (DfES 2006: 7). This phase encourages peer interaction by sharing texts and discussing what pupils like and dislike about the texts they are reading. In so doing pupils learn that their views count; that readers are allowed to have personal responses to texts and that these responses are valid. It will also highlight the fact that different readers have different responses and that the same text can evoke different feelings for different readers. If pupils are guided to interrogate the reasons for this, they will learn that personal responses are often influenced by individual experiences which cause readers to engage with texts in different ways.

Not only are pupils acquiring an appreciation of the particular effects created by authors and the means by which they do it, they are also learning about the social significance of texts as artefacts that reflect life and are interpreted differently by people who have different experiences of life. The sharing of texts is complemented by means of drama which, through the use of spontaneous speech, is likely to draw on the language and structures of texts already discussed by pupils. Drama can also be used as a way of exploring the kind of texts that might otherwise be relatively inaccessible to pupils. This is a matter I return to later in the book when discussing sensitive issues in literature. During this phase it is expected that pupils will use their implicit knowledge of texts; their emerging ear for language and their own jottings from observations in their writing. There will also be opportunities for pupils to write in role during drama sessions. This is also a matter addressed later in the book.

In the third phase of the model, pupils will be experienced users of talk in groups and will have acquired the ground rules for doing so. Exploratory talk requires pupils to be able to challenge and question one another's thinking in constructive ways, as the means by which collective learning is developed (Dawes *et al.* 2000: 4). In relation to texts, pupils are expected to be able to justify their responses. By making reasons more explicit and fine-tuning critical judgements whilst combining these with the developing ear for language, it is expected that pupils will have greater control over their own writing. However, unlike a purely technicist model, this approach enables the acquisition of explicit knowledge of language and of texts, and the simultaneous development of an intuitive feel for language.

The final phase is the culmination of all acquired knowledge and experience in relation to the text types that have been explored. It is the stage at which pupils make informed comparisons of their own writing and published sources. They are able to talk confidently about texts when questioned in depth, through dialogic talk and are able to make explicit their reasons for personal preferences and choices in both their reading and writing.

What this model attempts to do is place learning and the learner at the centre of the pedagogic process in a non-didactic manner, without losing sight of the important role of the teacher. The model scaffolds pupils' development of language by integrating all modes of language: reading, writing, speaking and listening in an holistic manner and places implicit knowledge of language before explicit identification of syntax and textual grammar. The role of the teacher changes at different stages in the process. The teacher is instrumental in creating the right conditions for pupils working through the phases. They have to exercise subject knowledge in the selection of texts, in their questioning techniques and the modelling of talk. They need to know how drama can be used to elicit language and thought and create strategies for pupils to interact meaningfully with one another. They also need a good knowledge of literature and the process of writing. Above all, they need the confidence to allow pupils time to experiment with language through extended sessions of reading, writing and talking; and to incorporate all modes of language in an holistic engagement with English, without being hidebound to a didactic model of teaching.

3

Who's talking now?

CREATIVE TEACHERS HAVE ALWAYS valued talk as a foundation for learning but this has not always been reflected in 'official' forms of the curriculum. In this chapter we consider:

- how modes of communication in the classroom influence the nature of learning and pupils' roles as learners;

- the dichotomised view of oracy and literacy;

- the erroneous nature of deficit models of language;

- an inclusive approach to speaking and listening, involving exploratory and dialogic talk.

Of all the language modes, talk, or speaking and listening, has been something of a poor relation in the teaching of English. Although its importance has been promoted by leading educationists and has been acknowledged in various influential documents, including the Literacy Strategy (DfEE 1998: 8), which advocated a greater use of interactive whole class teaching, involving discursive and 'high quality oral work', evidence showed that the range of opportunities for pupils to explore ideas and ask questions remained greatly restricted (Mroz *et al.* 2000 cited in Myhill and Fisher 2005). References to talk were never given the same status as reading and writing. Indeed the preference for the use of the term literacy, rather than English, in the 1990s and into the twenty-first century suggested that talk, in reality, had little value. This was perhaps due to the volumes of official documentation devoted to the teaching of reading and writing and the sparse wordage given to talk.

We might say that literacy became the hegemonic discourse that put talk in the shadows. However, with the advent of the second Literacy Framework (DfES 2006), talk was reinstated with four of twelve strands of English attributed to it.

Furthermore, the Framework declared that talk is the foundation of learning. The 'new' status that was given to talk, as a means of learning, was to be welcomed, largely because creative teachers had always recognised its value. Furthermore, they recognised that carefully planned teacher–pupil and pupil–pupil talk, enhanced the study of texts and was, therefore, an integral feature of literacy development. Skidmore (2003 cited in Myhill and Fisher 2005) suggested that where pupils were given opportunities for purposeful dialogue around texts they developed as more reflective readers. However, the vacuum created by its earlier neglect means that too few teachers were thoroughly equipped to plan for, and to implement, purposeful talk, and even less well equipped to assess it. Circle time and the use of talk partners are useful starting points but they are hardly extensive ones and talk, or oracy, which includes speaking and listening, needs to be used across the curriculum for different purposes.

As indicated above, despite its lowly status, oracy has been greatly valued in certain quarters and has been recognised as an influential tool for learning. It is possible to trace a line of influence from the 1970s to the present day. In Britain, leading advocates of talk for learning have included Britton (1970), followed by Barnes (1976), leading on to Edwards and Mercer (1987); and Alexander (2008). In this chapter, I explore what we have learned about oracy from research conducted by these educationists and consider ways in which talk can be integrated into creative classrooms. The way talk is used in the classroom has a tremendous influence over the nature of learning that takes place, and the ways in which teachers and pupils see themselves; their relationship to one another and their relationship to learning and knowledge. Using these ideas as a starting point, let me turn to Barnes, who was one of the first to identify the significance of talk and its power in classroom interactions to develop pupils' thinking and use of language.

Classroom talk and the nature of learning

In his seminal text, *From Communication to Curriculum* (1976), Barnes demonstrates how different types of classroom discourse are the precursors of different types of learning and thinking. Some forms are restrictive and restrain creative possibilities. These are usually ones that are teacher-dominated and result in learning that is tightly controlled and learners that are largely teacher-dependent. Conversely, more open forms of discourse; those which allow pupils to use language to explore and share their thinking lead to empowered learners, able to hypothesise, analyse and critique ideas. To conceptualise how types of learner and learning are constructed in classrooms I have created a model of Barnes' explanation in Figure 3.1. The model is dominated by the central rectangle, which represents the classroom. It is always going to be the case that the teacher

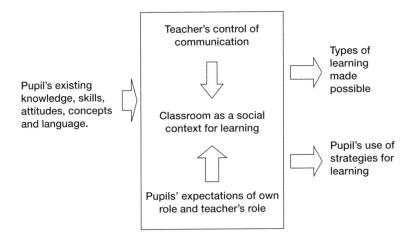

FIGURE 3.1 A model of classroom communication and learning

Source: Adapted from Barnes (1976: 32).

controls the types of communication that are possible. It is the teacher's responsibility to create a classroom ethos that sets the parameters of teacher–pupil and pupil–pupil interactions. Appropriate patterns of behaviour, including the use of talk, or types of discourse signalled by the teacher, create the social context in which learning is to take place. This in turn influences pupils' expectations and self-view as learners. A practical example might help to illumine what I mean. Edwards and Mercer (1987) note that talk in many classrooms is characterised by what is termed I-R-F discourse. The teacher is in control of who talks and when they are able to. She not only controls communication but also the transfer of knowledge and signals the type of knowledge required of learners. This discourse begins with *initiation* in the form of a question. This is followed by a *response* from a pupil; usually one selected by the teacher because they have raised their hand to answer. The discourse culminates in *feedback*, which may be a simple yes or no, to indicate whether the answer was correct or not. This pattern is repeated with further questions being asked. Such discourse may last for up to twenty minutes, depending on the age of the pupils. In their review of studies of I-R-F discourse, Myhill and Fisher (2005) refer to the work of Myhill (2002) and Marshall *et al.* (1995) which confirm the prevalence of I-R-F discourse. Questions asked by the teacher tend to require low order thinking and are largely ones that demand information recall or factual knowledge on the part of the learner (Moyles *et al.* 2001).

Ironically, the interactive teaching advocated by the literacy hour was interpreted by many teachers as meaning I-R-F discourse, a matter that Alexander (2008) challenged by advocating the use of dialogic, rather than interactive teaching. A small-scale study on the use of questioning in the literacy hour conducted by the Institute of Education revealed that teachers asked approximately seventy-five questions every twenty minutes. That is more than three questions a minute, which is indicative of the lack of thinking time given to pupils to answer questions. When the types of questions asked were analysed, not surprisingly the study found that 50 per cent required information retrieval from a text and 20 per cent required pupils to locate information in the text. Only 5 per cent of questions encouraged analysis, synthesis or evaluation; 4 per cent sought pupils affective response to the text or empathy with characters and 1 per cent of questions required pupils to justify their answers by giving textual evidence.

A comparison with the taxonomy of educational objective, Figure 3.2 (Bloom *et al.* 1956), demonstrates that 70 per cent of questions required low order thinking skills, while only 9 per cent elicited higher order cognition. If this type of questioning is replicated across the country, as is suggested by more wide-scale studies, the result would mean the nation's pupils were engaged in superficial learning during whole class interactive teaching of literacy. Furthermore, these types of questions signalled to pupils an extremely narrow view of reading, one that required the reader to comprehend what is read rather than to engage with texts with thought, feeling and personal response. Such a view of reading places the reader in a narrow and restricted affective and intellectual frame and is likely to engender dull responses to literature. This may be one of the reasons why the Progress in International Reading Literacy Study (PIRLS 2001) of thirty-five countries found that English school children were less likely to read for pleasure than the vast majority of their international

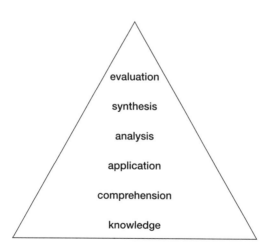

FIGURE 3.2 Bloom's taxonomy

Source: Bloom *et al.* 1956.

counterparts, despite scoring highly on reading for informational purposes. The Institute of Education study concluded with a set of recommendations to improve the quality of the teacher's questioning during the literacy hour. The recommendations encouraged teachers to:

- ask fewer, more varied questions;

- focus on higher order questions;

- elicit pupils affective responses to texts;

- focus on questions that model thinking process;

- use more small group discussion of texts.

Edwards and Mercer (1987) note that the overuse of questions in many professions is considered to be counterproductive to inducing talk. It is possible to see from research evidence that the I-R-F pattern of classroom discourse is a feature of English educational culture that is likely to lead pupils to view learning as the acquisition of facts and exercise of memory. The learner is likely to internalise a self-view as a passive recipient of the teacher's knowledge. The pupil–teacher relationship is, therefore, one in which the learner is heavily reliant upon the teacher for guidance and learning is viewed as a process controlled by the teacher, with knowledge framed largely as factual information.

Classrooms, talk and community

Returning to the Barnes' model which conceptualises classrooms as social arenas, where talk is dominated by the teacher there is often a failure to recognise the existing knowledge, skills, attitudes, concepts and language that children bring into the classroom from home and community. For such children, teachers implicitly signal that what they learn outside school has little or no value. In an attempt to challenge this perspective 'The Bullock Report' (DES 1975) suggested that no child should be expected to leave the culture and language of the home at the school gates. This often quoted statement referred to children for whom English is an additional language, but is equally applicable to all children. In the past, there was a tendency for some teachers in schools in poor socio-economic areas to apply a deficit language model to pupils, viewing them as having 'little or no language'. Such teachers adopted a remedial stance to language development and had low expectations of their pupils. In a well-known study, Rosenthal and Jacobson (1968) demonstrated that teacher expectations are extremely influential indicators of pupil achievement. Other studies indicate that where teachers perceive children to have poor language skills on entry to school, there has been a tendency for low levels of one to one teacher–pupil interaction, accompanied by the use of closed questions of the I-R-F type, with the result that pupils respond with monosyllabic answers. This type of discourse becomes a self-fulfilling prophecy, confirming the teacher's illusion of the child's language deficit. Such perceptions were found to be demarcated along social class boundaries with middle class pupils being privileged by teachers (Tizard and Hughes 1984). I provide a fuller discussion of Tizard and Hughes' findings below.

From the above discussion it is possible to see that classrooms dominated by teacher talk and teachers who accord little value to what pupils bring to school are likely to produce constrained types of learning and learners who have a narrow range of learning strategies. Conversely, where talk is seen as central to learning and teachers take time to nurture each child's 'personal voice', which includes the understandings the child brings into the classroom, there is the basis for creating positive learning based on effective social relationships (Clark 2001: 83). Clark adds that children need to feel valued as individuals if they are to be motivated to learn and that individual identity involves confidence in the teacher's acknowledgement of their personal voice.

Below, I explore what a more creative approach to learning, using oracy, entails. First, let us consider what talk is. That may seem a vacuous statement at face value, but given the tendency to perceive talk as a restricted, teacher-led routine requiring low levels of cognition, there is a need to explore and understand the reasons why talk has had such a lowly status in many English classrooms. The low regard for talk has perhaps been compounded by a common-sense perception of the hard-working class, as one characterised by individual endeavour on the part of pupils; one where pupils are inevitably engaged in silent writing and reading. Halliday (1985: 100 cited in Bunting 2000) considers that while written and spoken modes of language exploit different features of the linguistic system, talk should not be viewed as formless interaction, lacking logic and structure. Indeed, he forcefully states that a contrary view would be 'a myth – and a pernicious one at that, since it prevents us from recognising its (talk's) critical role in learning'. Bunting (2000: 34) suggests that instead of viewing talk and writing as separate forms, it might be more appropriate to consider the function and purpose of each in the context of social interaction. She asserts that some forms of writing are more speech-like in their purpose. These forms include informal letters, personal diaries and notes; whereas talk that is more like the written form includes, lectures and political speeches.

Speech, social class and ability

In an attempt to understand why talk has been seen as the poor relation of learning, it may be necessary to move beyond the classroom, to consider the social attributes of speech in society at large. Sociolinguists such as Trudgill (1975) have shown that the way a person speaks is a marker of social identity. Accent (the pronunciation of words) and dialect (vocabulary and syntax) characterise regional and social class origins, with some accents and dialects perceived to be more prestigious than others. Received pronunciation and Standard English are the accent and dialect, respectively, considered to be 'good' English; whereas many working-class and regional accents and dialects are perceived to be 'poor' English, or aberrations of the 'standard'.

However, Standard English is no more than a dialect that is no better or worse than any other dialect. Linguists conclude that all dialects are regular logical syntactic forms (Labov 1988). Views of different accents and dialects have their basis in social attitude rather than linguistic study. In our society, parallel to these attitudes to accents and dialects has been a view that prestigious dialects imply intellectual capability, while those who speak in ways perceived to be of lower status are intellectually 'challenged'.

A further dimension to this illusory dichotomy is the latent but influential belief that originates from eugenicist theories, which assert that different social classes reflect innately different levels of intelligence. One example of this pernicious belief was the tripartite education system and selection tests at eleven introduced in the 1944 education Act. The 11 plus, as it was widely known, was based on the spurious research of the eugenicist, Sir Cyril Burt. The fact that selection at eleven remains in some local authorities is indicative of the resilience of this outmoded strain of thinking.

Talk, social class and cognitive ability have been wrapped in a neat stereotypical package. Old ideas, no matter how ill-grounded, can be difficult to change, particularly when they are embedded in the 'common-sense' view of prejudice. They reveal themselves even today when individual teachers make statements along the lines of, 'these children have little language', or 'what can you expect of these children given where they come from?' Invariably when I have heard teachers say these things it has been with reference to pupils from working-class homes. The deficit view of working-class children's language was compounded by the work of Bernstein (1974) who suggested that the reason many working-class children failed in the school system was due to their mode of speech. He claimed that working-class families spoke a 'restricted code', whereas in addition to this code, middle-class families spoke an 'elaborated code'. The 'restricted code' was characterised by implicit language. The 'elaborated code', on the other hand, involved explicit speech, the kind of language expected in school for academic achievement. In some quarters, the links between social class, language and poor educational achievement formed a powerful, if erroneous, thesis that working-class children's language was deficient.

Deficit models of language have since been challenged by studies of children's language use both in home and school. Tizard and Hughes (1984) investigated the language of two sets of girls of Nursery school age. Although they found some marginal difference in the way language was used in the home between working-class and middle-class mothers and their daughters, there was a significant difference in the way teachers interacted with girls of different social class. It was found that teachers interacted more with the middle-class girls, asking them more open ended questions; whereas with the working-class girls they asked closed questions, requiring no more than single word responses. Labov's (1988) study of the oral language of young Black men in New York found that social context and differences of power in social interactions influenced the young men's responses. When the young men were made to feel at ease and were shown respect, their use of language changed from monosyllabic utterances to more extended ones. These studies have encouraged a view of language difference, rather than deficit. From this brief discussion, it can be seen that perception of language use is imbued with value judgements about the user's social and intellectual status. For this reason, language is never neutral or value free. Language always occurs in a social context; it is culturally bound and operates in socially constructed system of power.

As Barnes (1976) has demonstrated, classrooms are social arenas in which social relations are constructed by teachers who control the forms of communication available to pupils. Drawing upon the evidence provided by educationists discussed above, we might conclude that restrictive forms of classroom discourse are influenced by the teacher's perception of pupils' language abilities. Such perceptions may be influenced by social class prejudice. Similar prejudices might occur in the case of children who are developing English as an additional language. Prejudice of whatever type constrains learning and restricts the possibilities for creative teaching. For this reason, courses of Initial Teacher Education (ITE) need to engage student teachers in critical reflection of their own attitudes and perceptions of groups of pupils that have been marginalised in education. The prevalent use of I-R-F discourse maybe further compounded by traditional classroom cultures.

Speaking and listening in inclusive classrooms

Creative teachers take a critical view of language and embrace difference in their classrooms. They create an inclusive classroom ethos where difference is seen for what it is, difference. They recognise that children bring into the classroom a wealth of implicit knowledge of language, acquired from home, family and neighbourhood. They recognise too that children have constructed, in creative ways, their language in relation to popular culture. This is often evident in their use of rhyme, chants, clapping games and the subversion of popular songs. Grugeon's (2005) work has reflected this use of language by children and has shown how the school playground can be a purposeful site of pupil interaction. If handled sensitively, children's imaginative play, incorporating their control of the discourses of popular culture, can be a useful stimulus for further language development in the classroom.

Contrary to the predominant view of talk as discussed above, there has been a strong educational discourse in which the value of talk has been recognised as a powerful tool for learning. Collaborative talk, strongly advocated by Barnes (1976) is one means by which teachers hand talk 'for learning' to pupils, rather than dominate it themselves. Blatchford *et al.* (2003 cited in Myhill and Fisher 2005) note that in group talk power is more evenly distributed than in pupil–teacher interaction. Bearing in mind Labov's findings, we might speculate that those pupils who have a dislike of teacher-led whole class interactive teaching are given an opportunity to find their voice and express their ideas through group work. Collaborative talk involves pupils working in groups purposively discussing issues and solving problems collectively. Done properly, collaborative talk, requires very careful planning and preparation on the part of the teacher. The essential characteristics of good planning for collaborative talk involve careful consideration of group composition, ground rules for talk, rehearsal of discursive practices and tasks that require collective enterprise for their successful completion. When forming groups for collaborative talk, consideration needs to be given to the different learning styles of pupils and the ability of individual pupils to interact effectively with certain other pupils: the so-called social 'chemistry' of the group. In short, the group should consist of combinations of pupils who are going to interact well with one another. However, this means more than simply being able to hold a sustained discussion independent of the teacher, as is shown below. Effective talk in groups is only likely to occur if pupils have already devised and taken ownership of a set of rules for group discussion. Such rules might include the following agreements:

- to share ideas;

- to listen to each other;

- to take turns and talk one at a time;

- to respect one another's opinions;

- to give reasons and to explain ideas;

- to ask the reason 'why?' if we disagree with others;

- to try to agree at the end of the discussion.

Mercer (2000)

Once ground rules have been established, they need to be piloted and evaluated by pupils themselves in order to firmly embed their importance. Different types of pupil interaction need to be rehearsed. Pupils need to be prepared for occasions when they will be required to talk in groups. Such preparation can begin with circle time activities which inculcate a respect for the voice of others and the value of one's own voice, as well as the importance of turn-taking. The use of talk-partners is another effective way of introducing pupils to the value of talk. It enables teachers to ask questions that require different types of thinking. Questions need to be carefully framed in initial planning and asked using precise language, so that pupils are clear about what they are being asked to discuss. The time given to pupils to discuss an individual question will be dependent upon the type of question, the thinking it generates and the experience of pupils in the use of paired talk. The use of talk-partners encourages pupils to engage with their thinking and to articulate thought through spoken language. It also allows them the time to think and frame, or re-frame, their thinking before answering a question. Further opportunities to rehearse talk in carefully structured ways occur in plenary sessions where pupils review their learning.

Certain lessons lend themselves to other occasions for talk. Any lesson involving pupils demonstrating practical work, such as in P.E., Games and Drama, provide opportunities for pupils to evaluate what they have observed. Through evaluations, pupils are learning to exercise critical thinking by identifying what was positive in a performance but, more importantly, to explain the reason for their thinking. Pupils who have been well rehearsed in these structured but 'teacher-reduced' forms of classroom talk will be better prepared to engage in collaborative talk independent of the teacher, because they will have realised the value of talk for helping them to make intellectual realisations. The preparation of tasks for collaborative talk can be time-consuming. Even when they are not, teachers need to be clear about the learning they expect from pupils. Essentially, tasks need to be designed to give each pupil an integral role in the group's discussion and it is vital that the task cannot be completed without the engagement of all pupils.

From the above discussion it is clear that creative classrooms and creative teaching require greater emphasis to be given to pupils talking in small groups. However, not all group talk will be purposeful. Group talk may be no more than a replication of teacher talk with one pupil imitating the role of the teacher (Haworth 1999). In addition, certain forms of group talk have no greater value than I-R-F discourse. It is important, therefore, for teachers and pupils to be able to identify when talk is purposeful and when it is not. Mercer (2000) identifies three types of talk: disputational, cumulative and exploratory. Of the three, disputational talk is the least educationally valuable because it involves pupils in disagreement with one another with little or no justification given for different views. Cumulative talk is where pupils interact purposefully, moving talk forward, largely through agreement with one another. However, this type of talk does not necessarily lead to higher order thinking. The most valuable and creative form of talk is exploratory in nature. Mercer (2000) defines exploratory talk as that in which pupils interact critically but constructively, engaging each others ideas by jointly considering information. Differences of opinion are supported with reasons that may be challenged and re-challenged. Essentially pupils' reasoning is explicit through the discussion and knowledge is negotiated, leading to agreement in order to make collective progress. We might conclude then that exploratory talk is a form of collaborative talk that engages speakers in the pursuit of mutual learning and understanding by means of joint interrogation of information and ideas. Mutual understanding is achieved through discursive utterances that both challenge and justify reasoning.

Handing the control of talk to pupils can take a huge leap of faith for some teachers, particularly when working with younger pupils in the primary age range. However, several studies show that collaborative talk can be effective with a wide age range of pupils. Woodruff and Brett (1999 cited in Myhill and Fisher 2005) noted that Year 5 and 6 pupils were able to understand the concept of task-based talk as inquiry. Wegerif et al. (1999 cited in Myhil and Fisher 2005) confirmed that eight- and nine-year-olds, taught how to undertake collaborative talk, were able to make 'joint reasoning explicit'. Using circle time as a springboard for pupil initiated talk, DeSouza (2003 unpublished) found that Reception and Year 1 pupils, working jointly, were able to draw on a knowledge of world events to discuss their thinking.

Certainly the move to exploratory talk needs to be carefully managed. However, talk for learning can be implemented by planning for different types of collaboration. Strategies for talk include snowballing, jigsaw activities etc. Snowballing involves pupils talking in pairs about a subject, or problem. The aim is to reach a joint consensus. Pairs are then combined to form a group of four and the respective outcomes of paired discussion are compared. Reasons are given for the consensus reached and a new consensus is sought by the new group. Pupils should be made aware of the purpose of discussion, which may be the need to report back to the whole class. Feedback from each group may lead to further, whole class discussion, or it may result in the teacher scribing and summarising pupils' thinking.

Jigsaw activities begin with pupils working in small groups. Each group is given a text or part of a text on a subject being studied by the whole class. By reading and discussing the text group members acquire knowledge that no other group has. The texts are then removed from classroom circulation and the class is regrouped so that the new group consists of one member from all the other groups. The purpose of the regrouping is to enable pupils to share knowledge gained through the initial task of discussing the text in the first group. This is a particular useful activity for introducing or revising a subject because it enables pupils to gain collective knowledge quickly. This strategy does not necessarily involve exploratory talk but it does enable pupils greater ownership of knowledge than I-R-F discourse.

Assessing group talk

In order that teachers might successfully identify these different types of talk and the different roles that pupils adopt in group discussion, there needs to be opportunities to record and analyse collaborative talk. Initially, this will require audio or video recording group talk, followed by a transcription so that utterances can be coded. Both forms of recording have their advantages and disadvantages. The advantage of audio recording, particularly using compact, multidirectional recorders, such as an H2 Zoom portable recorder, is the unobtrusive nature of the activity. However, what audio recording loses and video gains are the paralinguistic features of talk. One significant difference between spoken language and the written form is the way we use our bodies to contribute to what is said, or how we respond to what is said. An expression, gesture, or the way a person moves during conversation signals meaning. These paralinguistic accompaniments to what is actually said, or to what is actually heard, can 'speak louder than words' and if we miss them, we may fail to appreciate the role that a particular group member has played in the ensuing conversation. Some children will speak more than others, but that does not necessarily make them better at talking. Sometimes the child who listens to others and then contributes may be the one who clarifies meaning, or who moves learning forward. Of course, an audio recording may imply the active listener but video makes their paralinguistic signals explicit. The main drawback with using video is that the presence of the camera may affect the natural behaviour of the group, unless pupils are so familiar with being filmed it is 'second nature' to them.

The recording and transcribing of group talk is a time-consuming process; too time-consuming for busy teachers to undertake on a regular basis. However, it could be undertaken as a continuing professional development (CPD) activity during one of the school's training days and followed up periodically as an assessment tool. Students at the University of Bedfordshire undertake such an exercise as a preparation activity for a written assessment on talk for learning. Students are provided with an analytical grid for coding utterances (see Table 3.1).

The names of pupils in the group are inserted in the top row of the chart. Utterances are then numbered on the transcript of the group's talk. Each child's separate contributions to the discussion are then classified alongside the

TABLE 3.1 Analysing and assessing talk

Types of Utterance/Names of pupils				
Questions				
Seeking confirmation				
Clarifying questions				
Hypothetical questions				
Statements				
Assertions				
Confirmation				
Tentative				
Managing task				
Disputational				
Cumulative				
Exploratory				

categories listed in the first column. This is done by writing the number of the utterance under the name of the child and alongside the relevant type of utterance. Some utterances may be coded twice. For example, a hypothetical question could change the direction of the conversation and might be judged to have assisted in the management of the task, or an assertion might also be coded as disputational talk. As with most assessment of language there needs to be a degree of qualitative judgement on the part of the teacher or student teacher. Once completed, the table can then be used to analyse both an individual's talk as well as that of the whole group. The following questions can be used to interrogate the data.

Analysing small group talk: key questions.

1   Is there a parity of types of utterance within the group or do certain pupils appear to use particular types of utterance?

2   Do the types of utterance being used change as discussion progresses?

3   Are the pupils exploring the subject matter and trying to justify their reasons?

4   Do particular pupils take charge of managing the discussion?

5   What does the pattern of utterances tell you,

   a)   about the talk of specific individuals,

   b)   about how this group interacts in discussion?

Which pupils make fewer utterances than others and why might this be the case? Is there evidence to suggest they are active listeners who make purposeful contributions at appropriate times? What does the analysis tell us about the nature of the group's thinking and learning?

What students find is that most utterances early in group talk tend to be classified as cumulative, but that as talk progresses utterances become increasingly exploratory. This suggests that pupils need time to develop purposeful conversation in group situations, with minimal teacher intervention. As well as its use as an analytical tool, the grid can also be used as self-evaluation by the teacher. Returning to Haworth's (1999) findings, teachers may perceive their own discourse reflected in the talk of their pupils. Where interactive teaching is of the I-R-F pattern, ameliorative action can be taken to change the nature of teacher talk and model for pupils more appropriate types of talk for learning. Drawing upon international comparisons of classroom talk, Alexander (2008) found significant differences in the value given to talk by teachers elsewhere, compared to teachers in English schools. In particular, he found that oracy and literacy were given equal importance and that talk was intrinsic to the development of literacy. A high proportion of learning involved talk and there was a good deal of talk about texts. Talk was used for formal assessments, whereas in England Standard Assessment Tests (SATs) assessments are exclusively written. Most significantly, Alexander found little evidence of I-R-F discourse in teacher–pupil talk. Instead, talk involved teachers using questions to develop pupils' thinking through extended interactions. Pupils were often given thinking-time before answering questions and wrong answers were used to develop understanding. In short teacher–pupil talk had a higher cognitive function than that allowed by I-R-F discourse. Alexander's findings are corroborated by studies in the USA and Australia where classroom practice was influenced by social-constructivist learning theory (Geekie et al. 1999; Many 2002), both of which are cited in (Myhill and Fisher 2005). The latter study also confirmed that through extended teacher–pupil talk meanings are negotiated, rather than given by the teacher.

Dialogic talk, as advocated by Alexander and referred to in the Primary National Strategy's Literacy Framework (DfES 2006), albeit without explanation, involves the development of understanding through collaboration and discussion. Teachers use language to model talk and its accompanying thinking processes.

This is done by means of teacher–pupil interactions that build a coherent and emerging sequence of enquiry and understanding. The emphasis on who talks most in classrooms is passed from the teacher to pupils, making what pupils say more important than what teachers say. In short, dialogic talk extends higher order thinking by being:

- Collectively framed – everyone learning together;

- Reciprocal – teacher and pupils share ideas and consider alternatives;

- Supportive – children articulate ideas and support one another to reach common understandings;

- Cumulative – teachers and pupils build their own and other's ideas into coherent lines of enquiry and thinking;

- Purposeful – talk is geared to specific educational goals.

In conclusion, the way that talk is modelled by the teacher and the time given to pupils to engage in talk influences particular types of learner and particular types of learning. The prevalent use of I-R-F discourse, with its tendency to focus on knowledge and comprehension-type questions, leads to superficial learning whereas dialogic talk, which encourages pupils to develop exploratory talk, creates learners who construct knowledge by means of negotiated meanings. Creative teachers, working in creative classrooms, will use talk for a variety of purposes. There will be occasions when the asking of closed questions may be appropriate but, in the main, creative teachers foster the use of dialogic and collaborative talk for learning. They also utilise the linguistic resources of pupils, rather than assume that some pupils have limited competence in language. As discussed above, pupils' social class backgrounds can sometimes lead teachers into stereotypical assumptions about pupils' ability to use language. The same point can be applied to pupils' ethnic backgrounds. Such prejudices hinder, rather than enhance, creativity and need to be challenged by personal self-reflection on the part of the teacher. Challenging one's prejudices is an essential component of teachers' professionalism.

In this chapter, some active learning strategies have been discussed but the examples given are by no means exhaustive. Any learning activity that requires pupils to collaborate in order to achieve a collective outcome is likely to engender purposeful talk. Drama, the subject of the next chapter, is an obvious aspect of the curriculum where pupils utilise and extend existing linguistic resources. Later in the book, when dealing with non-fiction, an example of a collaborative activity using short texts to complete the labelling of a diagram is given. In order to complete the task pupils must share newly acquired knowledge in order to come to collective understanding through talk. Learners who are empowered by the experience of negotiating meanings and exploring their own thinking, as well as that of others, will have realised the creative power of their own minds. Equipped with the knowledge of how to think, and the realisation that they are able to think for themselves, pupils are more likely to develop as lifelong learners. The same cannot be said of those schooled in I-R-F methods of educational discourse. If pupils are to make such a realisation it means that we, as teachers, have to talk less and enable our pupils to talk more. However, pupil talk must be purposeful if it is to be meaningful. Classroom talk needs careful planning and it is in the planning of talk that teachers exercise their creativity. Creativity at the planning stage enables pupils to be creative in the classroom.

'The play's the thing ...'

WITH DRAMA ONCE AGAIN on the educational agenda, this chapter explores the following:

- the nature of drama as an educational strategy;
- how drama brings the outside world into the classroom;
- reading and writing in role;
- using puppets to create narrative voices.

The place of drama in the English education system has had an uncertain development. After being the international leader in drama education during the latter part of the twentieth century (Heath and Wolf 2005), drama disappeared from the primary classroom for a decade or more following the implementation of the National Curriculum (DES 1988). Its revival occurred with the revised curriculum (DfEE/QCA 1999a) and its place in the primary curriculum was reinforced with its inclusion as a distinct strand in the Primary National Strategy (DfES 2006). Old debates located around the dichotomy of drama as performance and drama as process atrophied in the intervening years and with its reappearance these polarities became fused in what Clipson-Boyles (1997) refers to as 'new wave drama'. As discussed below, the revitalised version combined experiential modes of drama, sustained through improvisation (process) with the skills of theatre and drama as an art form (product). In the current climate drama can be viewed as both an entity in its own right and a means for learning. As a rich and diverse means of learning with no single pedagogic mode, drama provides teachers with a wide range of creative and highly flexible techniques, strategies and devices. It is a means for bringing the outside world into the classroom; it is shaped through collaborative action, making learning a social and inclusive experience; it stimulates the affective aspects of learners and, under the guidance of a teacher skilled in its techniques, it combines feeling, thought and language into a holistic form of meaning construction. It promotes both personal introspection and the potential for both self-awareness and social awareness, through the exploration of real human issues. These impressive attributes make drama a potent pedagogic process.

From its origins in early human behaviour drama has been mimetic in nature. It is an art form that draws heavily on the social world for its source of material. It is likely that the very earliest forms of drama involved dance and sound which were used to represent aspects of humanity's primary needs and rites of passage: hunting, birth, death. As artistic culture developed, drama evolved around its three elements of dialogue, character and plot and dealt with tensions and conflicts of the 'human condition'. As Heathcote (1978) succinctly puts it, 'Drama is a real man (sic) in a mess'. Taking conflict in the real world as its central dilemma, the dramatic representation seeks to play out the effects of that conflict on human lives (characters) and how they resolve, or fail to resolve that conflict. The conflict is represented by means of characters playing out their actions in a sequence of events (plot). Their thoughts and emotions are articulated through dialogue but in the stage play, as opposed to radio drama, dialogue is accompanied by spectacle. Drama is, as Martin Esslin (1987) puts it, 'a narrative made visible'. As such, then, it is not only words, but expression and gesture that combine to articulate dramatic meaning. Through drama, as in real life, we read meaning by simultaneous analysis of both the spoken word and accompanying paralinguistic signs (body language) that combine to make up the totality of human language. By standing outside a set of actions, as a viewer, rather than being immersed in them, as a participant, as is the case in real life, we are in the privileged position of being able to question matters with some degree of objectivity. This is the educational value of drama as product, or theatre. It is important, therefore, that children have ample opportunity to see good theatre, both in school and in their community. But the real value of drama is its application to the classroom for learning through action. Reflecting on Heathcote's perception of drama in education, Baird Shuman (1978: xi) says:

> educational drama as Heathcote perceives it projects a situation that poses a dilemma and the drama unfolds as the dilemma is examined by the participants in the drama, who are working toward a resolution. In so working, they escape from themselves into another being. Just as reading literature helps one to experience vicariously events, situations, and emotions which cannot be experienced at first hand, so does educational drama enable students to get inside the consciousness of other beings and to experience a critical segment of life as those beings experience it.

Drama, pedagogy and learning

So, drama provides the means for replicating in the classroom some of the dilemmas of real life. However, if taken no further than allowing pupils to merely 'experience' what it is like being in someone else's shoes in a given situation, drama may move no further than the affective domain. Experience needs to be reflected upon, analysed and evaluated for real learning to occur. This is where the dichotomy that once existed between drama as art, or product (theatre), and drama as process or experience (educational drama) has been replaced by a view that synthesises the two. This is because drama in education utilises techniques that combine the role of the pupil as both participant and spectator. These techniques arise out of the recognition that drama is a construct; a way of simulating the experiences of real life, without being real in themselves. Whereas early drama practitioners focused on affective responses by advocating improvisation in real time without identifiable outcomes, more recent approaches to drama recognise the pedagogic value of 'breaking' the drama at appropriate interludes to reflect on experience and affective responses (Fleming 1997). This puts the teacher in control of a process that allows pupils to both experience simulations of real life, or the enactment of texts and subtexts, by being 'inside' those events and to reflect on those experiences by standing outside the drama, viewing and commenting on it as a spectator might.

Pedagogic uses of drama consist of a repertoire of strategies to turn pupils from 'experience', or 'participants in role' (Bolton 1984) to reflection on 'experience'. Such devices as 'freeze framing', 'hot-seating', 'conscience alley' etc. enable the action to be interrupted, considered, discussed, challenged and used publicly as a means for collective learning. These devices combine affective responses of pupils with cognitive processes, including reflection, analysis and the evaluation of human behaviour and motives. This pedagogy places the teacher in a pivotal role by allowing her/him to frame, reframe and deconstruct the experiential contexts in which pupils are placed. As such, the teacher is located at the centre of a Vygotskian model of learning in which thought and emotion are used as the raw material for reflective discussion and the basis for the social construction of meanings.

Although this sounds like an elaborate pedagogy, the beauty of drama is that it can be exemplified in simple ways. For example, elsewhere (Grugeon and Gardner 2000), I relate an occasion when I went into role as a ten-year-old boy during circle time. 'Billy' talked about how he was tired of all the rows at home between his mum and dad; how he had to console his younger brother at night because the arguing prevented him from getting to sleep. 'Billy' had packed a little suitcase, hidden in his wardrobe. It contained simple things: his favourite toy, his toothbrush, a few clothes. As I drew to the end of this fictional anecdote,

I said, 'I was sure that one of these nights, when mum and dad were fast asleep, when there was silence, I would creep down the stairs, open the front door and step out into the darkness'. Words such as 'silence', 'creep' and 'darkness' were chosen carefully and, in good dramatic tradition, foreshadowed potential dangers. My final words to the class were in the form of a question, 'What do you think I should do?' My class of ten-year-olds responded with insightful comments, showing they had reflected thoughtfully on 'Billy's' plight:

'He should talk to his mum and dad, tell them how he is thinking.'

'If he cannot talk to his mum and dad he could talk to his granny, or an aunty and tell them.'

'Who will be there for his brother, if he goes?'

'He should stay at home, there are strange people out at night.'

Although the pupils were not themselves involved as participants in role, the use of narrative voice and teacher in role created sufficient dramatic exposition for their thoughts to flourish. This example demonstrates the flexibility and potency of drama. In all, the anecdote in role and subsequent advice from pupils took no longer than five to ten minutes, proving that drama does not require set lessons of extended time. The power of the strategy of teacher in role is demonstrated by the quality and sophistication of the responses of the ten-year-old pupils. Billy's dilemma was made 'real' for them. As the teacher, I created the context for their imaginations to make the situation meaningful. As such, the context connected with their own experience. What child has not wanted to run away from home at some point? How many children have heard their parents argue and have felt affected by it, vulnerable even? When one child said, 'I know how he feels', she demonstrated both her affective and cognitive similarity with Billy. It is not possible to know whether she took the advice of her peers and talked to someone about her feelings, but this brief circle-time discussion provided her with a potential avenue for the possible resolution to her concerns. This example also shows that learning can be tightly controlled by the teacher, yet also create the space for the pupil voice and the scope for their empowerment.

The meeting of primary and secondary worlds through drama

It is not my purpose in this book to provide a comprehensive list of the specific drama techniques available to teachers. Clipson-Boyles (1999: 136) provides such a list, together with brief examples of literacy events that can ensue from such techniques as 'guided action', 'tableau' or 'dynamic duos'.

Drama: a bridge between real and imagined worlds

Drama provides pupils with the opportunity to control the enactment of experiences from the real world. As such it is a bridge between what Auden (1954 cited in Carter 2000: 11) refers to as the primary and secondary worlds of the writer. The primary being the real world as it is experienced and the secondary being that which is imagined in the writer's mind, but which is firmly located in lived experience. Through drama, under the careful guidance of a skilled teacher, pupils are able to take experience from the real world and control it, shape it, re-create it, reinvent and interpret it. The drama becomes an artefact, an intermediary between reality and imagination, a material phenomenon that is very like the real thing, but is not quite like it. This materiality, a term used by Derrida, (cited in Carter 2000: 21) to refer to texts, if viewed by others, becomes an object capable of investigation, a spectacle open to critical scrutiny, both of itself, as an artefact, and as a representation of an aspect of the real world. When pupils spontaneously produce dialogue and action through improvised drama, they are making material their thoughts. This 'materiality' becomes a text to be read by those who have produced it, as well as those who become its spectators. In the next chapter, which examines ways of using film construction in the classroom, I provide an example of how improvisation might be used as the first draft of a scripted drama.

Drama, then, provides the means by which real lived experience can be brought into the classroom and used as a resource for learning. Learning may take place at several stages and different levels. For those engaged in the enactment, learning involves taking decisions and making choices about what to include and what to leave out. Such decisions are the first stage of the creative process of drafting a narrative, and because drama involves pupils working together in groups, learning is supported by means of collaborative action. The process of doing drama, of making considered selections as a group in order to shape a narrative, is akin to the writer undergoing the same process in isolation. As such then, drama is not only important for English as a subset of speaking and listening, it can be used as a device for rehearsing writing. We shall return to this point later when considering the practical means by which this may be done. For the time being let us explore further how the drama may, of itself, stimulate learning. Not only are pupils selecting from lived experience or observation of lived experience, in order to create a narrative, they are also making choices about the language that is appropriate to the characters they are representing. This involves choices at lexical and sentence level, albeit that we rarely utter sentences when talking, and ultimately these linguistic choices contribute to the shape of the whole narrative. The making of choices involves pupils reflecting on appropriate language and behaviour in a specific social context. When pupils make thought material through spontaneous speech during improvised drama, they are able to reflect upon speech, as text, and make instant judgements about the authenticity of what they say.

Implicit to reflection is the cognitive process of analysis; the un-picking of reasons why a character uses certain words and behaves in a certain way, and the reasons that might motivate a character to behave in a particular way. The end result of this process of doing drama is a product, an artefact, that can be made available to others in the form of a presentation. At this point a second stage of learning is opened up. In the form of a presentation, the drama invites an audience to spectate the unfolding of human action and language. Pupils as spectators, if encouraged to do so by their teacher, are able to evaluate, not only the quality and authenticity of the drama itself, but also the language and human action on which the drama is based. In this way, critical thought can simultaneously be given to the drama as art, that is the creative construction from real experience and its believability as an imitation of the real, or primary world, referred to by Auden, and to the human issues that arise out of the drama, which are drawn from the primary world of experience. To these ends we might ask pupils first to comment on how real or believable the drama was; how plausible was the behaviour of the characters; how authentic were their words. A second set of questions might be aimed at the issues that arise from the drama; the reasons why particular words were used; explanations for the reactions of certain characters and their motives for doing what they did; and judgements can be made – was the character right to act in the way they did; what might the consequences of their action be; how did language and behaviour affect others; what affect did it have on the spectator? Hence, drama as process and drama as product provide the means for a creating a synthesised resource that can be evaluated through collective scrutiny by pupils under the guidance of the teacher.

Exploring narrative and writing in role

In the chapter on story, I refer to epic narrative writing, using a little-known story called, *The Voyage of Prince Fuji* (Thorne 1980). One episode of story making, based on the book, involved pupils writing in role as the eponymous character, Fuji. The session was tightly structured, commencing with concentration exercises, followed by the identification of Fuji's significant character traits, which had been partially explored in the previous session. The purpose of requiring pupils to assume the character of Fuji, to sit and move as he might, was to refocus pupils' thinking of him as the central character and to allow them to get 'inside' the character's thoughts and feelings. Using the technique of 'thought-tracking', I moved around the room after telling pupils that if I touched them on the shoulder, I wanted them to tell me one thing about their character's personality. This opening to the session was consolidated at the next stage by pair work in which Fuji ordered one of his courtiers to collect a list of items he required for his voyage. At a relevant point, the action was 'frozen' and the courtiers view of Fuji was captured using the same technique. At this point in the session I adopted the role of the narrator, telling pupils that several days after embarking on his voyage, a terrible storm broke, tossing Fuji's ship about on the sea like a tiny cork. Using the whole class, we created a body sculpture of the ship and the raging sea breaking over the sides and used the image to once again capture pupils' thoughts about how Fuji might be feeling at this point on his journey. Predictions were made about what might happen next. Invariably, pupils predicted Fuji would survive the storm, but might be shipwrecked. These predictions provided the causal link for the next set of events. Fuji, wracked with pain and exhaustion, managed to swim to land, but which land? Not his own. He wandered for a day, venturing into a town, where he was immediately singled out as different. Soldiers arrested him and took him to the king, where he was ordered to explain his presence in the town. His audience with the king was improvised in small groups and selected pupils were asked to explain Fuji's feelings at this juncture, using the technique of 'hot-seating'. Their comments reflected Fuji's change in fortune and his sudden sense of powerlessness. The king decided Fuji was a spy and had him imprisoned. In his prison cell, sat alone in the darkness, he thought about how he had left his wife in search of adventure. His sense of isolation and the memories of his wife made him want to write to her. So, taking his pen and a scrap of paper, and finding a thin ray of light, he wrote her a letter. For the next six minutes pupils wrote in complete silence, without further prompting. Fortunately, Fuji was on good terms with the gaoler, who was persuaded to post his letter for him. The letters were passed from one pupil to another. Once in receipt of a letter from another pupil, it was read from the perspective of Fuji's wife. At the end of the reading, I asked pupils to tell me how Fuji's wife might respond to the letter and the reasons why.

Reading in role had established a context for interpreting what was written, just as writing in role created the context for framing language and thought for a specific, highly personal audience, and pupils responded to the affective qualities of the writing, commenting on how certain words and phrases had made them feel.

Within a dramatised episode of an epic tale, the four language modes of speaking and listening, reading and writing had been integrated, using narrative structure as the frame for developing affective responses and empathy. Talk in action had been used as a prelude to writing and kinaesthetic learning had contributed to independent thought, lexical and textual choices. For those pupils who are unable to write independently, Johnson (2000: 85) discusses how the teacher can act as scribe. She describes how, whilst enacting the story of the Pied Piper of Hamelin, pupils and their teacher wrote a letter to the Mayor of the town, as its citizens, demanding something be done about the growing number of rats that plagued their lives. By adopting the role of scribe, the teacher was affirming the role of the pupils as composers of text. This activity also provided a purposeful social context for the modelling of formal letter writing. These examples serve to illustrate how drama can be used to create imagined worlds in which pupils are able to adopt the lives of imagined characters and how within such imaginings literacy can be embedded in plausible ways.

Let the puppet talk

Some pupils are confident talkers, no matter what their age; others are not. Some children do not like to speak in large groups for various reasons; they are timorous, or they prefer to reflect on what others have said before speaking themselves. Some cultural practices encourage the view that children should speak only when invited to do so by an adult. Children for whom English is an Additional Language (EAL) may be reticent to speak publicly, preferring small group or paired conversations. Conversely, there will be pupils who come 'alive' through the oral mode; some for whom writing is a chore and the opportunity to literally 'speak their mind' enables them to show the power of their thinking. In any classroom there are likely to be pupils with capabilities that fall across a range of oral competencies and practices. Drama provides one means of equalising the potential for talk and for making it a satisfying experience for all pupils. In addition to the modes of drama discussed above, puppets provide a further means for developing language through action. Puppetry is an ancient art form with its origins in religious storytelling, but it transfers easily to the classroom and it is a relatively cheap resource to make or purchase. Puppets and the means for showing them can be made in Design Technology, although children can use them without such things as elaborate puppet theatres. Alternatively, there are several companies that produce well made, durable puppets. Contact addresses can be found at the end of the book. The use of puppets to retell stories already read to pupils has been adopted in Storysacks, although these tend to be for the younger age range. However, pupils across the whole primary age range can benefit from devising dramatic narratives using puppets.

Lloyd (1991), used his extensive knowledge of using glove puppets as a pedagogic resource in his school in Colaville. He outlines a five-phase approach to using puppets with pupils:

1 Phase One – Introducing glove puppets;
2 Phase Two – Creating the story;
3 Phase Three – Developing the dialogue;

4   Phase Four – Rehearsal in small scenes;

5   Phase Five – Performing.

In the first phase, children are given time to explore the puppets, to try them on, to 'bring them to life' by giving them a voice, animating them, and by engaging with other pupils in brief dialogues. The introduction need not be a formal one, on the part of the teacher. As pupils use the puppets, however, it is important that the teacher uses the time to assess how they interact with them and which children take readily to them and which one's may need further opportunities to use them. The second phase involves pupils deciding on a theme. It is likely that chosen themes will be influenced by prior knowledge of stories and children's popular culture. Alternatively, pupils may decide to retell an existing story. Each pupil selects a puppet they wish to use. Short snippets of the story are improvised and recorded. At this stage pupils begin to organise their thinking, with appropriate coaching from the teacher. Pupils who have little experience of performing in front of an audience may need to be reminded about such things as vocal volume and positioning, in relation to the audience. Without dominating the pupils' control of the story the teacher may also need to give advice about the pace and organisation of aspects of the story. The transcribed story is made into a class reader so that pupils can further familiarise themselves with their narrative. In phase three pupils work in pairs to dramatise parts of the written story. The focus is on developing the voice of the character; making dialogue flow; practising movements with the puppets; getting used to working in a confined space and working collaboratively with their partner. At the end of the session, time should be allocated for a brief evaluation of the work in progress.

Phase four is the main rehearsal stage when groups of pupils work together to tell the whole story. Moving from paired to group work requires careful management. Not only are pupils having to collaborate with one another in a confined space, they are having to learn that cooperation necessitates turn-taking, self-control and mutual support. Although difficulties arise, the group's enthusiasm is usually sufficient to overcome any hiccups. Further discussion to evaluate the work will help shape the story and its performance. The initial rehearsals are likely to require close attention from an adult but as the pupils become more adept support can be withdrawn. As far as possible the story and its telling should be 'owned' by the pupils themselves. Parallel to rehearsals pupils will need to gather any props they might need, prepare backdrops and choose appropriate music and sound effects. The final phase of the process is the actual performance. A performance is only ever going to be as good as the preparation that precedes it. It may be the first time that pupils have performed before an audience, which gives the performance an added dynamic. If all has gone well in rehearsals, the story will be well paced, fluent and have vitality. At the end of the show, there will be opportunities for pupils to get feedback from the audience.

Shadow puppets

Ewart (1998) draws on the tradition of Turkish shadow puppetry to do what Lloyd does with glove puppets. The Turkish shadow theatre dates from the sixteenth century and, at face value, appears to be a contradiction in Islam, which frowns upon the depiction of animate beings in art. However, the shadow puppet is accepted because its form is perforated and is not, therefore, an exact imitation of a lifelike being (Ewart 1998: 11). Shadow puppets are probably the cheapest form of puppet to make, requiring a sturdy stick and durable card, in addition to a light source. A translucent screen is useful but not necessary. Ewart offers further advice about helping pupils to construct the narrative and emphasises the importance of audience awareness. During the preparation for storytelling, with or without puppets, time needs to be given for pupils to discuss what makes a good story, but also what the storyteller needs to do to make the story interesting for an audience. As well as an introduction that sets the scene and introduces the characters to an audience, pupils need to be aware of character development and the use of repetition to remind the audience who the character is and the character's key traits. This can be done by the character speaking directly to the audience, although, in the case of shadow puppets this may need to be done by a glove puppet that is outside the action, acting as a kind of omniscient narrator. Ewart (1998: 74) advises that the best stories for shadow puppetry are those with a few, well developed characters. Shadow puppets do not offer the same physical flexibility as either glove or string puppets. However, Ewart suggests that performances need to be highly descriptive, which creates purposeful conditions for detailed language work.

String puppets (marionettes)

Different types of puppet create slightly different modes of presentation, requiring pupils to consider how best to tell the story using actions, words and special effects. Like shadow and glove puppets, performances with string puppets are usually 'framed' in a purpose-built proscenium arch, or screen. However, I have used string puppets perfectly well with pupils without a 'stage'. In one performance pupils used the carpeted area of the classroom to give a 'theatre-in-the-round' performance to their peers. As in the theatre of Bertolt Brecht, the magical element of the puppet disembodied from the puppeteer is absent because everyone can see the puppeteer pulling the strings and giving voice to the puppet, but this 'alienation effect', to use Brecht's term, did not detract from the power of the storytelling. In this particular case the puppets used originated in India, which enabled one pupil, whose family had their roots in Gujarat, to use her cultural knowledge to make the character she was playing authentic. She was also 'cast' as the expert during rehearsals and shared her knowledge with her English heritage peers who valued her advice. Not only did her oral language develop during the course of the puppet project, but so too did her self-confidence and esteem with other pupils. Sometimes it is the simplest of actions, such as the introduction of an artefact with a specific cultural location, that makes inclusive education a reality. In another instance, when working on a collaborative story-writing project, which I describe below; a particularly shy boy was overheard talking to his partner about dragons. He clearly knew a lot about them and I wanted him to share his knowledge with the rest of the class. He declined but agreed to tell his partner what he knew so he could impart the knowledge to their peers. When silence had been established, the partner began to tell the class about dragons but he made continual errors, causing the 'expert' to whisper the correct information. With each error the voice of the 'expert' grew louder until, frustrated by his friends failure to get the facts right, he turned to me and said, 'shall I tell them?'. He then shared his knowledge with the class without further hesitation. My experience leads me to the belief that creative classrooms are also inclusive classrooms. When pupils are given purposeful reasons to talk, when there is a real need for them to communicate, opportunities arise for them, to not only show what they know, but also to see that it is valued.

A rationale for working with puppets

Working with dramatisations of stories, using puppets, always creates surprises for the teacher. It offers a new way of working for pupils; a more kinaesthetic form of learning than is provided for by most lessons. It is possibly for this reason that some pupils are able to demonstrate, often for the first time, linguistic, organisational and interpersonal skills the teacher has not seen in them before. These revelations provide the teacher with fresh insights into the capabilities of these pupils and reference points for the direction of the pupil's further development. We might consider this point in the context of Vygotsky's (1962) Zone of Proximal Development (ZPD). ZPD refers to the difference between what a learner can achieve with support and what they can achieve without it. The ZPD is different for different learners on different pedagogic tasks. Essentially, what a learner achieves with support is indicative of their potential in the same area of learning. The physical use of the puppet; the active learning involved in story making and the collaborative nature of the task may all be contributory factors in helping specific pupils to demonstrate their ZPD, in terms of language use and narrative construction. In this way, the process of making the play and its performance could be regarded, not just as an end in itself, but as a form of formative assessment, or to use the more in vogue term, assessment for learning. Given the knowledge of the pupil's capabilities with language in performance, the teacher will need to devise strategies to help the pupil translate what they can achieve orally to achievements in writing.

We might pause at this point to consider why using a puppet might have helped a pupil demonstrate language abilities they have not shown before. Returning to Vygotsky, the conventional conceptualisation of ZPD involves a more expert 'other' assisting a learner to achieve, with support, what they cannot achieve independently. However, in this instance the pupil has worked with a puppet, not a more expert other. It is a well-known fact to language teachers that a learner's ability to understand language is in advance of their ability to produce it. We might say then that pupils have a repertoire of latent knowledge of language and that what they say, or write, is not indicative of their full language ability. Language development in the classroom is as much about creating the conditions under which pupils feel confident enough to draw upon their latent language, as it is about introducing pupils to new language. Vygotsky also refers to the learner's ability to internalise dialogue and it is possible the learner draws upon the repertoire of latent language to do this. We might speculate that the use of the puppet, because the pupil speaks through the inanimate character and must bring it to life, helps to externalise aspects of the pupil's latent knowledge of language, which is normally reserved for internal dialogue.

Our understanding from the field of second language acquisition is that the best way to help pupils develop another language is to create real purposes for communication, rather than to focus on the learning of the language itself. The use of the puppet in rehearsal does this by making learning stress-free. A further dimension to 'trigger' language is the dynamic interaction of peers through the collaborative process of story making. Hence, the physical and tactile nature of puppetry; the opportunity to practise language in rehearsal and the interactive nature of the learning process, all contribute to 'scaffold' learning and thereby enable pupils to utilise their latent knowledge of language. A pedagogic rationale such as this provides a strong theoretical basis for creative and imaginative forms of learning. We have considered puppetry in the context of English but what is said here is equally applicable to the teaching of 'primary languages'. A version of a story told in English could then be translated into another language and performed in that language. Alternatively, there may be a character in the play who speaks a language other than English. This would give an opportunity for bi or multilingual pupils to utilise their wider knowledge of language. It would also provide another opportunity for the teacher to see a further facet of a pupil's linguistic capabilities.

In summary, Figure 4.1 provides an at-a-glance model of the uses of drama. In essence, drama draws it's source material from the texts of real life, or from written, filmic or other visual texts. This source material is processed by pupils through pedagogic structures devised by the teacher. The outcome of this process

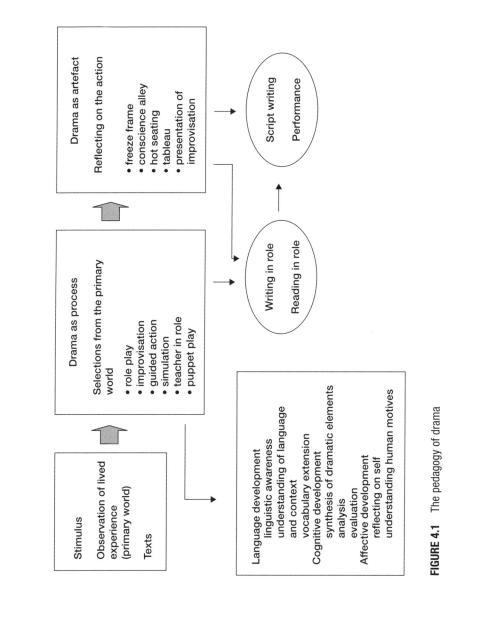

FIGURE 4.1 The pedagogy of drama

is an artefact, or text, capable of objective scrutiny by its creators and other pupils. Reflection and discussion may be the sole outcome of the use of drama. However, further products can be achieved by means of reading or writing in role, scriptwriting and performance. No matter whether the emphasis is on drama as a process in its own right, or is used to create an end product, the fact that it involves language, action and thought encourages pupils' linguistic, cognitive and affective development. Drama, then, is a superb multidimensional tool for thinking and learning and, as such, is a pivotal resource for creativity in the curriculum.

5

Scene one, take two

THIS CHAPTER EXPLORES the place of film in the primary classroom. It does so by:

- reconsidering the meaning of the term 'text' in the context of multimodal literacy;

- discussing the use of film as a creative resource for language and literacy development;

- providing several practical projects;

- introducing the language of film.

Once the domain of media studies in the secondary curriculum, film literacy has been promoted in the primary curriculum, largely by the British Film Institute.

In the twenty-first Century, the conventional meanings of terms such as 'text' and 'literacy' are being challenged. The term 'text' no longer refers exclusively to printed discourse and, likewise, literacy means more than the decoding and comprehension of conventional printed text. Indeed, Kress (2003) suggests that it is more appropriate to refer to literacy in its plural form, as literacies, and Bearne and Wolstencroft's (2007) work emphasises children's engagement with multimodal texts, that is texts which combine print and visual images. There is increasing recognition that children are immersed in a literate environment in which visual, auditory and printed information can be integrated into a single text, and that full comprehension of such multimodal texts requires the reader to move between modes, drawing connections between words, sounds and visual images.

The development of televisual and information technologies not only creates new types of text, but also new ways of reading and representing thought, which have implications for the way literacy is taught and the kind of literacies that are valid in the classroom (Kress 2003). Children bring into the classroom significant amounts of implicit knowledge of visual texts. It is a knowledge that forms a rich seam of potential for explicit learning, not only about how to read visual texts themselves, but it also provides opportunities for pupils to analyse how they process texts as readers and producers of text (Buckingham 1990). This involves classroom activities that encourage pupils to use their existing implicit knowledge of visual texts to explore the ways in which film conveys meaning. The practical application of film in the classroom is introduced by means of several film projects I use with my B.Ed English specialist undergraduate students at the University of Bedfordshire. Like other aspects of literacy, the study of film requires an appropriate language in order to describe and discuss items and processes. For this reason, a glossary of filmic terms has been included at the end of the chapter. If visual literacy is to become an integral feature of creative work in primary schools, we need to identify an appropriate body of subject knowledge and a metalanguage is an important first step.

Cinematic images: reading the signs

Film combines several semiotic systems, making it a rich, multilayered aesthetic medium. The study of semiotics involves an analysis of the relationship of signs and their meanings. In film there are at least four sign systems at work, often operating simultaneously. First, film draws on the aesthetics of pictorial art in order to create spatial relationships between objects, colour and perspective. Second, it uses dramatic conventions and the semiotics of expression, gesture, movement and body language. Third, dialogue between characters and other forms of verbal interaction utilise linguistic codes. Fourth, the musical score, sound effects and silence form aural signs or 'images'. If children are watching significant amounts of television and film each week, they are unwitting experts in reading the interplay of semiotic systems at work in film. However, children are often unaware of the semiotic skills they possess and often lack opportunities to describe, discuss and analyse what they see and hear.

Indeed, for some children their main source of implicit knowledge of narrative, character and setting may be through extensive exposure to films, watched on television or by means of DVDs. All too often children's exposure to television and film is disregarded as real knowledge because of a predominant discourse that is dismissive of children's popular culture. However, by watching films children are acquiring understandings of how human beings interact in communicative practice; they are learning that communication involves not just words but expressive paralinguistic signals through expression and gesture. They are learning too how the camera is the lens of narration. Film narratives share textual structures in common with print-based narratives. So, by watching films children are also acquiring knowledge of how stories are structured. They are also able to use their eye for detail, as viewers, in their writing, if they are made aware of the skill they have.

In his evaluation of the Story Shorts pilot project Parker (2002: 40 cited in Goodwin 2004: 138) notes how the 'deep links' between visual and print-based narratives enabled teachers to use pupils' implicit knowledge of film to scaffold pupils' writing development. Film makers use visual images in symbolic ways to suggest lateral meanings in the same way that writers use metaphor. The acquisition of visual literacy involves the ability to read these visual metaphors. According to the British Film Institute (BFI), by the time they are three children have learned the 'codes and conventions through which moving images tell stories' (BFI 2003: 3). A review of international research bears this out, to some extent. Close (2004) found that moderate viewing of age appropriate good quality television, among two- to five-year-olds, correlated well with levels of attention, comprehension, receptive vocabulary, aspects of expressive language, phonemic knowledge and knowledge of narrative. My own anecdotal observations of my son, Kiran, currently aged two, lead me to the view that young children are perfectly able to read the expressive symbols of televised drama. Whilst watching a scene in a hospital drama, (BBC 1 2008), in which a doctor, dealing with personal dilemma stands alone in a room, Kiran said, 'doctor hurt'. This one statement is indicative of a wide range of linguistic and semiotic skills possessed by this two-year-old. First, he showed great concentration to be able to follow a sequence of images that led to the scene in question. Furthermore, he was able to contextualise the scene in which the doctor stood, looking pensive. He read the doctor's body language and initiated an expressive utterance to give meaning to what he saw. The drama in question was by no means age-appropriate television for a two-year-old but had Kiran not been in the room we would never have witnessed his ability to comprehend the emotional state of the actor, nor his ability to use his emerging vocabulary to show understanding.

From this brief discussion, it is possible to see the value to teachers of harnessing the latent knowledge children bring with them into the classroom. I refer to this knowledge as latent or implicit because, like the acquisition of spoken language, it can be assimilated without explicit awareness of it having been learned. Hence, children can have knowledge of which they are not aware. The task of the teacher is to help pupils realise the skills and knowledge they already possess, enabling them to make what is implicit, explicit, so that it may be used as a means for conscious understanding and critical awareness. The development of visual literacy is, therefore, a valid enterprise in the primary classroom. It is valid in its own right but it is equally important for its application to conventional literacy too. In the next part of the chapter I want to explore the potential of film as a resource for learning. In order to do so, I am going to draw upon the experience of B.Ed students on one of my English specialist modules at the University of Bedfordshire. Students undertake several small film projects and use these to investigate the relationship of learning by means of film to other aspects of English, including speaking and listening, reading and writing.

Project one: narrative, subtext and scripts

In this project the camera is used as a means of recording action and sound with a view to writing a playscript. My starting point is a narrative text with strong subtextual scenarios. *The Finding* by Nina Bawden (1987) is a good example of a story with an exposition that is full of subtextual possibilities. The opening to the novel describes the Embankment on an early Sunday morning. A baby has been left in an untidy bundle at the foot of the Sphinx. We are told how a taxi driver found the baby and took it to the police station. Later the baby's adopted parents told him he was special because he was found. After reading the extract, students are asked to consider possible events outside the text. Working in small groups, they devise scenarios around key characters: the taxi driver, the mother who left the child, Alex, the boy who was left. The taxi driver scenario often involves him arriving home with the story of how he found the baby. The mother scenario might involve her in a state of angst talking to a friend, trying to come to terms with her personal dilemma of what to do with the baby. The scenario involving Alex takes place when he is eighteen and meets his biological mother for the first time. These improvised scenarios are filmed and replayed in camera. As they listen to their improvisation, students transcribe the dialogue onto the computer screen. The use of film provides the bridge between spontaneous speech, uttered during the improvisation and written dialogue. The improvisation provides students with a verbal first draft of the ultimate script. The movements and gestures of the 'actors' can be included in the script as stage directions. Once the improvisation has been transcribed, the text can then be redrafted, extended and shaped. In their evaluations of this process, students often comment on how the scripted dialogue has the spontaneity of authentic speech. This feature is often lacking when scripts are written in more sedentary ways, without recourse to drama. The process of working from a narrative text to a dramatic one is summarised in Figure 5.1.

If we apply this strategy for script writing to the classroom, we can see how learning can take place at various levels and at various stages in the process. First, when considering subtextual scenarios pupils are being asked to imagine what the 'lives' of characters might be like outside the text. However, to create these scenarios pupils need to draw on both their knowledge of the text and their expectations of how people might behave in specific situations. This approach is

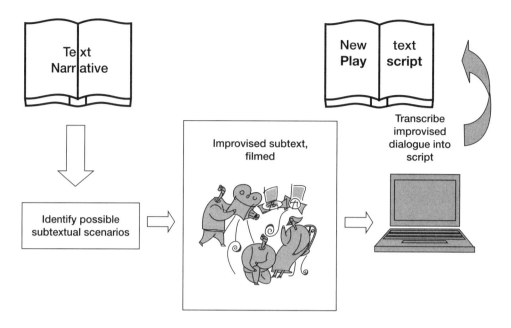

FIGURE 5.1 Narrative, subtext and script

likely to appeal to kinaesthetic learners because they have the opportunity to explore thinking through enactment. The use of drama as suggested above provides an active form of a directed activity related to text (DART). I refer to DARTs activities elsewhere in the book when considering approaches to non-fiction texts but, in passing, their essential purpose is to encourage pupils to read for meaning. The second area of learning occurs during the improvisation as pupils 'speak for' the characters they are representing. At this stage they are employing their skills as speakers and listeners by articulating thought as a specific character and responding to what other characters say. Their implicit knowledge of language is verbalised and captured on film. It thereby becomes a material product which can be scrutinised as a further aspect of learning. This third phase of learning occurs during the process of transcription from the video camera to the word processor but is most apparent once the dialogue has been transcribed. At this point spoken language becomes an artefact which can be analysed and critiqued. Although improvised speech gives the script authenticity, the transcription enables pupils to consider the appropriateness of every word uttered. Once committed to screen, therefore, the dialogue can be redrafted and 'polished'.

These 'improvised scripts' can then be bound either separately or collectively to provide reading material for other pupils in the class or can be reinterpreted for performance, as radio plays or stage plays. If pupils have taken different subtextual scenarios of the same text, it may be possible to combine the scripts of several groups to create longer plays. Assemblies and performances for parents provide pupils with ready-made audiences for their work. However, it is the process that is more important than the end product because it engages pupils in empowering practices as creators and shapers of language. It also gives pupils insights into how televisual dramas are constructed. In this way pupils are simultaneously engaged in learning about language and learning about cultural modes of representation. This kind of learning has implications beyond the classroom because there is the potential for pupils to apply realisations made during the process of scripting to their own cultural lives. Having been on the 'inside' of the construction of scripts for performance, pupils have the potential to be more insightful as viewers and spectators of televised drama, film and stage plays.

Project two: adapting texts to film

In a second project students are asked to self-select a 'chunk' of text from a novel and storyboard it with a view to reproducing the written text as a visual text. The first stage of the process involves identifying the number of shots required to represent the written text. This is done by using oblique lines on a photo-copy of the text to demarcate shots. An example is shown in Box 5.1 'Narrative to film adaptation'.

Box 5.1   Narrative to film adaptation

Extract from Yasmin and Neena

|

Yasmin walked slowly to school. 3/ It was a cold grey morning 1/ and the wind blew harshly. 2/ She could feel the bitter November air through the thin blue material of her shalwar. 4/ Above her, in the pale sky, three birds swooped 5/and landed on the rooftop of a nearby house. 6/ In the air their tiny dark bodies had looked like arrow heads darting about. 5/ She looked at them 7/ as she passed the house and thought that it would be exciting to be a tiny bird. 8/ She would fly into the grey, misty sky. She would hover above the houses and swoop down to the rooftops. She would glide on the breeze, with the powerful air filling her wings. It would be fun to be a bird, she thought. 9/

'What are you smiling at?' asked Neena 10./

'Oh, nothing,' replied Yasmin.11/

She was disappointed that Neena had spoken. Yasmin liked Neena. She was her friend, but the daydream had been enjoyable and Yasmin had wanted to fly away with her dream. Now Neena would want to talk about school and the day's lessons.

Yasmin looked once more over her shoulder 12/ to see the birds on the rooftop. 13/ They had flown from it and were once more flying freely in the sky. 14/ She watched them 15/ get smaller and smaller as they flew into the distance. After only a few seconds they were so far away that they were no bigger than full stops at the ends of sentences and they quickly disappeared into the mist 16./

In adapting the extract from 'Yasmin and Neena' (Gardner unpublished), it is anticipated 16 shots will be required. A storyboard would then be devised containing a frame for each of the 16 shots. After discussion about the type of shot required, each shot is drawn on the storyboard. The process of storyboarding necessitates further careful reading of the text. The fact the text will be made into a film requires pupils to both comprehend and visualise the images created by the text. It is in this process of mentally visualising the potential image on screen that pupils use their implicit knowledge of film, gained through countless hours of viewing television and DVDs. During this phase of the project, decisions are made about the appropriate sequence of images. In Box 5.1 the first sentence of the narrative becomes shot 3, and is preceded by two shots from the second sentence. It was decided the second sentence should be the first two frames of the film because it would enable an establishing shot to be made. This shot would set the scene and locate the action at a particular time of day and season. Further detail of how Box 5.1 could be translated into a visual text is outlined below.

Shot 1 – establishing shot of the scene, depicting the dull grey, coldness of the morning.

Shot 2 – medium shot of wind blowing an object e.g. paper bag, leaves, branches.

Shot 3 – close-up of Yasmin's shoes as she walks.

Shot 4 – medium long shot of Yasmin shivering as she walks.

Shot 5 – long shot of birds flying in the grey sky.

Shot 6 – panning shot following the birds as they fly and then land on a roof.

Shot 7 – this shot is divided into two further shots as follows:

- medium-long shot of Yasmin turning to look at the birds

- point of view shot from Yasmin's perspective watching the birds.

Shot 8 – close-up of Yasmin smiling and then drifting into daydream.

Shot 9 – image of a bird hovering and then swooping. The bird is different from the ones on the roof (e.g. a kestrel) to indicate fantasy.

Shot 10 – medium shot of Neena in the background and Yasmin in profile in the foreground as Neena speaks.

Shot 11 – medium shot of Yasmin looking away from Neena. Yasmin looks disappointed.

Shot 12 – medium shot of Yasmin and Neena walking side by side. Yasmin looks back over her shoulder.

Shot 13 – point of view shot from Yasmin's perspective of the empty roof.

Shot 14 – this shot is divided into two further shots as follows:

- close-up of Yasmin looking up to the sky

- medium shot of birds flying in the sky.

Shot 15 – close-up of Yasmin smiling and then narrowing her eyes to watch the birds.

Shot 16 – long shot of the birds as they fly away, getting smaller until they can no longer be seen.

In addition to the type of shot required, thought needs to be given to the duration of each shot. Some shots may be longer and contain more detail than others. However, real decisions about the duration of each shot can be largely left to the editing stage. In a sense, the amount of visual and aural data within different shots is similar to the different sentence types in written narrative. A brief close-up of a hand might be similar to a simple sentence; whereas a medium shot of five seconds, in which we see a character in a new setting might be akin to a compound or complex sentence. The juxtaposition of different shots within a sequence gives film both its textual grammar and its variety.

The completed storyboard acts as the filmic script when on location. That is not to say there will not be some alterations to what was initially intended. There may be environmental factors that affect how the film is shot and directorial decisions have to be taken on location. This makes film a fluid and dynamic medium in which to work and students soon become aware that solutions to problems often have to be quickly improvised. The pre-production and production stages of film making, important though they are, are not the end of the creative process. The post production aspects of editing and dubbing require the same eye for detail as the other two stages. The making of a film, even a short one, requires the synthesis of numerous skills. It may be that an individual pupil does not have the full range of skills required. However, the collaborative nature of film work necessitates that pupils pool all their resources in order to complete the project.

One drawback of working with film is the amount of time it can take to shoot the script. A short film of three to four minutes can take up to twelve hours to script, shoot and edit. However, the advantages of working with film are numerous and include several aspects of learning, such as:

- collaborative thinking

- problem solving

- the application of semiotic awareness

- the development of research skills

- the development of ICT skills

- creative thought

- critical thinking.

Collaborative thought

Learning through collaboration with peers involves cohesive group work in which a task can only be completed by means of mutual cooperation and involvement of all group members to achieve shared learning goals (Gardner 2002: 18). During the making of a film, there are numerous opportunities for collaborative talk. Corden (2000) has identified a range of positive learning outcomes which accrue from well structured collaborative group work. Drawing on evidence from a number of studies and his own involvement with the National Oracy Project, he lists cognitive development, exploratory talk, reflective and hypothetical thought as characteristic features of such work. In addition, he suggests collaborative group work improves pupils' behaviour, interpersonal and social skills, motivation and self-esteem, as well as positive attitudes to learning. This is an impressive list of educational attributes, providing a persuasive argument for requiring pupils to collaborate on the construction of film narratives. Some teachers may be apprehensive about allowing a group of quite young pupils to use a digital video camera with minimal adult supervision. However, my experience of working with pupils in Year 3 leads me to the view that the nature of the medium in which they are working, combined with a real purpose to work collaboratively, encourages pupils to behave positively.

Problem solving

During the creative process decisions have to be made. Problems arise that require the group to pause, reflect and initiate possible solutions. It may be that the group wanted to use certain props that are not available, or a particular location that is inaccessible. It could be that a particular effect they had hoped to create did not work and alternatives have to be found. At times such as these, groups have to devise their next best option without their intentions being overly compromised.

The application of semiotic awareness

When framing each shot, thought has to be given to the particular effects the group want to create on screen. It may be they want to convey the sadness felt by one character or the dominance of one character over another. They will have at their disposal a great deal of implicit knowledge about how expression and gesture signify emotion but they may also find other semiotic devices to convey such feelings; the use of colour or lighting, the application of particular camera angles, for example. The intention to create particular effects causes the group to find symbolic ways to construct meanings, and because film allows this to be done visually, pupils may unwittingly stray into the realm of metaphor. Once the image has been recorded, it then becomes a material product to be scrutinised and analysed by others. Hence, a film produced by one group is an aesthetic item that can be evaluated by others in the class.

The development of research skills

Film narratives can be set in different locations, or in the past. At the pre-production stage of film making there is a real purpose for undertaking research in order to create images that truly reflect the time or place in which the film is set. If a setting for a film is the war years of the 1940s, appropriate props need to be found in order to avoid anachronism; photographs of typical clothes worn will need to be scrutinised; popular music of the period listened to. All of these items are symbols of the time and by synthesising findings, pupils will give their film authenticity. By means of research and representation pupils emulate the processes of undertaking real historical research. A film project, therefore, lends itself to cross-curricular applications.

The development of ICT skills

In addition to camera skills, film technology involves the use of computer editing software; use of the internet for research purposes, including finding documentary evidence such as photographs and newsreels appropriate to the theme of the film; downloading music and voice-overs and dubbing them onto the film.

Creative thought

At every stage of the filmic process, creative thought is central. It is evident in the composition of the narrative; in the juxtaposition of images and of elements within each image or shot; in the depiction of character and the character's use of language; in choices about what to cut and where to cut in the editing process; in selections of appropriate music and even in the choice of font for titles and credits. Film is arguably one of the most creative of all art forms because it relies upon the synthesis of such a wide range of skills and other art forms for its realisation.

Critical thinking

Critical thinking encompasses the processes of analysis, synthesis, application and evaluation. In both the construction of film and the reading of film these processes are evident. In order to understand how film creates aesthetic effects, it is necessary to unpick the sequence of images, frame by frame, to identify how the various elements are synthesised. The BFI (2001a: 19) has suggested the elements of film suitable for scrutiny in the primary classroom are: sound, setting, story, colour, camera and character (the so called 3Ss and 3Cs). When viewing film it is advised that the class be divided into groups with each group focusing on a different element of the film. The Story Shorts teaching guide (BFI 2001a) provides detailed guidance and programmes of work in relation to five short films in an accompanying video compilation. The analysis of film is an important preliminary stage to film production because it enables pupils to realise their implicit knowledge of film by means of collaborative discussion. The production of film requires pupils to apply knowledge, skills and thought. Armed with knowledge of how such elements as the 3Ss and 3Cs function, pupils become critical viewers of film. For example, they become much more aware of how the position of the camera, in relation to subjects in shot, influences how they see and how the narrative is told.

Given children's extensive exposure to film, the use of film in the primary classroom provides one means by which implicit knowledge, acquired largely at home, can be utilised, thereby creating links between classroom learning and children's cultural experience. Film production involves pupils sharing their thinking, skills and knowledge to create a product. This requires active learning and collaborative group work; thereby making film a truly social means of learning. In the course of such work, pupils support one another as problems occur and decisions need to be made. The close relationship between filmic and print narratives enables knowledge of one medium to be transferred to the other, with effective results in pupil's development of conventional literacy. The development of visual literacy provides pupils with lifelong skills as critical viewers and, given that creative industries are becoming an increasingly important aspect of the British economy (Film Education 2008: 4), these skills may also provide pupils with opportunities to benefit from economic life too. Not only does film require creative processes for its creation and production, it gives teachers the tools to creatively combine different subjects disciplines at the same time as giving value to children's cultural knowledge.

The language of film: a glossary of terms

Absence/presence
Film narratives create illusions of time. This is known as temporal illusion in the sense that time, including past, present and, sometimes, future time, is contracted into a unity of time for the viewer.

Adaptation
Cinema has been made 'respectable' through the adaptation of classic novels for the screen. However, the nature of the different forms (literary narrative and film narrative) mean that the film version is never the same as the book. Each medium lends itself to different modes of representation. In a novel an omniscient narrator can take us everywhere, including the thoughts and feelings of different characters. In film the camera tells the story, which, because of the nature of the medium, has to be a sequence of images that are external to the characters. When watching film, we have to interpret the psychological and emotional states of characters through visual representation, rather than the descriptive commentary available to a writer of a novel.

Agency
Agency refers to the person or character who controls meaning making. Within the film it can be a character whose desire controls the direction the narrative takes. Outside the film it can be the director or the spectator. In terms of the latter, a similar process as that described in reader response theory applies in which the viewer (or reader of film) controls the meanings inferred from the audio-visual narrative.

Ambiguity
Ambiguity occurs where a double meaning exists.

Angles
180 degree rule
A rule which states a line of 180 degrees between camera angles in consecutive shots should not be crossed in order to maintain continuity.

30 degree rule
A rule which states that angles of less than 30 degrees should not occur between consecutive shots.

Atmos effect
A sound effect used to create a particular atmosphere: e.g. a hooting owl, or a gale.

Close-up
A shot framing the head from the neck up.

Colour
The use of colour in film can serve both a realistic function, in the sense of representing the world in its 'true' colour, and thereby contribute to the process of making the story real for us, and a symbolic function. Colour has been used to signify qualities or attributes of character. In Westerns for example the villain often wears black whereas the hero is dressed in white. As such the film utilises assumed cultural and ideological perspectives of the spectator or viewer.

Continuity editing
Seamlessly editing from one shot to another to give the appearance that editing has not taken place.

Crane shot
A shot with the camera mounted on a crane to create a sense of height or aerial movement.

Credits
List of people involved in the film which appears at the end of the film.

Cut
A term used in film editing where two shots are spliced together. A cut may have different meanings. First, it can signify a change of place or time and functions in much the same way as a paragraph in writing. There are four types of cut, as follows:

Continuity Cuts
As suggested these cuts maintain continuity by preserving the development of the narrative by making seamless transitions between sequences of shots.

Match Cuts
These occur within a single scene and involve the movement of the camera from one place to another whilst maintaining the visual–spatial logic of the scene. For example a long shot might be used of two characters in a park, followed by a medium shot of one of them.

Cross-cuts
These cuts tend to speed up the narrative by juxtaposing two sequences occurring in different places but at the same time.

Depth of Field
Refers to the focal length provided by a lens. A wide angle lens provides the possibility of keeping both the background and foreground in sharp focus. This type of shot is known as deep focus.

Denotation/connotation
In semiotics every sign has both a signifier and a signified. The signifier is the sign itself and the signified is its meaning. The semiologist Roland Barthes refers to two orders of signification. The first, denotation, is a literal reference. So the image in film of a cat, which is, of course, an illusion, because it is not the cat itself, represents a cat in real life. The second order, connotation, are culturally encoded meanings. So, the image of the cat on film might signify abstract qualities such as domesticity, or, depending on context, it could foreshadow a significant occurrence, such as the entrance of a character, e.g. cat woman.

Diegesis/diegetic

Refers to everything that is integral to the narrative. In film this includes images, dialogue, sounds of actions, props and objects. The musical score is considered to be non-diegetic, except when musicians are playing as part of the story.

Director

The person who makes artistic decisions about the translation of a script into a film.

Dissolve or mix

This involves two images on the screen at once; one superimposed on the other. One shot is faded in whilst the other is being faded out.

Dutch or canted angle

The camera is tilted to one side, making the image appear diagonally in the frame. This effect disorientates the viewer, leading to a sense of unease.

Editing

While some editing 'in camera' can occur during the shooting of the film, it is usual that editing takes place after filming. Many school computers include editing software, such as Moviemaker. This enables a film to be downloaded so that transitions, cuts, special effects and music can be applied.

Ellipsis

Ellipsis refers to periods of time that have been omitted from the narrative. This may be denoted by a particular type of cut, such as a fade or jump cut, among others.

Establishing shot

This shot shows the surroundings in which the action occurs. It tends to be early on in the film and serves a similar function to setting in the novel or short story.

Extreme close-up (ECU)

A shot detailing part of an actors face.

Extreme long shot

A shot in which a scene is shown from a distance.

Eye line

The direction in which a character is looking.

Fade

A fade can be in or out and can apply to either the image or to sound. A fade-in involves the gradual emergence of the image or an increase in sound, whereas a fade-out is the opposite.

Flashback

This involves reverting to a previous point in time in the narrative. Flashbacks are usually associated with a character revealing an event that is pertinent to their life. They represent subjective truth or the personal interpretation of events of that character.

Foregrounding

This refers to devices that bring to the attention of the viewer a particular element of the film. It may be that a particular character is foregrounded by means of medium close-ups in the foreground, or by means of the character's voice in a voice-over.

Frame

The individual image captured within the rectangle of the screen.

Genre

Type of film, e.g. horror, western, adventure etc.

Iconography

Icons are visual signs which signify specific genre. In a Dracula film, these would include the dark foreboding castle, the black cape, fangs and bats; in a Western, the stagecoach, six-shooter, spurs etc. Iconography has a connotative function by implying more than a literal representation. The dark cape implies more than just the character of Dracula, it signifies death, evil and the darkness of time, in that Dracula is several hundred years old.

Image

The smallest unit of meaning in film is the image (a single shot), which can operate on two levels of meaning: the literal in what it denotes and the symbolic in terms of its connotative meaning.

Jump cut

This is a cut between two shots of the same subject where the camera angle is less than 45 degrees. This type of cut leaves the viewer in no doubt that a cut has taken place; it therefore draws attention to itself. It gives the film a feeling of fragmentation which can suggest instability and dislocation in the narrative structure.

Line of action

This is an imaginary line along the sight line between two characters. In order to maintain continuity and cinematic logic the camera will not cross this line. So, all shots will be taken from one side of this line.

Long shot (LS)

This shows the subject from above head height to below the feet.

Low angle shot

This is a shot in which the camera is used to give the appearance of looking up at a subject or action.

Master shot (MS)

This is usually a wide angle shot in which all the action of a scene is depicted. It is usually cut together with other shots, such as close-ups etc.

Medium long shot (MLS)

This shot shows the subject from knees up.

Medium shot (MS)

This shot shows the subject from waist up.

Metalanguage

This refers to a language that describes language or theory.

Method acting

Based on the work of the Soviet director Stanislavski, the method actor acts naturally as a character, that is s/he attempts to become the character by drawing upon their own experiences to feel how the character would feel and think how the character would think. The most famous method actor was Marlon Brando.

Mise en scène

A French theatrical term, meaning what is put in the scene. In film it is all the elements of a shot, including the set, props and actors, as well as the use of lighting, colour and the way these elements are juxtaposed or choreographed.

Montage

A montage is a sequence of shots that collectively create a mood or express an idea.

Narrative

Narrative refers to the means by which the story is organised. Narrative cinema is concerned with telling a story in a 'real' world. All devices, including lighting, camera angles and sound combine to tell the story, which is driven by the motivation of a central character. Classical narrative cinema follows a triadic formula involving order/disorder/order-restored. In this narrative structure a harmonious situation is disturbed by some event that sets in train a series of cause and effect events leading to a sequence of problem/resolution scenarios, culminating in satisfactory closure at the films conclusion. There are many connections between film as narrative and the narrative of written stories and novels. This makes film a useful resource for making pupils' implicit knowledge of narrative, explicit. This explicit knowledge can then be used to develop and improve pupils' written narratives.

Off-screen

Action that is integral to the story but that takes place outside the frame.

Over-the-shoulder shot (OTS)

This is a shot in which one side of the head and shoulders of a character in the extreme foreground is framed so that the viewer sees what the character is looking at.

Pan/panning

This is a shot in which the camera moves, usually from left to right to capture a panoramic view of a scene.

Point of view (POV) shot

This is a shot in which the viewer sees as though through the character's eyes.

Post production

Once the film has been shot all work, including editing and dubbing, is referred to as being post production.

Reaction shot

This is a shot in which we see a character's reaction to something.

Reverse shot

Alternate shots in which we see the two points of view of two characters in dialogue are referred to as reverse shots.

Scene

A scene is a dramatic unit in a film. A scene is usually continuous in time and place.

Sequence
A sequence involves a series of shots in which a single action is depicted.

Shot
This is a single continuous image and is the basic unit of meaning in a film. A shot can be analysed in several ways: its length, its frame, or the way the camera is used to create the shot, and the *mise en scène*, i.e. the juxtaposition of elements in the shot.

Shot transition
The transition of one shot to another by means of a cut, dissolve etc.

Social realism
As in literature, social realism in film involves the realistic depiction of social and economic circumstances of a particular group in society, usually the working and middle classes.

Sound perspective
The use of a sound effect to create an awareness of physical space, e.g. a sound that is close up or distant.

Sound track
The sound track is all the sounds that accompany the visual aspects of the story, including sound effects, dialogue, music etc.

Storyboard
A series of drawings made before filming detailing the sequence of shots to be filmed. These show the types of shots, e.g. long shot, close up etc. and the *mise en scène*.

Subjective camera
This is when the camera is used to suggest the viewpoint of a particular character. The use of subjective camera implicates the spectator in the gaze since they view images from the perspective of the character.

Tilt
This is a shot in which the camera pivots on the horizontal axis, moving up or down.

Top shot
This is a shot in which the camera is directly above a character or scene.

Tracking shot

This is a shot in which the camera is mounted on a moving object or track, thereby creating a horizontal movement across a scene.

Two shot

This is a shot in which two characters are depicted in the frame.

Unmatched shots

This when a cut from one shot to another is used to disrupt continuity, thereby creating a surreal effect.

Wide angle shot (WS)

A shot in which all or most of the action is captured.

Zoom

When the focal length of the lens is altered resulting in a change in the size of the image. A zoom-in moves the viewer closer to a subject, whereas a zoom-out takes us further away. A zoom-in intensifies the voyeuristic gaze of the spectator.

The following sources were used to compile this glossary.

Hayward, S. (2006) *Cinema Studies: The Key Concepts (3rd Edn)*. London: Routledge.
BFI (undated) *An Introduction to Film Language* – CD ROM. London: British Film Institute.
BFI (2000) *Moving Images in the Classroom*. London: British Film Institute.

Further information and resources about film in the classroom can be found at the following websites:

www.peterborough.gov.uk – clips of children's films entered into the Local Authority's annual film competition.
www.filmstreet.co.uk – produces a regular newsletter.
www.teachers.tv – clips of children making films.
www.filmeducation.org
www.bfi.org.uk/education
www.firstlightmovies.com

6

Story, story, story

> In a way each of us is a story and all the stories
> we hear become part of our own story ...
> (Crossley-Holland 2002: 293)

THIS CHAPTER DISCUSSES the following:

- the importance of oral storytelling in the classroom;

- the function of narrative as a medium of learning;

- narrative as a cross-curricular resource;

- practical ideas for narrative writing.

I begin by considering the place of oral storytelling in the classroom, followed by a discussion of written narratives. In addition to what pupils may learn about narrative itself by creating their own stories, being read to, being told stories and by reading stories, they will learn much about the world through narrative. Narratives are one of the most enduring pedagogic tools. The application of story for curriculum development will be discussed with reference to particular texts. In discussing the place of story in the classroom, particularly story in its oral form, there will be inevitable links with much of what has already been said about talk as a means of learning. In reading this chapter, therefore, the reader will need to make continual mental cross-references to what has been said about speaking and listening. There will be an analysis of story structure beyond the usual advice of 'a story must have a beginning a middle and an end . . .' and a practical example of a story-writing project will be discussed.

In the chapter on talk, reference was made to Clarke's assertion that to value the pupil as a learner it was essential that teachers create classroom environments in which the 'personal voice' of the child could be nurtured. Carter (2000: 14) states that, '... the tendency and ability to tell stories is within us all.' However, Grugeon and Gardner (2000: 40) are careful to point out that while a narrative imagination may be an inherent aspect of the human mind, as suggested by Hardy (1977), storytelling, 'is an art which we have to acquire, practise and polish'. In Chapter four we considered the use of puppets as one means of helping pupils develop their oral storytelling. Another means is the use of film, which was discussed in the Chapter five.

Storytelling then provides one means by which the personal voice of the child can be developed and valued. Stories encompass a wide range of narrative forms from the brief anecdote to the epic narrative poems of the Ancient Greeks. Homer's *Iliad* and *Odyssey* were not written and could not, therefore, be read but were told to audiences. These oral recitations necessitated strong powers of memory on the part of the storyteller. For this reason Carter (2000: 18) advocates storytelling in the classroom as a means of developing pupils' verbal and non-verbal memory, as well as their ability to structure narrative, develop characters, and acquire a feel for narrative pace and momentum. He adds that to remember a story, the storyteller should visualise narrative events rather than try to remember the actual words. The ability to construct mental visual images is an essential attribute of fluent, independent readers and writers. If this skill can be developed through oral storytelling, it may assist the development of comprehension skills because pupils' are better able to 'see the story in their heads'. Similarly, if pupils are able to visualise what they want to write, descriptions of characters, settings and other elements of narrative may be much more finely drawn. In this respect, the practice of oral storytelling, involving the visualisation of a known narrative and the practice of sharply observing their world, as suggested in the model, 'An integrated approach to English' discussed in Chapter two, appear to be complementary activities, likely to strengthen pupils' visual recall. Jennings (1991) acknowledges the importance of the ability to visualise the narrative but goes further than mental recall in her evaluation of the educational benefits of storytelling. She asserts that the storyteller uses higher order thinking skills in order to enthuse the audience. In particular, she identifies the following cognitive features of storytelling:

The ability to reflect on content and control the subject matter;

The integration of emotional responses to be conveyed to the audience;

Analysis of the story and the selection of its salient feature;

An evaluation of the story's worth for audience appeal;

Consideration of a method of presentation suited to both the story itself and the audience.

(Jennings 1991: 11)

These skills are transferable to narrative writing; they encourage control of the kind of choices that writers have to make when constructing narratives. Both oral and written stories require the narrator to move between different levels of the text simultaneously. The unfolding plot is told by means of sentences and words that fit the emotional tone created by changing events and their effect on characters. And all of these features are influenced by the genre of the story. The kind of words and sentences used in the telling of a ghost story will be different from those used to tell a humorous one, but common to both will be the narrator's awareness of audience and purpose for telling the story. In addition, Jennings notes the value of storytelling for empowering pupils: developing their linguistic skills and use of the four modes of language, reducing inhibitions and creating group cohesion.

The use of visual memory to tell stories rather than memorising the actual words is one reason why storytelling involves a unique version of the story at each telling. Another is the nature of performance and the interaction of the storyteller and the audience. Although the storyteller is drawing upon a known narrative structure and may use words used in previous recitations of the story, each telling is, to some extent, improvised. The most spontaneous elements of storytelling are likely to occur at those moments in the story when the audience is most emotionally charged. The storyteller senses the emotional cadence of the audience and chooses language to accentuate the affective response. Anyone who has performed before an audience will recognise that different audiences respond differently; some will be more serious than others; some will laugh in all the right places. It is this affective relationship between an audience and the performer that influences the way in which the performance is delivered. In Chapter three mention was made of the paralinguistic features that accompany talk and contribute to the meaning of what is said. These features, in the form of gestures, expressions and general body language also apply in the case of oral storytelling. A good storyteller will utilise all their rhetorical skills; words, silences, repetition, facial expression, hand gestures and body movements to draw the audience into the imaginative world of the story and carry listeners through to its climax and conclusion.

If we take Carter's advice and teach pupils to visualise stories rather than learn the words of the story, we encourage them to utilise their personal linguistic resources in each retelling. Because these personal linguistic resources are derived as much from home and community as they are by language acquired in the classroom, oral storytelling implicitly signals a value for the child's cultural background. Shirley Brice Heath (1983) drew attention to the way in which literacy practices are culturally embedded and that for some children the oral tradition is the primary means by which they acquire narrative skills.

The traditions of oral storytelling survive in many of our minority ethnic and traveller communities. Stories of social life reflect the cultural and experiential world of the child. One of my students, fresh from a school placement where she had taught a large number of pupils from a traveller community, reported enthusiastically how one of her six-year-old pupils had told her how he had tracked a rabbit, caught it, skinned it with his own knife and prepared it for the evening meal. The story served an important social function and both teacher and pupil learned something from the telling of the story. The teacher gained a valuable insight into the world of the child and discovered skills she would never have realised without the story being told. For the boy, it was an affirmation of the value of his story because the teacher had listened. But that is only the tip of the iceberg because further implicit affirmations were made by the telling of this story in the classroom. It was an affirmation of the child's social world and therefore, affirmation of his personal identity, embedded as it was in cultural practice.

As Houlton (1985: 14) observed, 'to value language and culture is to value the child'. In addition to saying something about the identity of the speaker, stories about personal experience also 'signal the speaker's view of the way the world is' (Rosen 1993). Storytelling then, provides one way in which we, as teachers, get to not only hear the voice of the child, but also acquire an understanding of the person the child is. Simultaneously, it is a means by which the child gets to hear their own voice and to develop their language as a personal resource for social interaction and meaning making. Even at the level of pupils' personal adventures and exploits, storytelling changes the classroom dynamic represented in the adaptation of Barnes' model (Chapter three), by handing talk to pupils, thereby giving them fresh strategies for learning.

Narrative as a pedagogic tool

As well as giving a voice to pupils, storytelling is one of the oldest and most powerful means of teaching anything (Carter 2000: 24). Throughout history and across all cultures adults have used stories to tell younger generations of their heritage. Story is the means by which the social world is revealed to children and given coherence (Egan 1988; Bruner 1990). Through story, otherwise unrelated pieces of information can be connected in a way that makes it easier to remember information than if taught as discrete facts (Cooper and McIntyre 1992;

Howe 1999). Story is, therefore, a powerfully effective means by which teachers can construct meaningful contexts for learning; scaffolding the acquisition of knowledge and concepts by helping pupils to come to cognitive realisations through narrative associations (Grugeon and Gardner 2000: 58). There has always been a rightful place for story in the primary classroom. However, its importance was lost in the curriculum congestion caused by the imposition of the literacy and numeracy strategies (DfEE 1998) on the National Curriculum (DES 1988). The reading and telling of complete stories tended to be pushed to the margins of the school day. Curriculum change in the middle years of the first decade of the twenty-first century, which resulted in many schools reverting to the kind of thematic approaches to curriculum design and delivery that existed before the implementation of the National Curriculum, signalled the opportunity to revitalise story, both as a tool for learning and as a pivot for thematic teaching.

Narratives are multidimensional teaching tools; they lend themselves to the development of a range of curriculum areas. Stories occupy time and place; they can involve physical, mental, emotional and sometimes spiritual journeys; characters are presented with problems that force them to make choices, requiring moral or ethical decisions; they include patterns of changing emotional intensity, atmosphere, suspense, climax and anticlimax; and they create 'secondary worlds', virtual realities that provide readers with views of the world they may never witness, other than through story. We will revisit this latter point in Chapter seven, which considers the work of writers who deal with sensitive issues of global significance. For the time being, I want to explore the potential of narrative for teaching aspects of the curriculum.

Time and place

All narratives are set in a time and place. The temporal setting, unless it is a science-fiction story, provides opportunities to explore the historical period in which the story is set; while the location, or locations, of the story can lead to the teaching of geographic concepts. Of course some novels lend themselves more to historical investigation than others: the historical novel is an obvious case. Rosemary Sutcliff's, *The Capricorn Bracelet* (1973), set in Roman England, is typical of the genre for upper Key Stage 2 pupils. Sutcliffe draws on historical fact to create a narrative interpretation of the key events in the period. Not only is the narrative a means of taking pupils into the social reality of life at the time and helping them to visualise what Roman Britain might have looked like, it can be used to help pupils conceptualise what the study of history entails.

History should not be mistaken as the uncritical recount of past events. Historians attempt to make accurate judgements about the past in terms of what happened; how things happened; why they happened and what the concomitant effects were. They hypothesise about the past and interrogate historical data in an attempt to justify their interpretations (Grugeon and Gardner 2000: 67). The historical novelist also uses information about the past to construct their narrative. In some cases this data may be entirely secondary, or someone else's interpretation of the past. So, we can never take the historical novel at face value and accept it as a narrative facsimile of the past. The value of the historical novel is its capacity to take us into the past and show us what life might have been like, but additional investigation is required to fully appreciate how accurate the novelist has been. Allied to the reading of a novel set in the past, teachers can engage pupils in the process of doing history by investigating other sources of information about the temporal setting of the novel, in order to make critical judgement about the historical accuracy of the author.

In addition to interpretative skills, history also entails an understanding of concepts such as chronology, causation and change, the nature of historical inquiry and the way in which the past is communicated. This latter point raises the issue of bias in the reporting of the past. A history of the Crusades of the Middle Ages is likely to read differently from a Christian perspective, compared to that of a Muslim one. It is important, therefore, to use various versions of the same event or period, so that pupils come to realise the past can be presented differently. So, the reading of history itself should not be undertaken uncritically. We should always ask ourselves, from whose perspective is a particular account of the past being written. It may be that the writer did not intend bias but that their view is prejudiced by the sociocultural and political lens through which they view the world. So, any investigation of the past is also likely to generate further questions and interrogation of the recount of the past. We may view the historical novel as a particular form of recount of the past, bearing in mind there is a difference between how a novel is structured and how history is presented in other formats.

Novels can help to bring the social world of the past to life. Kevin Crossley-Holland's 'Arthur Trilogy' (2001, 2002, 2003) and *Gatty's Tale* (2006) are excellent examples. By means of sparse use of language and often poetic imagery, the sights, smells, tastes, social relationships and general feel of medieval England are re-created. Crossley-Holland intersperses the diction of his novels with the language of the past. Archaic words from the period such as; marl, twitchell, vellum (clay, a fork in the road and parchment, made from the skin of a calf, lamb or kid, respectively) emerge unexpectedly to add to the flavour of the past. For the teacher of English, these are lexical reminders that languages change. Within an historical perspective we might consider what English looked like at the time, how it was written, who wrote it, what form it took and how it was spoken. Aspects of such study might include the etymology of words – identification of words that have fallen out of use and the possible reasons for this – as well as investigations of English orthography – how the spellings of words have changed over time and the reasons for this.

The study of diachronic change in English, at word level, is an important aspect of knowledge about language (KAL) which was raised by Richmond (1990). In some instances, specific words relate to the names of artefacts that are no longer in use and their makers who are no longer employed. A study of nouns can lead to an understanding of diachronic language change as a result of technological innovation. In our own time, the English language is undergoing rapid change, partly as a consequence of the growth of televisual technology. New words are being created, definitions are being modified, either because meanings have changed or additional meanings are attributed to words, and the spellings of existing words are being altered. The language of the computer has introduced words such as 'program' and 'disk' – words that have specific meanings but which are so close to the pre-existing words 'programme' and 'disc' that, over time, the newer spellings may cause the older ones to fall into disuse. It should be remembered that 'programme' and 'disc' themselves became widely used nouns as a result of technological changes in popular culture. This link between language change and technology can take us back into history and the vagaries of the English language. O'Rourke and O'Rourke (1990: 270) remind us that before William Caxton established his printing press in London in the year 1476, he had been working in Holland. His familiarity with Dutch words and lack of familiarity with certain English words resulted in a Dutch influence of some English words. For example, he wrongly assumed the digraph 'gh' existed in English as it did in Dutch. Hence girl was written as 'gherle' and goose as 'ghoos'. As we know the spellings of these words have changed over time. However, certain other words have retained their Dutch influence. Such words include; ghost, ghoul and ghastly.

Research with narrative

The identification of artefacts referred to in the text could be used to create a visual museum of pictures, if the actual artefacts are not available from the local museum. Pupils can use research skills to locate information about the artefact and present it in a form that suits an audience of peers. Mini-group research projects could culminate in the compilation of an interactive classroom display. Such information might include: what the artefact was used for; who might have used it; how it was made; how or why it was invented and why it fell out of use. By attempting to answer questions such as these there is the possibility that pupils might realise that reasons for historical change can involve cultural and technological innovation too. If pupils achieve an understanding of the interrelationship of various forces in historical change, then they will have engaged in deep-level learning about causal relations that is likely to equip them with important lifelong cognitive abilities and knowledge. Returning momentarily to the discussion of the role of collaborative talk in the classroom, covered elsewhere in the book, pupils are more likely to make these connections if they are given opportunities for constructive discussion around the questions raised above. If the actual artefact is available we might engage pupils in a consideration of its significance, or the construction of a plausible narrative of the object.

The use of stories to enter into past time comes with a pedagogic warning. Stories have the power to captivate the reader or listener, especially those who have not yet learned to discern what is real from what is fantasy. Most teachers have heard a child ask 'did it really happen?' after being read a good story. There are particular types of story that appear as authentic versions of the past and, while they may contain 'grains of the truth', they nevertheless include the embellishments of 'poetic licence'. Myths and legends are two examples of the kind of stories I am referring to. So that pupils do not accept particular stories as true accounts of the past, it may be necessary to create a critical frame by asking pupils to consider whether the events in the story really happened, whether the characters really existed, why they think the story was told and what evidence there is to help them decide whether the story or parts of the story are true (Grugeon and Gardner 2000: 69). The essential point about using novels set in the past is that they do not necessarily need to be true to the facts of historical events but they do need to be authentic to their time, that is free from anachronism.

A novel location

The places referred to in novels, especially actual places that are set in past time (even relatively recent past time), change. Comparisons of places, using documentary, cartographic and pictorial information, enable a study of the changes that have taken place. This can lead to the more important question of the reasons why change has occurred, taking us into the realms of human geography. There may be commercial or economic reasons for the process of change. In the Britain of recent times, let alone the distant past, towns and cities that once employed thousands of workers in heavy industry have undergone tremendous physical changes as the British economy has moved from its once strong manufacturing base to one where the service sector has flourished. Hence, large factories, steel works, smelting plants, iron foundaries, dockyards, shipyards and farmland have given way to warehouses, small business units, housing estates and supermarkets. Although some places have remained relatively unchanged over the last forty years, the use of buildings within communities may have changed. The migration of people who have different religions, modes of dress and diets to those who originally lived in an area, may result in changes in the goods sold in certain shops, changes to the denomination of churches and chapels, or even the religion worshipped in them. Demographic changes such as these have further links to Religious Education and the study of language. With the inclusion of 'primary languages' in the curriculum there is the opportunity to learn a 'community language' alongside a European one.

If the study of places goes no further than a simple comparison and description of the changes that have occurred, important learning opportunities will have been missed to engage pupils in an understanding of the interrelatedness of historical, geographic, economic and demographic change.

Many, if not all, stories involve physical journeys around a single location or across several locations. Some writers make this apparent in their work by providing a map of the physical world in which the narrative is set. Hence, Tolkein provides us with a map of Middle-Earth at the beginning of *Lord of the Rings* (2001). Where writers do not do this, it is possible to use pupils' comprehension skills to construct a map of the narrative action. For younger pupils, narratives with relatively simple journeys within a single location might be applicable. Suitable texts include *Going on a Bear Hunt* (Rosen 1989); *Each Peach Pear Plum* (Ahlberg and Ahlberg 1982) and *Rosie's Walk* (Hutchins 1992); older readers will, of course, require more complex journeys. These may be within a single location or could involve multiple locations. Parallel to the identification of the places in the story and the realisation of the spatial layout of the narrative map, a study of 'real' maps could be made. Understanding of coordinates, cartographic symbols, cardinal points and keys could be used in the construction of pupils' own maps, depending on the age of the children. This is another way in which literature and geographic concepts might be integrated in a creative, thematic mode of curriculum delivery.

Novels set in locations outside Britain provide a 'window onto the world', transporting pupils to places they may never have been. Good stories, with well developed depictions are able 'to evoke the imagery of place through the power of their telling' (Grugeon and Gardner 2000: 73). We should not forget that writers such as Beverly Naidoo and Elizabeth Laird are as assiduous in their study of places, as are Sutcliff and Crossley-Holland of their study of the past. Before writing *The Garbage King* (2003), set in Addis Ababa, Elizabeth Laird was well travelled in Ethiopia and had spent time with street children there. Similarly, Beverley Naidoo's novels provide authentic geographic representations of Lagos (2000) and Kenya (2007), as well as those set in her native South Africa (1985; 1989; 1995; 2001). Of course these novels do not just depict places; they represent the lives of those who live there. The opening two lines of *The Garbage King* say as much about the life experience of the protagonists as they do about the novel's initial setting:

'There was no light in the shack, none at all, except when the moon was shining. Mamo could see chinks of it then, through gaps in the corrugated-iron roof' (Laird 2003: 1).

Avoiding stereotype

Where novels set in countries other than Britain depict extreme poverty and human suffering, we need to be careful not to reinforce what may be pupils' stereotypical preconceptions of this being the natural order of life in these countries. Child poverty and child labour outside Britain may well have their roots in historical and recent actions and events perpetrated by European and North American countries. These kinds of realisation take us into current affairs and politics, which in some quarters, may be considered politically sensitive. I shall deal with sensitive issues in children's literature in a later chapter but, in passing, it may be opportune to say that not to refer to the causes of poverty is equally political because both to say, or not to say, influences pupils' assumptions of why the world is the way it is. So, even a refusal to acknowledge the root cause of poverty can be a political action. In addition, most countries are socially demarcated by an unequal distribution of wealth, with the poor often living alongside the rich. It is important that pupils see a distant location in its entirety, so that they are left with an holistic view of the country, rather than a partial one, for the reasons given above. It is important, therefore, that narratives presenting a particular and partial view of a distant place should be supplemented with additional teaching materials that provide a broader view.

In addition to providing a backdrop for teaching about the physical features of a distant location, the value of narrative resides in its capacity to show pupils what it might be like to live in a specific location. Human geography then raises issues about social conditions that provide key questions for further investigation, discussion and deeper understanding of world affairs. Some of the central questions of our age – international debt, mass migration, sustainable development and global warming – can be stimulated by the study of a distant place and the effects that poverty, drought, famine, war and natural disasters have on populations. The way in which these issues are presented in the media often imply they are recent ones, but many of them have much longer histories than discussions of current affairs suggest. The story, *The People Who Hugged Trees* (Rose 1990), a fictionalised version of real events and real people, is a case in point. Set in Rajastan over 300 years ago, the story tells of how a woman by the name of Amrita Devi challenged the maharajah when he sent his men to cut down the tress that protected her village from the encroaching desert. Realising the environmental importance of the trees, Amrita Devi was one of the first 'eco-warriors' as she encouraged the villagers into direct action by hugging the tree trunks to save them from the axe. On meeting the maharajah, she was able to persuade him to her view and the trees were given a 'reprieve'. Both they and the villagers were saved.

Stories such as this one provide the cohesive fabric for comprehensive and coherent knowledge made from the threads of history, environmental studies, multicultural education and current affairs. They also provide recursive links to geography through a study of such aspects as soil and coastal erosion and to biological science through an investigation of plant growth, photosynthesis and the symbiotic relationship of flora and fauna. Equally, a study of environmental issues can be complemented by stories from Native American folklore, which are seeped in respect for the environment and recognition that all living things are part of one family of being. To harm one member of the 'family' risks jeopardising the whole family.

Narratives are even more powerful if they are actual life stories, told by children and young people from the location being studied. Producers of 'location-packs' tend to include these real life stories as an integral part of teaching material. Huckle (1997) advocates that by studying the lives of young people in distant places, it is possible to create a 'critical school Geography' if pupils are encouraged to compare their own lives with those being studied. Life stories and fictional narratives provide the means by which lives in distant lands can be transported into the classroom to enable greater insight into the reasons why life is as it is for other children.

Narrative, curriculum and knowledge

Novels set in past time and different locations provide us with opportunities to move easily between different aspects of the curriculum, whilst maintaining coherence and continuity of theme. It has been noted that a subject-based curriculum, because it divides knowledge, skills and concepts into discrete compartments, can restrict the learner's ability to transfer knowledge from one subject to another. This is because knowledge is demarcated along arbitrary subject boundaries. By making cross-curricular links possible, narratives create the means by which holistic knowledge is made comprehensible through the synthesis of skills, concepts and understanding. This form of curriculum design and delivery creates the potential for a completely different type of knowledge to that produced by a subject-based one.

The way in which societies construct knowledge influences the way their members see the world. It has been suggested that in the West we tend to have a bipolar approach to knowledge; that is, we see knowledge and concepts in opposition to one another; things are either this or that, rarely are they seen as a combination of more than one element. There are ways of thinking that challenge this perspective. Postmodernism is one such mode of analysis that attempts to deconstruct global theories, but we only have to look at the terminology used by key commentators when they talk about world affairs, to realise that the Western world view is often a dichotomised one. For example, military action abroad has been justified by some Western leaders in terms of the 'free world' defending freedom. By implication, there is, both an 'unfree' world, and the West has a monopoly on the concept of freedom. Of course, such rhetoric may be viewed as a front for ulterior motives but it works as a persuasive device because, by and large, Western populations accept it without question, apart from a minority who voice opposing views.

This discussion may seem tangential to the one begun about the thematic curriculum, but the point is that knowledge and the way knowledge is created is culturally bound. Knowledge itself can influence our view of the world, but so too can the process by which knowledge is constructed. I am suggesting here that an effective thematic curriculum; one that integrates knowledge, rather than treats it as disparate facts, skills, concepts and understanding, may lead to young people seeing the world in a less dichotomised way and enable them to make critical judgements about the world. I am not alone in considering the interrelationship of the curriculum to society. Gaine and George (1999: 68) state it is through the curriculum that a society tries to create an image of itself – its past, present and future. The statement is made in relation to the need for a more multicultural curriculum. The point that needs to be made here, in relation to narrative, is that the use of texts depicting Britain and the world with a richness of cultures will create a different image and a different way of viewing that image to a continual diet of texts that are purely ethnocentric, that is ones that view the world only from the perspective of our own society and its dominant culture.

The application of narrative to the Arts and Humanities components of the curriculum is often easier than it is to either Science or Mathematics, but it is not impossible. In the early 1990s several Local Authorities in England launched projects in which scientific investigation, observation skills and prediction were prompted by the use of stories and drama (Grugeon and Gardner 2000: 60). Around the same time Stannard (1989, 1991) published his 'Uncle Albert' stories which explained Einstein's theory of relativity. Strube (1990: 54 cited in Grugeon and Gardner 2000), asserts that the familiarity of a character in a story creates an 'intimate acquaintance' which engages the reader, enabling scientific concepts to be shared. Because children are introduced to stories from an early age, narrative is familiar territory; it is a known context within which fresh knowledge can be woven.

Stories can be used to frame scientific questions, particularly when the writer or storyteller has been overzealous with 'poetic licence'. How many times have we heard the story of Goldilocks and the Three Bears? How many times have we heard, in one version of the story, that mummy and daddy bear had larger bowls of porridge than baby bear but that daddy's porridge was too hot, mummy's porridge was too cold, whilst baby's was just right? Is this fictional information scientifically plausible? The question can be investigated by applying methods of scientific inquiry. Pupils can make porridge, put it in different sized bowls, and record the changing temperature of each bowl. They will discover that the porridge in the smaller bowl cools faster than the other two, making the story factually incorrect. Alternative versions of this part of the story can then be devised (Grugeon and Gardner 2000: 63).

Although narrative and mathematics require different types of thinking, it is possible to embed arithmetic or mathematical problems within stories. When my youngest daughter, Nanaki, was unsure of her ability to recall her multiplication tables, I incorporated them into a bedtime story. The giant who lived at the top of a steep hill was a very forgetful character. After a hard day at work he often forgot to do his shopping. So, in the morning when he awoke, he had no breakfast and had to amble into the nearby village to buy some food. But, being forgetful, when he went to buy bread he discovered he had left his money at home. The baker, who was very busy, did a deal with the forgetful giant. If the giant could tell him how many loaves he had baked, he would give him a loaf free of charge. The baker said he had made seven trays of bread with six loaves on each tray. The story was suspended as I helped Nanaki to decide which multiplication table she needed to work with and what existing knowledge she had about multiples of six or seven. The story provided a context for us to work collaboratively to solve the problem presented to the giant. Of course, what I did was to help her identify what she already knew and use this to deduce the answer. The story, and the giant's need for breakfast, provided a more meaningful context for finding the answer than the usual decontextualised recitation of multiplication tables.

Children may find it easier to deal with mathematical problems through the medium of story because the narrative creates a fictionalised distance between the problem to be solved and any 'fear' of mathematics they may have. The problem is an inherent aspect of the story and the narrative cannot continue unless the problem is solved. It is the continuation of the story that is the imperative with the mathematics being a minor detail. The advantage of storytelling over story reading is that the storyteller has control of narrative detail and can adapt the story to include the latest aspect of mathematics to be solved. It is useful for the teacher, therefore, to have a repertoire of oral stories that can be adapted, as needs arise.

A thematic approach to teaching then opens up the possibility of putting a particular text at the heart of medium-term planning and integrating specific subject content around prominent elements of the narrative, including its thematic concerns. However, it is highly unlikely that a single text will serve all curriculum areas and there may need to be individual planning of some subjects in order to realise full curriculum delivery. It is also important that with a thematic approach the academic features of each subject discipline are retained. The National Curriculum (DfEE 1988) introduced the idea of studying subjects using similar processes to those used by, for example, real historians, real scientists, real designers. These processes, which include investigative, interpretive and analytical skills need to be retained because they are exactly the skills that lead to higher order thinking; they also involve processes that make learning active and interactive. In short they are the ingredients of creative approaches to teaching and learning. Some children's novels lend themselves more than others to cross-curricular teaching. Dick King-Smith's *The Merman* (1997) is one text that almost appears to be written for the purpose. Its central character, Zeta, befriends a merman who teaches her a range of subjects from Geography to Mathematics.

Knowledge of story structure

For decades pupils have been given a simple formula for their story writing; their narratives must have a beginning, a middle and an end. It is time this simplistic view of narrative was replaced by a more detailed account of narrative structure; one that informs teachers' subject knowledge so they are able to give pupils better guidance about story writing. We might think of the three components of beginnings, middles and ends as the narrative superstructure; each with its own sub-components. Within the beginnings of stories, there are three such sub-components; the aperture, exposition and inciting moment. Each has a specific function in the telling of the story and each contributes to the engagement of the audience, whether they be listeners or readers. The aperture consists of the opening to the story. It often signifies the type of story to be told. For example, the opening, 'Once upon a time . . .' immediately informs the audience they are in the realm of fairy tale. The reader is able to draw upon a tradition of fairy tales, which ignites their predictive faculty and frames their thinking within the genre to be read. Of course, many apertures are less obvious of genre than this but they nevertheless signify some feature of the story, through the clues they give.

The exposition consists of all the information a reader needs at the beginning of the story to begin the process of mental visualisation that is necessary to become engaged with the narrative. Such information includes; the setting, both in terms of location and time, introduction of the protagonist and other major characters and initial details about the relationship of characters to one another. Additional information is, of course, imparted throughout the story. The final element of the beginning of a story is the 'inciting moment', an event that 'kick-starts' the action, driving the narrative forward. Without an inciting moment, the story would come to an abrupt end.

The middle section of a story is its longest part and includes three further elements – the developing conflict, climax and denouement. A story must have tension or conflict caused by a problem or series of problems that have to be overcome. In some traditional tales, the protagonist is sent on a quest to perform three tasks. Each task involves overcoming an obstacle, which creates tension and conflict; each task is harder than the previous one. This stage of the story is also known as the 'rising action'.

The emotional cadence of the story rises to a climax where the tension is at its most intense. The denouement soon follows and involves a final event that begins to draw the story to its conclusion. The end of the story has two elements, although some stories have three. The final suspense involves the resolution of conflicts which leads to the story's plausible and satisfactory conclusion. Stories such as parables and fables, where a moral tale is told, often include a third element called a coda. This is a final statement to reinforce the lesson to be learned from the story. Some fables signal the coda in an obvious way, using the words, 'And the moral of this story is . . .' However, a more sophisticated coda may be couched in a more symbolic way. To summarise, then, the various components of a story are:

- The Beginning

    the aperture

    the exposition

    the inciting moment

- The Middle

    the developing conflict

    the climax

    the denouement

- The End

    the final suspense

    the conclusion

    the coda

Sophisticated narratives manipulate this structure, making the story less linear than the above description suggests. Some stories are made more complex by the parallel delivery of two stories in one, by means of a plot and its concomitant subplot. Some stories are tightly structured and every detail contributes to the telling of the narrative; others are loosely structured and involve description and figurative detail that is not essential to the development of the narrative.

From storytelling to story writing

Ultimately, pupils have to be able to transfer their knowledge of stories, whether that knowledge is gained through storytelling, reading or other media, to writing. No matter how good the pupil is at telling a story, he or she must be able to demonstrate similar competence in the written mode because academic success is still measured by means of the pupil's competence in literacy. The evidence suggests that time spent developing stories orally and hearing stories has a positive impact on pupils' ability to write stories. Working with bilingual pupils, Bassi (1999: 99) found that the practise of storytelling, combined with strong oral input at the drafting stage of story writing, did enhance the quality of stories pupils wrote. Initially, she encouraged pupils to tell the class their story idea. This was followed by pair work in which pupils collaborated to draft their stories. At this stage pairs composed plots, described characters, created and resolved problems and devised effective conclusions. Once the groundwork had been achieved through oral composition, pupils then wrote their stories and finally read them to the whole class. Feedback was then given to the writer by their peers. In her evaluation of the classroom-based research, Bassi (1999: 109) came to three main conclusions about the influence of storytelling on writing. First, through storytelling pupils develop ideas, their own voice and an awareness of their own power. Second, effective story writing is produced in relation to the quality of what children are exposed to through oral storytelling, reading and visual literacy. Finally, in order to properly judge the pupil's ability as a writer, the teacher must read beyond surface features (spelling, handwriting and punctuation) to consider such items as variations in phrase structure, thematic variety and textual cohesion.

The difference between transcriptional and compositional skills was pointed out by Smith (1982) but there is a stubborn tendency in educational culture to view writing ability in terms of the pupil's neatness of handwriting and accuracy of punctuation and spelling. This view is often reinforced by parents. However, as Smith asserts, compositional skills are at the heart of what makes good writers and good writing. In working with pupils as writers, the emphasis, therefore, needs to be placed on the development of pupils' ability to construct a good story. However, when presenting written texts to an audience, there is a secondary need, which is the ability to make the text understandable to the reader in the writer's absence. It is at this point that the importance of transcriptional skills needs to be considered. The development of both compositional and transcriptional skills should be orientated to the needs of the audience. Pupils, therefore, require authentic audiences to write for, with opportunities to receive constructive feedback on their writing. The need to communicate meanings effectively provides the rationale for the writer to improve the quality of what is written and how it is written.

The epic story

Returning to the story *The Voyage of Prince Fuji* (Thorne 1980), referred to in Chapter four, I want to describe a project in which this beautifully illustrated epic story, involving the eponymous character's travels across several lands, was used as the stimulus for a writing with Year 4 pupils. The first four illustrations were used to write an aperture and exposition. In the first picture, Fuji is standing in a garden with a woman at his side. In the next he is setting sail. The third picture shows a storm tormenting Fuji's boat, which appears frail against monstrous waves. The fourth picture depicts terrified expressions on the faces of two sailors as they clutch the ship's mast, tilting towards the onrushing sea. At the foot of these last three pictures, the woman in the first picture is knelt embroidering the tapestry of Fuji's voyage. The implication is that she received news of the shipwreck and was recording the event. These fragments of the original, combined with a request to reconstruct the story of Fuji's voyage became the impetus for an extended story-writing project with a Year 4 class. At the outset, pupils were told they would be reading their finished stories to pupils in a Year 6 class. This information caused a few audible gasps. The thought of writing for an older age group appeared daunting. However, the challenge proved effective when, seven weeks later, each pupil read their story to an older counterpart. Year 6 pupils were asked to comment on what they liked about the stories and whether anything about the writing surprised them. The feedback given to the writers was probably among the most memorable they were to receive in their whole school careers. Comments of 'I did not think Year 4 would know the words they have used' and 'these are really good stories' left the writers shining their egos. The impact of the project had long-lasting effects. I am told by the parent of twins, who were in that class of Year 4, that even at university they remembered the 'Prince Fuji work' and how it had helped them improve their writing.

This comment alone makes reflection on the project a worthwhile undertaking, particularly if processes can be replicated for use in other classrooms, to the benefit of other pupils. It should be noted that this work was undertaken before the implementation of the first National Literacy Strategy in 1998, and that the prescriptive content and structure of the strategy would not have made the project possible. The fact that I now feel able to write about the work with some confidence that it may provide a useful contribution to the practice of other colleagues is indicative of the current sense of 'back to the future', and the end of an arid period in the teaching of English.

In the first workshop, pupils were given a picture of Prince Fuji and asked to describe him and to speculate on the kind of person he might be. Keywords and phrases were recorded for use later. However, as some of the first descriptions of Fuji included stereotypical language, pupils were given time to consider alternative words and phrases. The refusal to record stereotypical language to describe Fuji's features implicitly signalled the thoughtful approach we expected pupils to adopt during the project. In addition, pupils were asked to consider the verb tense they should use when writing. It was generally decided the story was set in the past because of the clothes the Prince was wearing. The geographic location for the beginning of the story was also discussed. When it was agreed this was to be Japan, a map of the country was given to pupils so they could identify coastal towns that they might name as the port of departure for the voyage. These questions and accompanying resources helped to give the story authenticity.

At the beginning of each writing workshop pupils were reminded of the intended audience. In the second session, I used the four pictures to construct a rationale for writing as well as a stimulus for the story's aperture and exposition. The title of the story was introduced in the initial workshop along with my explanation of how the book came to be lost. A number of pupils were unfamiliar with the word 'voyage', so a definition was elicited. The class' task was to reconstruct the story, using the plot of the original. The use of the original plotline helped to scaffold pupils' own narratives and relieved them of some of the cognitive load involved in the complex process of writing. Writers across the ages, including Shakespeare, have used existing narratives to tell stories, so why should we expect pupils to be original all of the time. Originality can be expressed through the narration, that is how the narrative is told, rather than in the narrative itself, which is what the story is about (Genette 1972). Using an existing narrative as a skeleton structure provides pupils with the thinking space to give to other aspects of composition such as development of character, description of setting and narrative tension.

Working in pairs, pupils were given the four pictures and an opportunity to discuss them. Some guiding questions were also given. These were:

- Who is in the picture?

- What might be their relationship to one another?

- What are the characters saying to one another?

- How do they feel?

- What do they see and hear around them?

The questions were designed to encourage pupils to discuss the expository elements of the story; that is, the introduction of the main character, Fuji, and the setting. Pupils also implicitly recognised the inciting moment, Fuji's decision to embark on a voyage, and produced plausible reasons for the journey. As decisions were made they were recorded in note form alongside each picture. These planning notes were then used to begin independent writing. First drafts were then shared with a 'writing partner'. As the class was not used to discussing their work and giving evaluative feedback, a guidance sheet, divided into two sections, was provided to aid discussion. The exact questions used to guide pupils can be found in Figure 6.1. Essentially, the first stage of the process of evaluation involved making judgements about compositional aspects of the writing in relation to what the writer wanted to tell the audience and the feelings, in the reader, the writer intended to evoke. The second stage focused on the transcriptional aspects of writing, in terms of making meanings clear to the reader. The sequence in which pupils were asked to judge each other's writing implicitly reinforced our view that composition was more important than transcription, but that consideration of how the writing was to be presented still

Stage One

With a partner follow the guidance.

Your task: read your work aloud.

Partner's task: Listen carefully to the story.

Both of you: try to answer the following questions.

1. Do you think the writing is interesting/ enjoyable?

2. Is there anything missing in the writing?

3. Is there anything which is not clear or accurate?

4. Can you suggest any helpful words or expressions?

5. Can you suggest a more suitable beginning or ending to the piece?

6. Do you think it is too long, or too short?

7. Can anything be missed out?

Write suggestions on a separate piece of paper.

Stage Two

With your partner read through your writing again.

Try to answer the following questions:

1. Are there any spelling mistakes? If so, underline them in pencil.

2. Check the punctuation. Are full stops, capitals and commas in the right places? Correct them in pencil.

3. Show in your writing where you want to make alterations.

4. Ask the teacher at this point if you feel you need more help.

Rewrite the piece by yourself, using the advice you have been given.

FIGURE 6.1   Pair drafting

had value. The pair drafting sheets were used throughout the project as a means of helping pupils refine their writing.

In the original story, Fuji encountered a dragon on his trek through China. In order to introduce this episode in the story I drafted a letter that Fuji wrote to his wife. The letter, deliberately incomplete, read:

My Dearest Beloved,

For many days we journeyed across angry seas that rose above our heads like monstrous watery mountains. At the height of the terrible storm three of my best sailors were swallowed up in the jaws of a huge wave. I feared for my own life.

Thankfully, I survived to tell the tale of that terrible voyage. I have so many tales to tell you. The next, upon reaching China, is more dreadful still. But for all that the Chinese are a most civilized people and we have much to learn from them. Soon I shall leave for . . .

The style of writing, embedded with simile and metaphor, was reflected in the writing of many pupils in the class. Through the letter pupils 'tuned into' Fuji's voice. The letter was accompanied by a picture of a Chinese dragon and pupils speculated that this is what the next terrible tale involved. When humans meet dragons it leads to one thing, conflict. True to form this was not a pleasant dragon. Keen to avoid a quick skirmish before Fuji moved on, I wanted to slow the narrative at this point to encourage pupils to develop atmosphere and tension. A grid sheet (Table 6.1) was given to pupils along with a set of descriptive words (Figure 6.2). In pairs pupils decided on appropriate words to use and completed the grid sheet. This activity generated questions about the meaning of certain words. It encouraged the use of dictionaries and thesauruses, which lead to vocabulary extension. The more adventurous pupils sometimes chose to use synonyms they had discovered in place of words on the sheet. On completion, pupils were asked to describe, using one or two sentences, the place where Fuji discovered the dragon. They were also asked to consider how he came to encounter the dragon; was it by accident, or was he searching for something the dragon might be guarding? In their writing they were encouraged to show how the dragon and Fuji reacted to one another on first meeting and what happened next. The dragon was a fantastic beast and the importance of describing it in detail, as a record for the reader, was emphasised. The grid sheet provided pupils with a lexical 'prop', which enabled them to concentrate on creating imagery and tension through sentence construction. Writing is a complex multidimensional process and many young writers need to be supported with aspects of their writing so they can devote mental energy to other aspects of the writing process. In this instance, the process of making word choices was separated from the process of making sentences. Pupils were reminded the reader would need to know the outcome of the encounter.

TABLE 6.1 The dragon: description grid sheet

The dragon's	head	eyes	horns	teeth	nostrils	breath	claws	tail	back	torso	front legs	back legs
Colour												
Size												
Shape												
Texture												
Temperature												

Size

big large enormous gigantic thick small

little tiny minute slender narrow thin lean

broad wide tall long short stubby

Colour

red ruby blood-red

crimson scarlet rose

orange copper apricot

creamy white ivory

silver grey gold ochre

saffron yellow gilt

Texture

smooth silky
sleek polished

valvety glossy
slippery soft

sharp rugged
gnarled knurled

scraggy prickly
rough uneven

wrinkled scaly
knobbly knotty

Shape

round curved hooked bent oval

almond circular crooked crinkly wavy

curly cavernous hollow barbed snake-like

serpentine straight square pointed jagged

triangular tapering spiky conical flat

Temperature

hot warm fiery hot as a furnace

aglow glowing blazing like a volcano

flaming ablaze smoking smouldering

unquenchable cold cool chilly ice-cold

FIGURE 6.2 Describing the dragon: word sheet

Writing in this episodic manner meant that sections of the story appeared disjointed. We discussed this point and devised a set of suggested discourse connectors, which can be found in Figure 6.3.

Some writers progressed with their writing at a faster pace than others. That is not to say that those who progressed more quickly were the better writers, although the 'slower' group did include all of the pupils who found writing difficult. This group also included those writers who painstakingly crafted every sentence before moving on to the next. We might call such pupils 'perfectionists'. To allow the slower group time to complete the first stage of the story, time was built in to allow them to catch up. The faster group 'remained' in China and was introduced to the Terracotta Warriors and the Grand Buddha. Sat in groups, pupils were given large colour posters of the warriors and the Buddha. They were also supplied with Chinese artefacts. After discussing the pictures and artefacts and considering their relevance to the story, pupils then described their chosen images and wrote their first drafts. Pair drafting followed, which included consideration of how to connect the new episode in the story to the previous one.

The words in the box below will help you move from one event to another in your story

Later...　After a while...　Then...　Next...　Shortly after...　Before too long...

Soon after that...　Soon...　Suddenly...　All of a sudden...　Time passed...

Sometime later...　Eventually...　By evening...　Later that day/night...

On the following day...　The following morning...　The day after...

On the second/third/fourth day...　Before too long...　A week went by...

Here are some examples of how to use the above words and phrases:

Shortly after leaving the shores on his homeland, Prince Fiji sailed into a terrible storm.

Suddenly a storm blew up.

Later that day the sea grew rough and a storm tossed Prince Fiji's ship from side to side.

FIGURE 6.3　Story connectors

To stimulate discussion and thought around the next stage in the story, a second letter home was mentioned. However, this time pupils were not given a copy of the letter, just a summary of its contents, which were:

- a reference to the land he next visited;

- a description of how he travelled from the coast to inland regions and how long the journey took;

- descriptions of some of the sights, sounds and smells he experienced en route;

- accounts of some of the people he met en route;

- a reference to a lucky escape on his return journey to the coast.

Accompanying the synopsis of the letter were pictures of Mughal paintings depicting regal scenes; line drawings of farmers working the land; a poster of the interior of a mosque, ornately decorated with geometric patterns and arches; and a map of the Indian subcontinent. It should be noted that the pictures were chosen to reflect the backgrounds of the Muslim children in the class. Had they been Hindu or Sikh, alternative appropriate religious icons would have been selected.

　　The final episode of the epic journey took Fuji to Tanzania in Africa. Again, pupils were given pictures and artefacts of the country. These were carefully selected to depict the country's rich cultural heritage, architecture, dress etc. in an attempt to challenge any stereotypical misconceptions pupils might have about Africa. Alongside this episode we taught the pupils about archaeological evidence that suggests the East African Rift Valley is the place where humanity was 'born'. It was here that Fuji made an important realisation and where the climax of the story occurred. The end of the story was left for pupils to decide. Most had him return to his homeland for a happy reunion with his wife, the woman in the first picture. Some left the story open for other adventures to be told as Fuji continued his epic journey, others concluded with Fuji being wiser than when he embarked on the voyage.

The 'Fuji epic' was a carefully scaffolded writing project involving seven workshop sessions over as many weeks. Pupils were given a structure for the plot; a variety of stimuli for each episode in the story; examples of stylistic possibilities through examples of Fuji's letters; and possible words that could be used in the story. In addition, there was a 'dictionary' of names. Examples of Japanese, Chinese, Indian and Tanzanian names were given to pupils so they could give characters authentic cultural identities.

When I set out on the 'Fuji project' I had intended to focus on story writing. However, when I analysed what we had done during the seven weeks, I realised that working with epic story writing had a number of additional advantages for teachers. It enables the teacher to control certain variables in the writing process such as word choices and plot, thereby relieving pupils of some of the cognitive load and enabling them to focus attention on other variables such as descriptions of setting and narration of the story. The journey taken by the protagonist can include the homelands of pupils' families, which enables the teacher to reflect the cultural mix of the class. It also encourages pupils to demonstrate cultural knowledge, which may be new to the teacher, and allows them to write within a familiar 'cultural frame'. Whole class interaction, collaborative group work, paired talk and independent writing were synthesised in an evolutionary and holistic process which made sense to the pupils. In this way the development of writing was a social event rather than a wholly individual one with pupils supporting one another's learning in a carefully structured progression of the story.

Parallel to the writing of the story were elements of other subjects. Geography was evident in the inclusion of several maps and references to climate and the landscapes of places visited by Fuji. The story was set in the past, which necessitated research on the history of the places visited. The study of artefacts and pictures encouraged pupils to consider the cultural significance of the items which gave the whole project a strong multicultural dimension. Religious icons initiated talk and thinking around their symbolic significance and meaning to worshippers. Each episode of the story was accompanied by an illustration. The product of the workshop session, the finished writing and illustrations, were made into a book, which gave each child's work a status they had not previously known. The writing had begun with a purpose, to re-create the lost story of Fuji, and the writers had been given an authentic audience. These factors seemed to both stimulate the imaginations of pupils and cause them to orientate their work to the intended readers. The fact they were writing for an older age group encouraged them to 'raise their game'.

In this chapter we have seen how story in all its forms, whether it be oral storytelling, story reading or story writing, is a powerful medium for learning about the world, past and present. We live our lives through narratives. Narratives connect us to who we are and help us make sense of life. As such then, narrative can affect us emotionally as well as intellectually. As we shall see in the next chapter, which deals with sensitive issues in literature, story can also take us into worlds we may never personally encounter and enable us to become embroiled in the 'virtual' narratives of others. Narrative then, has an abiding place in the curriculum, both as a means of self exploration and as a pedagogic tool.

7

Reading outside
the box

THIS CHAPTER EXPLORES the following:

- the role of the reader and reading as an active creative process;

- moving pupils' beyond their reading 'comfort zones';

- dealing with sensitive issues in children's literature;

- ways of identifying different types of reader and their needs when encountering new texts.

A good story possesses the power to absorb us as readers, to enthral our senses and take us into imaginary worlds. Children's literature abounds with good stories. However, there may be a tendency to view children's stories as simply a literature designed for children's entertainment. For example, some may view illustrations in picture books as a means to make books attractive to children, or as the visual representation of the text; a means to aid comprehension. While this may be one function of the picture, it is a simplistic interpretation of the nature of picture books. We see, for example, in the work of Anthony Browne (1992, 1994, 1997), simple texts enhanced by multilayered, polysemic visual images. His illustrations do not simply reflect the text; they go beyond it by taking the reader into a symbolic world beyond the word. Like all good texts, they imply subtextual possibilities or make subtle connections with cultural artefacts such as King Kong in 'Voices in the Park' (Browne 1999). Such intertextual links enable the reader to read within and beyond the text. This kind of reading requires the reader to apply their worldly knowledge in conjunction with the text in an active process of meaning making. In this chapter I want to explore the relationship of fictional narrative to the real world and consider how to deal with writers who reflect uncomfortable scenarios in their stories. Part of this exploration is a consideration of the position of readers in relation to such texts and the kind of preparation that might be required to help readers to access literature that may be outside their 'comfort zone'.

Fictional and social narratives

The study of children's literature then involves the analysis of internal features of the narrative, as well as meta-narrative structures and their interconnectedness. In this context, meta-narrative refers social, cultural and even political narratives outside the text. Stories do not exist in isolation of the social or cultural contexts in which they are made, or read. They are created by writers who are themselves implicated in a social universe, who draw on the social world for their material. As stated earlier in the book, the authors Phillip Pullman and David Almond attest that all writers are 'magpies'. Taking this to be the case, it follows that all narratives are in some way intertextual; that is to say all narratives are influenced by other narratives, fictional, personal and social (Worton and Still 1990). In his work Almond (1998, 1999, 2003), draws heavily upon autobiographical experience and personal lived narratives of childhood in north-east England. Pullman often uses literary sources as the inspiration for his work. In the case of *I Was a Rat* (2000), it was the traditional tale of Cinderella; *Clockwork* (1996) was inspired by the gothic tales of the Germanic tradition and his Dark Materials trilogy alludes to Milton's *Paradise Lost*.

The relationship of children's literature to the social world is expounded by Stephens and McCallum (1998: 3–4) when they state that in contradistinction to narratives for adults, children's stories are far more intertextual because, to a far greater degree, they involve the retelling of stories. They assert that the repetition of children's narratives, subject to individual modification, serves an important sociocultural function; it is the means by which a society imparts its core values, heritage, collective allusions and experience to the young. Thus, the individual narrative of story is framed by a social meta-narrative that defines acceptable behaviour in the young and proscribes unacceptable behaviour, thereby affirming the moral code of a society. However, the retelling of a story is never a simple replication of the original version. In some instances, as is often the case with traditional stories, the original version is not known to the teller or writer and the retelling is based on multiple retellings of that original. As such then, the story is reworked by the author but is done so within the context of social meta-narrative; the pre-text, or version of the story that pre-existed the retold version and the reconfiguration of the narrative, which Stephens and McCallum prefer to call 'reversion' because the retold story is never quite the same as previous versions, since it is imbued with fresh significance by the author.

Roald Dahl's version of 'Little Red Riding Hood' (2001) is a case in point. In this version of the story, a story that has undergone thousands, if not millions of retellings, Little Red Riding Hood is not the vulnerable, naïve girl of the traditional story, but a street-wise, no nonsense, sassy female, who has her wits about her. Dahl has her pull her gun from her knickers and shoot the wolf in a humorous and surprising 'twist' on the original. On one level we might read this 'reversion' of the customary tale as parody, which, of course it is, but parody operates within the strictures of a moral code, albeit sometimes at the margins of acceptability. The climax to Dahl's version of the story is framed both by the original, its pre-text, and by current social discourse or meta-narrative. Dahl has Little Red Riding Hood pull the gun from her knickers, rather than say the basket she is carrying to Grandma's, partly for its risqué connotation; a connotation in keeping with the sado-erotic nature of the original story, which is about rape and the vulnerability of a pubescent girl to the sexual predatory nature of a certain type of man. The deliberate use of the word 'knickers', which has an explicitly feminine connotation, is a reminder of the sexual nature of the 'pre-text' but the reversal of violence, with Little Red Riding Hood as the perpetrator, rather than the wolf, taps into a feminist discourse, a meta-narrative, in which the protagonist is no longer a defenceless little girl but is an assertive, self-determining young woman who is quite able to defend herself. It is worth recalling that in the original version, both Grandma and Little Red Riding Hood are rescued by the woodcutter, who is absent in Dahl's version, thereby accentuating the dominance of the female.

Dahl's parody not only requires the reader to know the traditional story, 'the pre-text', but to also be aware of feminist ideology and the growing body of literature in which gender reversals subvert male dominance, a characteristic feature of traditional tales, which are themselves based on traditional gender relations. Without feminist discourse the humour might be lost and Little Red Riding Hood's action of revealing her knickers to withdraw the gun might be viewed as distasteful. In this example we can see how a retold story may be signified by social discourses that may not have existed at the time of previous 'tellings' and is, therefore, altered, either explicitly or implicitly, by sociocultural references.

For every good story there are at least two possible ways of analysing it. The first is within the story itself, and the second is in terms of its significance in social context. In the first analysis the student is concerned with such features as characterisation, plot, narrative, the author's use of language and thematic concerns. The second type of analysis requires these elements to be considered within the broader social frame. It is a frame bounded by society and culture with their concomitant socio-political concerns. Butts (1992: xiii) makes the point that literary genres, such as the adventure story, the school story and fantasy have emerged as the result of specific social, cultural and historic situations. Within this social frame then are both the text and the reader. In this chapter I want to explore the relationships of both texts to readers and texts to the social world outside the text, of which the reader's lived experience is an integral part.

Reading within the 'comfort zone'

Unless they are shown alternatives, pupils' choices of what to read are often fixed securely within the parameters of their own comfort zone; that is, they readily read topics and authors with whom they are familiar and with whom they feel safe. Often choices are influenced by the popularity of certain authors whose work has been privileged by the persuasive hype of advertising. Consider the media coverage of the publication of each Harry Potter novel and the eager parents and children who formed long queues outside bookshops to acquire the latest edition. What J.K. Rowling did was raise interest in reading for a lot of children and if Harry Potter led them on to reading other books, then it was a job well done. However, unless they are guided to do so, pupils may not challenge themselves as readers. In addition to those children who only read within their comfort zone, there are others who do not read for pleasure at all.

In this chapter I want to explore possible ways, first, of encouraging pupils to read and, second, to be more adventurous in their reading by introducing them to writers and novels they might not encounter unless it is in the classroom. The particular novels I will discuss deal with issues that might be considered sensitive. They are novels that weave within their narratives authentic problems of the human condition; that is, real concerns and dilemmas experienced by their child protagonists. Before introducing these novels, I consider what the process of reading entails, drawing upon reader response theory, which positions the reader as an active maker of meanings, guided by the text. A second element of reader response theory concerns the experiences readers bring to the text in order to construct meanings. Texts may be sensitive for a variety of reasons: they may deal with issues that are political in nature; raise moral, social or emotional problems; they maybe graphic in their depictions of characters under emotional duress, or touch the lives of certain readers in raw and painful ways because the reader's personal narrative closely resembles that of the protagonist. These kinds of sensitivity require delicate handling by the teacher. In recognition of this point, I propose a model for identifying the positioning of different readers in relation to issues raised by the text. The model is then used to suggest possible ways in which teachers might work with pupils to develop their thinking around such texts.

Arising out of the above discussion there is perhaps an assumption that all teachers have a comprehensive knowledge of books for children, but pupils may not be alone in selecting books from a narrow range of well-known authors; many teachers too are often unaware of the full range of books for children and young people that are available. In a study of 1,200 primary teachers, Cremin *et al.* found that although the majority of primary school teachers read for pleasure on a regular basis, their choice of books to read in the classroom was greatly influenced by the books they had read and loved as children. In addition, their knowledge of current authors and poets writing for children was limited (Cremin *et al.* 2008). The corollary is that in our classrooms a canon of populist texts is paraded as children's literature. Given that the majority of primary teachers are white and female and that, as Cremin *et al.* point out, their knowledge of children's literature is largely based on their own reading experiences as children, these texts are likely to be restricted to children's classics, and authors who appeal to a white female readership.

Elsewhere, Cremin and Powell (2008) suggest the current curriculum emphasis on the teaching of decoding and comprehension skills has marginalised consideration of the affective and attitudinal aspects of the reader. Yet, much research indicates that effective teachers of reading have a wide ranging knowledge of children's literature and use this knowledge in the classroom to motivate developing readers (Meek 1998; Medwell *et al.* 1998; Martin 2003: Cremin 2007). Furthermore, there is a strong association between children's attitudes to reading and their reading attainment (Twist *et al.* 2006). It would seem, therefore, that if we are to motivate pupils to read and encourage them to engage with texts in thoughtful ways, we need to provide a wide reading repertoire; one that takes pupils beyond their comfort zone and challenges their preconceived notions of stories that they find 'cosy'. However, before that can happen, teachers themselves need opportunities to explore books and novels by new authors, as well as ones that are not readily found on the shelves of mainstream bookshops. To do this they need access to specialist knowledge. The school's own literacy coordinator may be able to provide such knowledge but here are others outside the school setting who spend their professional lives engaged with children's literature. Librarians in the local School Library Service are ideally placed to advise teachers about the ever growing range of books for children. Some libraries have their own websites that provide reviews of the kind of quality books that may not reach the High Street bookshops. An example is the Bedfordshire Library Service's virtual library, which has an easily navigable children's section with links to other sites, including those of the major children's book awards. Web addresses for these sites can be found at the end of this chapter.

Types of reading and types of reader

Taking pupils beyond their comfort zone and into uncharted territory may pose some risks. As we have seen above, effective reading involves more than the simple decoding and comprehension of literature; it requires the reader to become cognitively and emotionally involved with the text. This may lead to emotional sensitivities being exposed in relation to some texts by some readers. Therefore, in moving beyond the cosy familiarity of customary reading, we need to give thought to the role that the reader plays in the process of reading. Smith (2005) has identified four processes of reading that frame different types of reader. The way a reader engages with a text may be influenced by their conception of what they think reading is and what readers do. As Heath (1983) has shown, reading is a social practice and personal reading habits are cultural behaviours learned from the social contexts in which we learn to read.

Smith states that in contexts where the emphasis is on decoding and word recognition, pupils may become 'implosive readers'. By this she means readers who adeptly read the words on the page but do not make connections beyond the text, or think beyond the text. For such readers, she explains the text 'collapses in on itself' (Smith 2005: 15). Her second category of reader is characterised by 'tangential reading'. Tangential readers are influenced by certain triggers in the text that encourage them to follow lines of thinking that are tangential to the text but only tenuously related to it. The result is that this tangential thought takes the reader's mind away from the text and does not allow them to connect experience from outside the text with events inside the text. Hence, reading becomes 'fractured'. A second type of 'fracture' occurs with Smith's category of 'ricochet reading'. Like tangential reading, a thought is triggered by a stimulus in the text, which then triggers associated thoughts, as in stream of consciousness, but these thoughts bare little relation to the text. Unless they are taught otherwise, none of these three types of reader will develop into the ideal reader, adopting what Smith calls 'balanced reading'. Balanced readers are able to use personal experience, knowledge of other texts and their own emotional response holistically in order to interpret what they read. This kind of reading involves the recursive flow of the reader's thinking within the text and beyond it, and back again, as the reader reads and reflects on what is being read, making the links between the real world and the virtual world of the text. Smith acknowledges that this type of reading takes practice and proposes classroom reading practices to encourage 'balanced reading'. As with the model proposed in Chapter one exploratory, group talk is central to the process of stimulating pupils' thinking in relation to texts and to encouraging more balanced reading habits. This approach to reading requires teachers to 'stand back' and allow pupils the time and space to share their thinking through collaborative group work. This positioning of the teacher is the hallmark of creative teaching and learning (Burnard *et al.* 2006).

Literature circles

One means of formalising collaborative group work in reading is the use of 'literature circles'. The literature circle is a means of embedding group talk around texts in order to create a learning culture in which reading is promoted and children's views are valued. The literature circle involves a group of pupils reading the same book independently and then joining together to talk about the book. King and Briggs (2005) explain that because literature circles encourage pupils to share their thoughts about a text they have read in common, it stretches their thinking and encourages a deeper reading for meaning. By sharing their thinking and by seeing how other readers read, membership of the literature circle can lead readers to develop more 'balanced reading' habits. In so doing, therefore, the literature circle encourages pupils to enter the text more deeply than does isolated, independent reading; it challenges pupils to support their views by going back into the text to find evidence to substantiate thinking; it allows pupils to see that emotional responses to texts are valid and allows pupils to make interconnections between texts and real issues in their lives and in the world generally. However, the latter is only likely to happen if the texts that pupils are given connect authentically with their lived experience or relate to issues in the real world. As Carter states, 'A work of literature . . . will only be great as a text for children if it concurs with their interests, psychological needs and potential for understanding' (Carter 2000: 77).

Encouraging reader responses

In this sense then, effective reading requires the reader, not necessarily to judge what the writer meant by aspects of the text, but how the text made them respond. In addition, it requires the reader to reflect upon their response and question why they responded in such a way (Iser 1980). This approach to reading recognises the role of the reader as an active participant in the construction of meaning around a text, and views reading as a creative process. In this line of thought, a text comes alive only in the act of reading. Readers construct meaning by viewing the text through their own interpretive lenses. One such lens is personal experience; the accumulated events and incidents of one's own specific real life narrative. Smith (2005: 6) refers to this kind of affective response to reading as the 'intimate' response. Texts with which readers can strongly identify tend to have close parallels with their own lives, and meanings are derived from a transaction between lived experience and the 'virtual reality' of the narrative (Rosenblatt 1995, 2005).

What is being described here is Reader Response Theory, of which both Iser and Rosenblatt are advocates. Reader Response Theory provides primary teachers with a liberating and creative approach to the reading of literature in the classroom, because it acknowledges that the act of reading begins as much with children's own lived experience, as it does with the text itself. It provides the means by which reading can be located within what we know about how children best learn; that is, by building on prior knowledge and experience. As such then, the epistemological basis of Reader Response Theory resonates strongly with constructivist theories of learning. This approach challenges the dichotomised view of reading as, on the one hand, the ability to recognise words on the page and, on the other, to comprehend what is being read. The Simple Model of Reading (Rose 2006), which has become the orthodox approach to teaching reading within the Primary National Strategy, fails to acknowledge the role of the reader, reducing the act of reading to the application of a set of taught skills. What Reader Response Theory allows us to do is put the reader, and his or her affective responses to texts, back into the equation.

By acknowledging the importance of the reader and by valuing his or her experience, which influences how responses to the text are arrived at, there is a greater possibility that pupils will see the relevance of reading to their own personal experience. By enabling pupils to make connections between texts and their own lived experience, relevance and the advocacy of personal response is likely to lead to a greater value being attributed to books by the reader. In this way, reading is likely to be a more meaningful and satisfying activity for more pupils than is suggested by the findings of the Progress in International Reading Literacy Study 2006, which found that there had been a decline in reading attainment among English ten-year-olds over a five year period (Twist *et al.* 2006).

I refer above to readers bringing their lived experience to the text and using this personal experience as a 'lens' through which they construct meanings. This individualised, unique experience might be regarded as a 'small interpretive lens'. I use the analogy of a lens to suggest that the reader's experience influences the way they 'see' the text. Seeing involves signification. By that I mean that the reader attributes to various stimuli in the text, meanings that are triggered by their own experience of life. However, individual experience is mediated through larger lenses that play a significant function in shaping an individual's social experience. Smith (2005: 6) refers to this level of interpretation as the 'extra-personal', which includes the identity of the child and his or her lived experience. Elsewhere, I discuss how an individual's experience of the social world is mediated through differing levels of identity. In addition to the personal self, there is a communal self, which includes the matrix of experience acquired through social interaction at the level of community. This includes interactions with family members, school, the peer group and interactions with others during the course of daily life by virtue of being a member of a community. Beyond the communal self is the social self. This concept of self includes ascribed identities such as the individual's gender, social class, 'race', ethnicity, sexual orientation and the degree to which society restrains the individual's movement in the environment and access to social institutions. These larger social categories provide the basis for the creation of group identities, which alter the way groups of people and, therefore individuals, are positioned in the social world, causing us to experience that world differently (Gardner 2007: 17). To these categories I have assigned the term 'large interpretive lenses'.

Allied to our own unique way of seeing the world (small lens), we share in common with others in our social group common ways of seeing the world (large lens) because of the way we are positioned socially by virtue of our membership of these larger social classifications. Hence, when we read, we bring both unique experience and social experience to the text. This view gives rise to the possibility that there may be, for example, a gendered construction of meaning around a text. In which case, it is possible that boys and girls read a given text differently and, therefore, construct meanings that are, to some extent, shared by individuals of the same gender but are different from individuals of a different gender. The same principle applies to all the categories referred to above. However, individuals are not positioned solely by means of one social category because each of us is a member of several categories simultaneously. So, in addition to having a personal narrative (small lens), aspects of that narrative may be influenced by the larger social experience of being, say, a particular gender and a particular ethnicity (large lenses). In addition to social experience, is the reader's knowledge of other texts, which not only include printed texts, but visual and aural ones also. As discussed elsewhere in this book, many children have extensive knowledge of film and for some, their experience of narrative structure, characterisation, depiction of setting and other elements of story will be derived solely from watching visual texts. This visual literacy is as important to these children as book reading is to others. The fact their knowledge has been acquired through watching television or videos does not make it any less valid than does knowledge acquired by means of the more orthodox process of reading print-based narrative.

It is possible then to see that the meanings the reader attributes to a text are mediated through several lenses simultaneously: by the text itself; by one's gendered experiences; by virtue of one's ethnicity; by one's social class etc. and by one's personal experiences, as well as one's knowledge of other texts. This discussion is summarised visually in Figure 7.1, 'An active model of reading'. Looked at in this way, it is possible to see the reason why readers interpret the same text differently, thereby making the reading of a specific text an experience that is unique to each reader.

Reading with a focus on the reader

Good literature involves the unravelling of complications around the human condition; that is, the problems human beings experience as protagonists in a

Reader   Interpretive lenses   Text

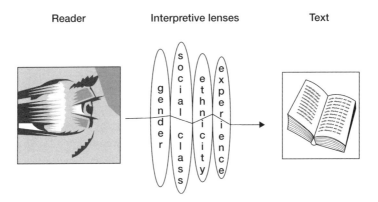

FIGURE 7.1   An active model of reading

complex social reality in which human emotions and relationships are often challenged by competing pressures. In order to deal with social and emotional issues in a text, the reader needs to be an active constructor of meanings; meanings that are derived from the reader's interaction with the text and their own current and past experience. This conceptualisation of the reader as an active constructor of meaning provides the potential for a creative and liberating engagement with texts in the primary classroom. It means that teachers can start from the perspectives of their pupils and show them that their lives are valuable aspects of the reading process by validating the importance of their lived experience.

This perspective on reading contrasts markedly with orthodox ways of reading narrative texts. For many of us schooled in the kinds of textual analysis required to successfully pass public examinations, reading involved the deconstruction of texts to discover what the writer meant and how the writer achieved his or her ends by means of the use of literary devices. This view of higher order reading and the comprehension of texts is reinforced by curriculum guidance in the Literacy Strategy, which implicitly emphasises the function of genre study. An approach such as this marginalises the reader and promotes a reductionist view of reading, based on the proposition that a text can be read in the same way by all readers and will be interpreted in the same way by all. In contrast then, Reader Response Theory, because it recognises the centrality of the reader's experience as the basis for the reader's interpretive frame, opens up the range of possible reading activities to be utilised by the teacher, not only to engage pupils' interpretations of texts, but also to encourage them to read in the first place. Some suggested approaches can be found in Box 7.1. However, this is not an exhaustive list.

Box 7.1 Interacting with texts: creative ideas for the classroom

The following ideas and strategies have been devised to help pupils in KS1 and KS2 interact with written texts. Some strategies are well known but I have tried to suggest ways in which they might be adapted. The activities are designed to encourage close reading of a text by means of a related practical activity. The aim is to improve pupils' higher order reading skills (i.e. inference, deduction, evaluation etc.) as well as encourage a personal interpretation of the text. Traditional forms of comprehension activity rarely achieve these aims because it is possible to answer many comprehension questions without fully understanding the text. This is not intended to be either an exhaustive or prescriptive list but it provides a starting point for creative thought and new activities or adaptations of the ideas outlined below.

Sequencing

Sequencing is a well-known strategy but a variation is offered in point three, which is intended to encourage pupils to use their knowledge to suggest possible subtextual scenarios.

1. Represent the main elements of the narrative pictorially. Present the pictures to pupils in random order.
2. Ask pupils to put the pictures in the correct sequence and explain what is happening in each picture.
3. Variations might include the following:
    a) using the pictures to give an oral telling of the story
    b) asking pupils to add their own pictures to fill in some of the gaps in the story, e.g. continue the story, show what happens when a character is outside the action etc.
    c) write captions to accompany the pictures.

Reading games

Set out as in a board game, the main elements of the narrative are represented pictorially or by means of simple text on selected squares on the game. The game is played by each player throwing a die. When a pupil lands on a relevant square they have to tell the others what happened in that part of the story. If text is used, it might be in a cloze form. The pupil has to complete the cloze. The interactive nature of the game can be developed by including cards that require the pupil to apply their own experience to the text (see the example provided at the end of the chapter). If we apply the idea to *The Other side of Truth* by Beverley Naidoo (2000) (see review in Box 7.2), the rubric on a card might ask the pupil to recount a time when they were lost like Sade and Femi were. The question could be framed in the following way: 'How did you feel when you were lost and how do they think Sade and Femi might have felt and what were they thinking when they were lost?

Textual maps

Most stories involve action across several locations. Even when a story is set in one geographic place, the writer describes the setting, giving the reader a mental image of the spatial juxtaposition of objects or environmental features. Such descriptions can be used to create maps. The map might be an end in itself, alternatively further work can be developed once the map has been produced. For example, pupils might write brief explanations of the relevance of the location or object to the story or, if the location is a real place (e.g London or Lagos) they might undertake further research to learn more about the location. In this way a narrative text can be used as stimulus for cross-curricular work. The map can also be used as a prompt for an oral retelling of the story. Once pupils have experience of maps related to texts they have read, they could be encouraged to devise original maps of their own stories, based on their own experiences and places they know well. This could be an activity in its own right, or it might be extended by an oral story telling using the map. It could also be used as a planning tool for story writing.

Charting the journey

This may sound similar to the textual map and some versions may share a resemblance. However, all stories involve some kind of journey beyond the physical one. It might be a journey of discovery; a moral journey or the transformation of a character, usually the protagonist. Pupils begin by drawing a road and plotting on the road at appropriate distances from one another, signposts signalling the key points on the character's journey. Alternatively, geographic landmarks might be used to signify key points: a mountain or river might represent a significant obstacle on the journey, or a trophy might be used to represent a significant achievement. Pupils demonstrate understanding by explaining why they have used particular symbols or signs and how they are relevant to the story.

The reader's journey

In this activity the reader is asked to map their journey through the text, noting their thoughts and feelings at certain points in the story. As with the textual map activity, these significant moments for the reader can be represented pictorially with pictures subsequently used by the reader to explain how they felt and why, or to elaborate on their thinking. It is at these points of connection with the text that readers' own personal narratives are likely to be most significant.

Point of view chart

A point of view chart is a simple grid. The name of each character is listed horizontally and vertically, as shown below;

Point of view	Sade	Femi	Papa	Reader
Sade				
Femi				
Papa				
Reader				

Pupils use the text to gather evidence to show what view each character has of other characters and themselves by recording information in the appropriate box. The reader is included because they too will have a view of characters. They might also be encouraged to consider themselves as a reader and comment on how they think they read the book, or what experience they think they brought to the text. The information might then be used as the basis for a character study of one character. An alternative to an extended prose character study is a pictorial representation. Pupils draw or paint the character to be studied and then devise symbols to represent other characters' views of the chosen character. Alternatively, around the image of the character are posted brief reviews of the character by other characters and, or, other readers in the class.

The application of Reader Response Theory, as a purposeful perspective to encourage pupil engagement with texts, presupposes that teachers recognise the possible interpretive lenses through which their pupils are likely to view a specific text. Based on what teachers know of their pupils, this knowledge can be used to estimate the proximity of each reader's narrative (both small and large lenses) to that of the text and its inherent themes and issues. Some texts are likely to converge strongly with the personal and social experience of certain pupils in the class, whilst significantly diverging from those of others. For example, children whose parents have separated and are living with one parent are likely to view the circumstance of 'Andy', the protagonist in *The Suitcase Kid*, who lives alternately with both parents (Wilson 2006) differently from those who reside in one home with both parents. This interplay of social experience and the dilemmas experienced by characters in texts is the ground upon which meanings are constructed differently by different readers. However, this 'ground' also provides a fertile plain for readers' discursive activity around the text. Those who have 'insider' knowledge are in a position to share with those who do not. However, personal experience is unlikely to be shared if the emotional groundwork has not been established by means of a safe classroom ethos. The model presented in Chapter one provides a theoretical framework for integrating pupils' collaborative talk around texts and their life experience.

Dealing with sensitive issues in children's literature

Narrative has been seen as a 'safe haven' in which pupils can engage with 'dangerous emotional or moral' issues, allowing them to discuss the problem affecting people (Fines 1992 cited in Dean 1995: 8). Viewing human dilemmas, concerns and problems through a narrative voice may help to give emotional 'distance' to issues in children's lives, enabling them to view matters in a more objective manner. However, some issues may be too emotionally 'raw' for some pupils to deal with in isolation of teacher intervention. Similarly, some issues may be so far outside the experience of our pupils that they require some kind of 'lead in' activity to acquaint them with the emotional or moral terrain of issues in the novel.

In Figure 7.2, 'Texts and readers' prior knowledge', I have proposed a model for locating the relationship between issues that arise in a novel and the extent to which the reader has prior knowledge of those issues, or the knowledge a reader uses to make sense of the text. The model is a synthesis of thinking derived from

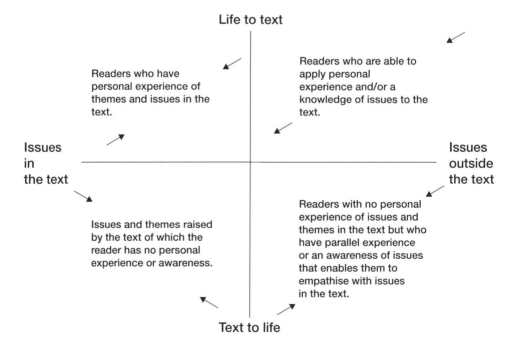

FIGURE 7.2 Texts and readers' prior knowledge

Reader Response Theory and our understanding of the way in which a reader's interpretive lenses are influenced by the prior experience they bring to the text. However, the reading of a text is recursive. Not only do readers bring prior knowledge of the world to the text, but the text also reflects aspects of lived experience, since it is a partial construct of social narratives and a partial construct of the writer's imagination. Hence we may view reading from two dimensions: life to text and text to life. In order to demonstrate the possible relationship of readers' experience and issues in the text, I am going to explain Figure 7.2 and then draw upon three children's novels that contain sensitive issues. By a sensitive issue I mean an event in the narrative, or a thematic concern, that might be seen as being sensitive in emotional, moral social or political terms. The three texts, *The Colour of Home* (Hoffman 2002); *The Other Side of Truth* (Naidoo 2000) and *Iqbal* (D'Adamo 2004) have been selected for the quality and power of their narratives, as well as the themes they include. They are also books that do not readily appear on the shelves of many mainstream booksellers. Figure 7.2 needs to be read in conjunction with the reviews of the three novels in Box 7.2.

Box 7.2   Reviews

1. Review of *The Colour of Home* by Mary Hoffmann, illustrated by Karin Littlewood

Initially, *The Colour of Home* appears to be a simple story about the first day at school of a migrant child. On the afternoon of his first day at school Hassan paints a picture of his family and his home in Somalia; the sky was blue and cloudless; his house, a brilliant white; the sun shone brightly; there were nine people in the picture.

'"What a lovely picture, Hassan," said Miss Kelly. "What beautiful bright colours!" But Hassan hadn't finished.'

At this point in the story the full dramatic horror of Hassan's past is revealed as he adds red and orange to the roof of the house. The sky turns to a murky purple and another person is added. The new figure holds a gun. The white walls of the house are spattered with red and one person in the family group is removed.

'"Oh, Hassan," said Miss Kelly. "It's all spoilt. What a shame." Hassan didn't know what her words meant, but he heard the sadness in her voice and knew that she understood his picture.'

This is a moment of irony rarely found in children's stories and it signals an opportunity for the teacher to explore how contrary meanings are created in texts.

Only after the arrival of a Somali interpreter is Hassan able to relate to his teacher the true meaning of his painting. 'When he finished, Miss Kelly had tears in her eyes.'

Mary Hoffman rarely writes a story that is anodyne and The Colour of Home is no exception. Deep feelings are evoked in this narrative and the reader cannot help but become emotionally charged by events and the response of the characters to those events. Hassan lived through atrocity, which is depicted in his painting, touching the heart of his teacher and the reader. Although the story reveals negative aspects of human behaviour, it also demonstrates the individual's resilience in the face of adversity. Hassan paints a second picture of the house for his mother. Once again it is bright and beautiful but on this occasion it remains bright and beautiful and is hung proudly in his new home, at which point Hassan begins to see all the other bright colours in the house.

The use of the painting is a clever device for introducing a flashback in the narrative. There is a lot for teachers and children to explore in this book, both in terms of literary and social issues. On a socio-political level the story provides an antidote to the negative media headlines about refugees and asylum seekers. Children will appreciate the very human dimension of Hassan's story. The changing emotional texture of the book is sensitively reflected in Karen Littlewood's colourful illustrations.

2. Review of *The Other Side of Truth* by Beverley Naidoo

From its tense and tragic opening this novel grips the reader, taking them on an emotional journey from conflict-ridden Nigeria to London, and an uncertain future for its two protagonists.

Sade and her younger brother Femi are the children of an outspoken journalist who believes that telling the truth is sacrosanct. His repeated criticism of the Nigerian Government of General Abacha is followed by the revenge killing of his wife, which is witnessed by the two children. With the prospect of further threats to the family, the children's uncle arranges for them to be smuggled out of the country to the home of Uncle Dele, a lecturer in London. However, Uncle Tunde's good intentions backfire when the children are abandoned at Victoria Station by their 'courier', Mrs Bankole. Alone in an unfamiliar country and unable to find their absent uncle, the children are taken into care by social services. Fearful of the repercussions for their father, the children remain silent about the nature of their arrival in Britain, until Mrs Appia, their social worker, informs them that she has met their father in a detention centre in London. There is an emotional reunion but the family live with the continual threat of deportation and the prospect of further harassment in their home country.

This novel does for Key Stage 2 what Mary Hoffman's *The Colour of Home* does for Key Stage 1; it gets behind glib newspaper headlines and political soundbites about refugees and asylum seekers. By means of intricately woven threads of human experience, this novel reveals the vulnerability of people living in fear. From the very outset, terror strikes at the heart of the family and it would take a reader with a heart of stone not to be moved by the unfolding narrative. The story is told with touches of poetry, the language of which reflects the cultural context of the twelve year old protagonist, Sade.

Beverley Naidoo's characters have emotional and psychological depth which brings to their relationships the authenticity of lived experience. The reader is drawn into their world and like them, cannot escape the range of emotions they experience. Thematically strong and topical, *The Other Side of Truth* is not so much a good read but more an experience which, though painful, should not be missed.

3. Review of *Iqbal* by Francesco D'Adamo

Francesco D'Adamo's third novel for young teenagers and his first to be translated from his native Italian into English, is a powerful and moving account of the courage and tenacity of the novel's eponymous protagonist. Iqbal can be read as a novel in its own right, but the fact it is based on a true story gives it political as well as literary significance.

Set in Lahore, Pakistan, the story exposes the harshness of life for children 'sold' into indentured labour by families, too poor to repay loans to the money lenders. As Francesco D'Adamo states in his introduction, which offers a brief explanation of child labour,this is 'a fictional account of a real person'. Told through the voice of Fatima, a child labourer herself, the reader is drawn into the squalid world of Hussein Khan's carpet factory, where children are chained to their looms and work long hours to earn a rupee a day. Their fate seems hopeless until the arrival of Iqbal, a boy with a passion to be free. What makes Iqbal's quest for freedom remarkable is his accompanying altruism; he not only wants his own freedom but that of other children too. With the aid of the Bonded Labour Liberation Front of Pakistan, Iqbal succeeds in freeing his fellow child labourers from Hussein Khan's factory. But he is not satisfied with that, he wants to free children in other factories too and becomes an ardent activist in the fight against the bonded labour of children. He draws world attention to the enslavement of children in the carpet industry, which makes him quite literally a target for the carpet mafia. One day, whilst cycling in his home village, Iqbal is gunned down by men in a passing car.

This is a compelling story of courage and determination. It is a story made all the more poignant by the fact that Iqbal was a real person, that this fictional version included real events. At the age of 13 the real Iqbal Masih was murdered because of his involvement in the movement to rid the world of child labour. Whilst reading this novel one cannot escape the connection of parallel narratives: that this is a story of a story. Older children and young teenagers will not fail to feel pathos, pity, horror, and perhaps anger, at the plight of Iqbal and his fellow workers.

The vertical axis of the model in Figure 7.2 represents the relationship of 'Life to text' (top) and 'Text to life' (bottom). The horizontal axis represents how issues may be inherent to the text (left) or represented in real life (right), either in general ways, or in the specific experience of the reader. Using this model, there are four possible ways in which readers might be viewed in relation to the text.

Life to text / Issues in the text

The top left quadrant represents those readers whose personal life trajectories or aspects of their life experience correlate strongly with the text. These readers are likely to identify closely with the narrative and its characters. In most instances this indicates a positive reader-to-text relationship. However, there are times when the relationship between the reader's experience and the text may coincide so strongly that reading becomes too emotional and the reader has to break away from the text. One such instance might be bereavement. At the beginning of Beverley Naidoo's novel, *The Other Side of Truth*, the two child protagonists witness their mother's death at the hands of a gunman. It is a scene that becomes a refrain through the use of flashbacks and memories. Children who have recently experienced bereavement are likely to find this scene upsetting and may need to be sensitively prepared for meeting this text. This novel, along with Mary Hoffman's, *The Colour of Home*, deals with issues around asylum and the separation of children from family, home and all that is familiar to them. These texts will resonate with those children who have migrated to Britain, who have had to endure extreme hardship and who have witnessed atrocities.

Readers with a strong affinity to a novel's thematic concerns will be able to make clear connections between the text and real life. Through discussion, they will be in a position to bring the text 'alive' for others because they will be able to demonstrate how issues inside the text are not just fictionalised ideas but resonate outside the novel in the real world.

Life to text / Issues outside the text

Another category of reader includes those who have similar personal experiences to the protagonist in a novel but do not closely share their narrative. In relation to the two novels already discussed, these readers may have experience of migration and feelings of loss without having experienced the kind of atrocities and hardship that some asylum seeking children may have. This category of reader is located in the top right quadrant of Figure 7.2. Also in this quadrant would be readers who are able to bring their lived experience, or an awareness of issues outside the text, to the text, even where the issues in the text are dissimilar to those in the reader's head. In these cases the reader is making connections by applying their worldly knowledge in order to make unique interpretations. An example of this kind of reading might be where a child has a strong sense of moral justice, possibly acquired by means of parental influences or strongly held beliefs. Although such a reader is unlikely to have any experience of child slave labour, their general sense of moral justice is brought to bear on their reading of Iqbal. Their affective response to the awful plight of the children in the novel is what engages them with the text. They are drawn into the text and through the narrative learn about aspects of real life of which they were previously unaware. Or if they were aware, then the narrative provides a more personalised emotional frame than factual information.

Text to life / Issues outside the text

In the bottom right quadrant issues in the text resonate strongly with issues outside the text. While readers may not have direct experience of the issues raised in the text or direct experience of those same issues in real life, the text provides the means for raising readers' awareness. Readers are able to use their life experience to empathise with the protagonists and their dilemmas, because aspects of their life and/or knowledge run parallel to the fictional narrative. An example might be where pupils have a knowledge of the existence of child labour, such as that depicted in Iqbal, but it is through the text that the issue is brought to life. In this instance the text raises the consciousness of the pupil to the human significance of child labour and thereby gives the issue outside the text greater meaning for the pupil.

Issues in the text / Text to life

The final quadrant deals with issues and themes in the text that the reader has no prior knowledge or experience of and that the reader cannot relate to real life issues. The text may be read for its own sake but opportunities for associated work around the text are restricted by the reader's lack of knowledge or life experience. This is the least educationally viable position for readers to be in. However, if a teacher feels there are pupils in this position ameliorative action can be taken. It is a case of providing the reader with some form of secondary experience so that they may then relate to the text in a more meaningful way. As discussed elsewhere, drama provides a superb means for enabling pupils to gain an insider view of issues. Based on practical experience, Barrs describes how texts that children might find difficult to relate to can be pre-empted through drama:

> the introduction of the text itself was delayed until the fictional world and themes of the story had been prefigured through drama. This had a big impact on the children,

who seemed to relate much more closely and personally to this text because they had already 'lived through' some of its events and situations.

Barrs (2000: 57)

In this way, we are able to move readers from the bottom left quadrant into one of the other quadrants, thereby making the text more accessible to them because they are able to apply 'secondary' lived experience in order to help them construct meanings and make sense of what they read. Hence they move from being passive readers, who are reliant upon the text, to active ones who are able to synthesise experience of issues inside the text with experience of similar issues outside the text.

If teachers have knowledge of both the lived experience of their pupils and their pupils' awareness of issues that emerge out of narratives introduced to the class, then they have the basis for planning associated learning around texts that enables pupils to share their responses to their reading. In some instances there may need to be a lot of preparatory work, through drama, discussion and research prior to reading the text. This is particularly so where pupils are being introduced to issues of which they have little or no experience. Conversely, where it is thought pupils will readily identify with issues in the text and are able to bring a good deal of lived experience to their reading, discussion might be located at intervals during the reading of the text and, or, at the end of the text.

In this chapter it is suggested that reading should be viewed from two perspectives; first, what the text offers to the reader and, second, what the reader is able to bring to the text in order to actively construct meaning. Hence the reader and, from the teacher's viewpoint, a knowledge of the reader's experience of the world, is an important prerequisite in designing the reading curriculum around novels shared with groups of readers or with the whole class. In the course of their school life pupils should have opportunities to experience novels that closely reflect their own lived experience, as well as novels that introduce them to issues and perspective of which they may have no, or little, prior experience or knowledge. The point about readers experiencing novels that reflect their own lives raises a further issue. Despite the long-standing nature of Britain as a multi-ethnic society, there remains a dearth of novels for children at Key Stage 2 which reflect this fact. Consequently, teachers of pupils from minority ethnic groups may experience great difficulty finding texts that positively reflect the backgrounds and lived experience of their pupils. This presents a problem that can only be effectively resolved by publishers commissioning works that redress the imbalance. The lack of such texts is relevant to the needs of majority ethnic pupils because they also need to experience narratives inhabited by characters of different ethnic backgrounds, including protagonists with strong character profiles.

A model has been devised to assist teachers to locate the starting points of readers in relation to both issues in the text and their life experience. In so doing, it is suggested that readers need to be encouraged to read texts beyond their comfort zone, taking them into unfamiliar territory where they encounter issues that may be new to them.

Web addresses

Achuka – www.achuka.co.uk

Includes reviews of children's book, including shortlisted books for the Marsh Award for Children's Literature.

Bedfordshire Virtual Library – http://www.galaxy.bedfordshire.gov.uk/cgi-bin/vlib.sh

Click on Children and Teens section. The Book Zone has links to age related booklists and children's book awards with reviews of the winners.

Booktrust – http://www.booktrustchildrensbooks.org.uk/Home

Includes reviews and recommendations of children's books.

The Carnegie Medal and Kate Greenaway Medal for Children's Books – http://www.carnegiegreenaway.org.uk/home/index.php

Includes reviews of current and past winners of these major children's book awards. Shortlisted books are nominated by librarians.

Costa Book Awards – http://www.costabookawards.co.uk

Has an award for children's books and includes reviews of winners.

Federation of Children's Book Groups – http://www.fcbg.org.uk

Includes a monthly newsletter of activities around the country involving book groups. The Federation also publish several very useful booklists.

National Literacy Trust – http://www.rif.org.uk/bookreviews/bookreviewsindex.htm

There is a drop down box that enables you to search for reviews of authors and titles of books.

Red House Children's Book Award – http://www.redhousechildrensbookaward.co.uk

Includes brief reviews of current and past winners dating back to 1981. The site also offers a monthly newletter.

Writeaway – www.writeaway.org.uk

There is a longer review of this site in the useful contacts section at the end of the book.

8

Poetry

IN THIS CHAPTER poetic language and the poetic 'voice' is discussed by exploring the following:

- what poets say about poetry as a way of getting to the heart of what poetry is;

- nurturing children's poetic language;

- ways of approaching the writing and reading of poetry in the classroom;

- a language for discussing poetry.

To begin the chapter, here is a previously unpublished poem that attempts to say something about the elusive nature of poetry itself.

> Words slip the leash and bound,
> To a fern wooded twilight, yelping,
> Startled wings lift from boughs, and beat.
> A tiny fluttering beneath camouflage.
>
> The mottled evening, grey
> Unyielding, cloud and stasis.
>
> Sniff, poised, caverns in undergrowth,
> The dark scent of some small bellied thing,
> Consoled in ignorance of what it is.
> And then, to a command, turns back on itself.
>
> The master's soothing hand;
> The rigid noose of leather.

Poetry is one of the most neglected areas of the English curriculum and yet it can be one of the most inspiring, creative and deeply rewarding aspects of English.

Indeed, Brian Cox (1989) saw poetry as a 'vital resource', one that should be at 'the heart of work in English'. However, many people seem to refrain from engaging with poetry, unless it is easily accessible or in comic form. For these reasons, I have chosen to devote a substantial chapter to poetry. In the chapter, I touch on two reports, one from Ofsted and the other the Clwyd Poetry Project, and highlight their findings. I discuss the nature of poetry by drawing on what poets themselves say about it because it seems to me that if we are going to significantly improve the quality of pupils' writing, we should listen more to our writers and less to the politicians who are driving the educational agenda. Practical ways into poetry reading and writing are suggested and the chapter ends with a glossary of terms that teachers need in order to describe and discuss poetry with their pupils, especially their own poetry. As in previous chapters, I suggest that textual analysis and the identification of technical language should start with the pupil's own writing. If pupils are able to demonstrate versatility in language to the extent that they naturally use poetic devices, and teachers are able to comment upon their work, using precise technical language, then not only is the writing and the writer being shown respect, pupils are introduced to the metalanguage of poetry through concepts they are already able to use. This approach may prove to be more beneficial to children's development as writers than an overemphasis on textual analysis, which, it is suggested, does not improve pupils' appreciation of poetry or their ability to write it (Fogg and Taylor 1992: 19).

The poetic voice of the child

Like people's reactions to Marmite, responses to poetry often involve strong feelings in adults and young people. These feelings can often be negative. When I ask student teachers of their experiences of poetry at school they invariably say they did not like it or could not write poetry. This is partly because poetry is often seen as a difficult form in which to write, and an incomprehensible form to read. Yet Carter (1998: 2) asserts 'a child is born with a poetic voice' and that teachers should be as concerned with 'letting loose each child's poetic voice' as they are with introducing poetry to them. In order to illustrate Carter's point about the poetic voice of the child, consider the following:

> Bruises hurt,
> They are like mold
> On the skin.

This short poem was written by my eldest daughter, Ashrup, when she was four and a half years old. I had shown her a technique for writing poetry, which I describe later in this chapter, but the words and sentiment were entirely her own.

The poem is clearly driven by the personal experience, common to young children, of being bruised as a result of childhood games and underdeveloped gross motor skills. I had not shown her what a simile was yet, the simile came naturally to her. She begins with a matter of fact statement, 'bruises hurt', but then moves from one sensory experience to another, shifting her expression from a personal statement to the more general visual representation of a bruise, by means of the comparison with mold. We get an instant image of the colour and texture of a bruise through this comparison. This demonstrates the sophisticated way in which young children are able to use language and should remind us that at the heart of language is the desire to make meanings for oneself and for others. Ashrup's poem is also testimony to Carter's astutely observed claim that children are born with a poetic voice.

Poetry, pedagogy and the primary classroom

So, what goes wrong in schools when it comes to poetry? Why is that at eighteen plus most students are averse to poetry, particularly writing it, when evidence suggests it is likely that it once came naturally to them? And, if as student teachers they have negative views of poetry, what chance is there that they will handle it well with children in their own classrooms? Ofsted (2007), in its survey of poetry in schools, concluded that although the teaching of poetry was slightly better in primary than secondary schools, it often remained underdeveloped. Reasons for this included teachers' own lack of subject knowledge; an undue focus on the improvement of writing skills; and didactic teaching, located around the identification of figurative language and poetic form. Inspectors noted that children in primary schools were more positive about poetry than their secondary counterparts, suggesting that by the time they get to university most student teachers have been 'turned off' poetry by often arid teaching. The survey also found that the same poems tended to be studied and there was insufficient attention given to classic poetry, or poems from a range of cultures. However, good teaching of poetry stimulated excellent responses from pupils. One source of inspiration came from the inclusion of poets themselves as resident writers in schools. Where this occurred, Ofsted commented, it 'provided a good opportunity for pupils to discover their own voices as writer' (Ofsted 2007: 3). Given the above discussion, we might want to replace the word 'discover' with 'rediscover' but the key point here is the implicit recognition that finding one's own voice is essential to a writer. This point applies to all writers, whether they are children or 'professionals'. This tiny comment in the Ofsted report resonates with the model presented earlier in the book where I suggest that the key to developing children's writing is by means of strategies to help them acquire their 'voice' and an ear for language, rather than by engaging them in repetitive exercises, requiring them to deconstruct sentence and textual structures and to identify specific parts of speech or, in the case of poetry, figurative language. It is a point reflected by Benjamin Zephaniah (cited in Saguisag 2007: 26) when he says, 'children's passion for poetry is being killed by dissection and over-analysis'.

Although Ofsted found the teaching of poetry generally to be the weakest part of the English curriculum, good practice inspired excellent pupil responses. Often good teaching involved the use of drama and role play; cloze procedures, in which pupils collaborated to choose a word to fit a deliberate gap in a poem; sequencing activities; prepared readings of poetry and 'translating' the poem in another form, such as through music or a film. Some of these findings are in accord with those of the Clwyd Poetry Project launched by Dennis Carter in 1992. Like Ofsted, the 'project' found that ways of helping children into poetry and through poetry was by means of representing poems in practical media such as, drama, dance, art and music. By re-creating poetry in these ways children were simultaneously engaged in comprehending their meanings (Carter 1998: 17). If we accept that reading is a transaction between the writer, the text and the reader, the act of re-creation through various media invariably engages pupils' responses to the poem and, therefore, the meanings they bring to the work. These practical ways of encouraging children to respond to poetry might be seen as reader-response in practice. As we saw in Chapter six, reader response theorists advocate that readers bring to a text their own personal experience and ways of seeing the world and that these influence the text's meaning. I shall return to the work of the Clwyd Poetry Project later in the chapter but it may now be opportune to consider what poets themselves say about poetry as a way of getting closer to what a poem is, and why poetry deserves a higher profile in the English curriculum.

Poetry and the poetic voice

On the relationship of poetry to the poet, W.B. Yeats (1966: 15) wrote, 'A poet always writes of his personal life'. Fogg and Taylor (1992: 7) comment on poetry as a 'verbal art form which shape and form personal feelings'. In a similar vein Larkin stated that a poem transferred emotion, first formed in the poet, to the reader (Larkin 1956 cited in Holt undated). Not only does this imply that poetry is perhaps the most intimate of all written forms, but that in classrooms poetry writing needs to begin with children's own experiences of life. The Scottish poet, Jackie Kay, sees poetry both as an egalitarian art form and as a means of articulating the inarticulate: 'Poetry is important because it manages to say in words things that you can't otherwise say ... (it) expresses for us what usually cannot be articulated. Poetry gives a voice to the voiceless' (Kay 2008).

The intensely personal aspect of poetry is apparent to young people when they are shown how to really engage with and use it to explore their personal, social and cultural worlds. In their evaluations of a poetry project with the poet, Ann Sansom, children wrote of how poetry had helped them learn about themselves. Some talked of it being a release of strong emotions and how these could be expressed in a 'new and sensational way' (Sapiano 2008). In the 1970s the teacher and poet, Chris Searle (1975) saw poetry as a means of his pupils giving voice to the social and cultural conditions of their lives in East London. When he was sacked for publishing their work they went on strike until he was reinstated. Teachers who value their careers may regard this citation as a disincentive for working too deeply with poetry. Both Jackie Kay and Chris Searle touch on the creative energy that can be unleashed through poetry, enabling children to realise its intensely personal force, as well as being a means of expression about their lives.

A word of warning perhaps needs to be cast at this point because my own experience suggests that some aspects of personal life are so close to us as individuals we cannot write about them, or if we do, we may not want others to see them. Some of the pupils in Clare Sapiano's (2008) class said in their evaluations that they liked the respect teachers accorded their work by recognising the need to gain permission from them before reading poetry in their journals. Pupils in the class had the right to select the poems they wanted to share publicly. In order to write about personal experience there needs to be a degree of emotional detachment or distance. If we are too emotionally bound up with the experience our words are often stifled. Detachment or distance may be created by the passing of time, making it is easier to write about past experience than the more recent past. Exploring personal experience through alternative media such as drama, dance, art or music, as suggested in the Clywd Project (Carter 1998), may provide the degree of detachment that makes the subsequent writing of experience possible. The modes of expression provided by these alternative media may also 'trigger' aspects of language to be subsequently used by the writer. For example, if children have retold the narrative of personal experience in dance, the very movements used to convey particular aspects of the experience may lend themselves to the language of expression used in the poem. Words such as glide, swirl, leapt, pirouette may enter the poem because they have been associated with the experience through its re-enactment.

On the language of poetry the words of T.S. Eliot suggest that children do not require extensive vocabulary work before engaging their poetic voices. Eliot (1966: 58) says that the language of poetry 'must not stray too far from ordinary everyday language'. Each child then has within their grasp the linguistic means for poetic expression and it is this 'voice' of the child to which teachers should concern themselves (Carter 1998: 2).

Eliot's contemporary, Ezra Pound (1966: 32) provides us with additional guidance concerning the language of poetry when he writes, the poet should 'use no superfluous word, no adjective which does not reveal something'. Here Pound is suggesting the brevity of language in poetry and implies its distinction from prose, as discussed below. This brevity leads to what Bruner has called 'semantic squeeze' (cited in Gamble and Yates 2008) because if the use of language is sparse, meaning is condensed. Poetry uses language in more economic ways than prose because it seeks to express disparate images, feelings or thoughts in a single phrase or line. Certain parts of speech, so important to prose, serve only to hinder expression in poetry. One of the initial problems with poetry in classrooms is the tendency for pupils to write poetry as they would prose, by adhering to conventional sentence structures. Schmidt (undated) states that 'prose uses the medium of language while poetry serves language and explores it'. Poetic expression is often most effective when certain word classes are left out: overuse of prepositions, conjunctions and articles can make a poem sound immature, insincere and lacking in authenticity. In poetry, words are often polysemic. That is, they convey several meanings simultaneously. Gamble and Yates (2008: 166) note that this 'compression of language ... means many poems offer themselves up for different interpretations'.

Poems are also poly-sensori in that they can appeal to our intellect and emotions simultaneously. They have rhythm and sound. For this reason, poetry must be spoken rather than read. When introducing poetry in the classroom, whether it is children's own work, or that of other writers, it needs to be heard, and prior to reading, it requires rehearsal in order to hear the authentic voice of the poem and rejuvenate the marks on paper. Poetryarchive, an online resource with an education section, has recordings of poets reading their work. The web address and further details about the site can be found at the end of this book in the Useful Contacts section. Using the Primary National Strategy's interactive planning tool (online source), it is possible to paste the recording into a lesson plan and play it by means of an interactive whiteboard. If the school is unable to organise visits by poets, this is one way of bringing readers and writers together and can be supplemented by interviews with poets, which are also accessible on the site. Combining the reading of a single poem with the views of the poet can help to demystify poetry, especially if the poet is talking about the experiences that influenced the poem.

When talking about poetry we often refer to imagery and the way the language of a poem evokes particular images. Ezra Pound (cited in Stead 1967: 99) offers a definition of 'image' which accords with what he says about poetic language: 'An "image" is that which presents an intellectual and an emotional complex in an instant of time.' Alongside brevity of language then is unity of time, suggesting that a poem is a concise or compact reworking of experience. Inclusive of experience is personal observation.

Dylan Thomas said that he wanted to write poetry because he fell in love with words (1966: 195). If we can encourage our pupils fall in love with language and help them to weave through their language the rhythmic play of words, or to see when they are already doing it, their language and *the* language will be all the richer for it. Poetry then has the unique potential to enrich, extend and enliven children's language and thinking. However, Ofsted (2007) noted that teachers sometimes accepted pupils' first drafts, and unfinished poems as final pieces, largely because they were unsure of how to help pupils develop their writing. Like prose composition, poetry too needs appropriate feedback from teachers and the time for pupils to redraft their work. This is probably best achieved by means of immediate feedback whilst pupils are engaged with their poem, rather than at a later stage, as a retrospective. Dylan Thomas (1966: 196) likens the reworking of a poem to the shaping of an artefact in the workshop: 'What I like to do is to treat words as a craftsman does his wood or stone ... to hew it, carve, mould, coil, polish and plane them into patterns, sequences, sculptures, figures of sound expressing some lyrical impulse ...'.

Poetry, language and thought

Echoing Dylan Thomas' allusion to the poet crafting words into sonic shapes, Wyse and Jones (2008: 262) state, 'Poetry offers degrees of intensity, subtlety and artistry which are unique to the English curriculum'. Poetry is a powerful medium for the exploration of the internal mental and affective landscape of the child; it is also a powerful medium for the exploration of the musicality of language. As such, it is a means for both giving voice to the child and for equipping the user with greater mastery of language. It is my contention that good poetry writing teaches pupils how to become artists with words, carefully reading the detail of what they observe, whether that be externally, in relation to an object, or internally with reference to a thought or feeling.

What these poets suggest is that poetry writing and reading require a particular type of thinking and language use. It is perhaps the uniqueness of the type of language and thought conveyed through poetry that causes Grace Nicholls (1988) to say that 'poetry helps us see the world through new eyes'. In terms of thinking, poetry encourages the use of lateral conceptual connections; the association of disparate images, thoughts and feelings. While all language is about the construction and communication of meaning, poetic language differs from conventional prose, the form of written language we spend most our time coaching children to write, in a number of ways. A significant difference is in the way communication is structured. Kress (1994) states that the sentence is essentially a concept appropriate to the written, rather than spoken form of a language. Poetry, however, deconstructs everything we tell children about how to write; the sentence and conventional syntax are not necessary for poetic expression, primarily because, as is suggested above, poetic language has to communicate a feeling, thought or idea through the concise juxtaposition of images, both aural and visual. When approaching poetry with pupils, therefore, we need to be prepared to drop the shackles of syntax and allow them to be spontaneous with words.

Inside the poem: a writer's journey

What follows is a personal view of how poetic expression has come to me. I reflect upon the inspirational spark that has fired some of my own work, some of which has been written for my pupils; some of which has come out of the very lessons I have taught. In sharing the stimuli for my own writing, I hope to demonstrate that the starting point for poetry has different beginnings and that, for any one poet and, therefore, for any one pupil, there is no single route into a poem, or through a poem.

The following poem was written alongside a class of Year 6 pupils as they wrote similar poems on the theme of bullying and name calling. Poetry writing on this theme occurred during an extended project on the subject, which began with the significance of pupils' own first, family names, and nicknames. We then considered pupils' feelings about names, who used them and how they were used. We explored sexist and racist names and the language of abuse used towards people who are disabled or who have learning disabilities. This was a multisensory project which predated the National Curriculum (DfES 1988). Written work was deliberately minimal in order to maximise opportunities for speaking and listening through such strategies as 'circle-time' (Moseley 1996), role play, freeze-framing and simulation activities. Writing occurred in the spaces left between speaking and listening. What we discovered was that the multi-sensory work had so enlivened pupils' thinking and feelings, the writing they produced showed greater depth of feeling, a greater command of language and was more evocative than writing produced by conventional means. The poem I wrote was a synthesis of the pupils' voices during the project. Its content and the language came from the discourse of the speaking and listening activities; its form from the rhythm of Rap music, which was popular with the pupils.

The Child who Stands Alone

Don't let the bullies get their way,
Don't keep silent have your say;
They want to make you feel weak and small,
So tell someone or you'll feel awful.
Your name is your name, wear it with pride,
Don't be abused, it'll hurt you inside.
Stand up, stand up, don't lose face,

If they attack your class, sex or 'race'.
The bully looks big and shouts a lot,
But when you get to it they're not that hot.
So don't stand alone and be afraid,
Don't let your life a hell be made
By the bully, the one who calls you a bad name,
Bullying is serious, it's not just a game;
So don't silently suffer, find your voice,
What you want to be called is your choice.

The 'spark' for the next poem was my own children when they were young, combined with some misconceptions expressed by my pupils in relation to our topic on light. Young children are full of questions about the world around them. The kind of questions children sometimes ask influenced the form and content of the poem; its language is indicative of the naïve views children sometimes have of the natural world.

Shadows

Where do shadows go when the lights are out?
Do they slide under the gap beneath the door?
Do they slip between cracks in the wooden floor?
Do they curl into a ball and fall asleep?
Or through the open window into the night time creep?

Where do shadows go when the sun goes down?
Do they seep like rainwater into the ground?
Do they hide for you to seek where they cannot be found?
Or are they in a sea of darkness suddenly drowned?

The poem, 'Mother's Tales', was the result of childhood memories triggered by a particularly still, grey, autumn afternoon. The first line is both a literal reference to the sky and a symbolic one, as I recalled, as a young child, my mother on wash days at her boiler and mangle. I was particularly fond of sitting by the fire staring into the luminous caverns that opened up between the coals as the throbbing glow slowly burned. I don't ever remember my mother sitting my sister and me on her lap, telling us tales, but the reference is indicative of the affection our mother always gave to us and the line, 'You dandled us with tales', typified her love. In the next line my thinking changed. The 'Coal cracked jaws grinning', is both a reference to the outline shape of the coal, eaten away by the fire and an oblique reference to the stereotypical witch of fairy tales. The alliterative 'coal cracked' reminded me of the witch's cackle and it led, almost in a stream of consciousness to the 'rising latch' and the woodcutter; a reference to my father coming home. He was a builder, not a 'tree-surgeon' but the term woodcutter carried a more romantic image; fitted the tone of the developing poem and was in keeping with the manual nature of his work. I thought of the woodcutter who kills the wolf at the end of the tale of 'Little Red Riding Hood' and the theme of the fairy story is picked up in the final stanza.

The next stanza is much more prosaic. In the kitchen at our house we had a drop-leaf table with a red gingham, formica surface. It was where we ate all our meals except Sunday dinner and tea. In my working-class vernacular, dinner is what the middle classes refer to as lunch and tea is dinner. There was a great deal of love and care in my home but we were not well off and sometimes my mother ate little so we could have more. The final stanza is an implicit 'thank you', embedded, once again, in the allusion to fairy tale. 'Red-hooded hopes', is indicative of the naïvety of children dreaming of who they want to become. In my dreams I was going to be a professional footballer. With the love of family all the harshness of the world was shielded from us. In folk tales, the wood or forest represents the unknown, the often sinister and dangerous world of beasts and the supernatural. It is the place where mishaps occur to children. Snow White was separated from her father and taken to the forest; Hanzel and Gretyl were lost in the forest and strayed upon the witches cottage; and Red Riding Hood, strayed from the path in the forest and encountered the wolf. The final stanza then is indicative of the protection given to us by my mother.

Mother's Tales

Through grey washed winters
You dandled us with tales,
Warm by the hearth-light;
Coal cracked jaws grinning,
'til the rising latch signalled
Cold after labour, the woodcutter.

Shifting to make a place
At the drop leafed formica,
Where yours was shared
To make a meagre, plenty.

You made childhood,
Red-hooded hopes, unhindered to pass
The forest's awesome darkness.

If we trace the development of 'Mother's Tales', a poem that took about ten minutes to write, we can see how my mind was working as a writer. The poem began with a visual stimulus, the grey sky, which triggered a memory. But it was more than that; once begun, the words took me back into my childhood. I was there, sat in front of that fire. I was a child again and significant moments floated into my consciousness. I was walking in my house, seeing the objects that are mentioned. It was a waking dream. Images triggered words and words triggered images, in a recursive manner. My thinking processes meandered between the romantic memory of the warmth and glow of the fire, to the coldness of winter and the frugal existence of our family. And, woven between the two is the intertextuality of fairy tale. There is an holistic semantic about the poem, contained as it is in the imagery of childhood. However, as a writer I was not conscious of how the poem was created. I was too busy living in the words and images; it is only as a reader that I have been able to analyse its evolution.

This gives rise to a key point about how we might respond to children's own work. As teachers, we invariably mark and comment upon the product of their writing, but we rarely investigate the processes of their work, the thinking that goes into the construction of their writing and the cognitive associations they make. If we encourage pupils to reflect upon their writing by genuinely discussing with them how they wrote, we will learn a great deal more about their creative thinking and about them as learners. This seems to me to be of far greater value to the teacher and the pupil than explicit teaching about metaphor and simile, or the deconstruction of a particular poetic genre. It is vitally important too if teachers are to help pupils to develop as writers, that they are themselves writers. It is a point that I make elsewhere in the book and is, therefore, something of a refrain. If the teacher as writer is able to talk to pupils about their own thinking processes whilst writing, they are in a position to model from the inside the writing process, rather than deconstruct, externally, the product of a piece of writing, recommended by the latest literacy framework. For this reason, I think that courses undertaken by student teachers should include a module that engages them in developing and analysing their own writing. My colleagues at the University of Sunderland, where I am an external examiner, have such a module. Some of the students' poetry is deeply personal and their reflective journals demonstrate the affective journeys they have undertaken as writers. In my view these students will be far better equipped to guide children's writing and have greater empathy with the subject than others taught solely on a diet influenced by the mechanics of the Literacy Framework.

The final poem I want to share began with a voice and was driven by that same voice. The way in which this poem was written shows that there can sometimes be a dramatic stance in writing. In 'Mother's Tales', I shifted between the role of myself as a child and myself as an adult, reminiscing. In the next poem, 'Dreaming of Darkness' I was entirely someone else, or rather, it was like there was a voice dictating the words that I should write. I will leave you, the reader, to explore the poem before I add my comments. What do you make of the poem? What meanings do you read into it?

Dreaming of Darkness

I wait for the darkness,
to rest my tiredness down
and with weary fingers,
pluck the Blues from dead strings.

I long for the darkness,
deep desire of black night,
smooth impenetrable night;
night of unfathomable stillness.

I yearn for the darkness,
embrace me this night,
enfold me in satin silence,
instil me with your peace.

I lust for the darkness,
that I may lay me down
upon your dark body,
and caress the blackness therein.

I ache for the darkness.
no fear of you beholden in me,
no whip crack smacking glare
bursting from the noon day heat.

I listen for the darkness,
humming sweetly through cabin walls;
crickets chirp in dark thickets,
night, swelling with songs of freedom.

I recall the darkness,
dreams fade to darkness,
dreams of a barefoot boy, running
homeward, across lush savannah.

The voice inside my head was that of a slave and the rhythm of the words move to the cadences of a Caribbean or African American accent. For the reader's information, I am not Black. So where did the voice come from, if not from my own experience? The only way I can answer that question is by saying that since taking an option module on Black American Literature as a student, I have been drawn by the power and pathos of writers such as Langston Hughes, Eldgridge Cleaver and James Baldwin. I have been appalled by the history of slavery and disturbed by the injustice of racial prejudice. My first encounters with racism were through literature at secondary school; first, when reading *To Kill A Mockingbird* (Lee 1966) and later, Wole Soyinka's poem, 'Telephone Conversation' (1991) . This point, I think, demonstrates the ability of literature to take us beyond ourselves and introduce us to experiences, worlds and landscapes that we might otherwise never experience. Good literature engages us emotionally, as well as intellectually. It forces us to see the world a little differently and we are never quite the same person who puts the book or poem down, as the one who picked it up. It was, I think, these excursions into Black American literature and my anti-racist activities throughout adulthood that brought this voice into my consciousness. But there is another aspect to the poem, encapsulated in the repetition of the word 'darkness'. English is riddled with negative connotations of the words, 'black' and 'dark', and with positive connotations of the words, 'white' and 'light'. The poem resists this bipolar discourse by reversing these connotations. In each stanza 'darkness' is associated with something positive, be it rest and peace in the first two, affection and love in the next two, absence of pain in the next and freedom in the final two. For the slave, night brings calm, peace and solace; whereas the only oblique reference to light, as in the use of the word, 'glare', is associated with the pain of a lash – 'whip crack smacking glare'.

Teachers as writers

It is my firm belief that teachers of English, and that means all primary teachers, should develop their own writing, starting with modules on 'creative writing' in Initial Teacher Education (ITE) courses. The important thing is not that all primary school teachers become great writers, but that they develop their confidence as writers and fine-tune the ability to reflect on their writing, in order to gain an insider view of the processes that writers engage with. This kind of subject knowledge is likely to enable more teachers to be better equipped to model writing for pupils. If, as students, they have internalised the importance of reflection and discussion of their work with their peers, these discursive practices are likely to be transferred to their pupils. Cremin and Powell (2008) note the importance of making classrooms 'communities of writers' but such a reality will be a truncated one if the teacher is outside 'the community'.

Ways into poetry writing in the classroom

In this next section I move from a discussion of poetry to some practical means of exploring poetry with pupils, first as writers and then as readers. Some of the examples given here are ones I have used personally, others are drawn from the work of other teachers. The first example is an extended project I undertook with Year 6 and 7 pupils. It uses the strategy I referred to above when talking about my daughter's poem.

Observation and 'wordstorming'

The strategy I am about to describe fits the initial stages of the model presented in Figure 2.4, in Chapter two, in that it encourages pupils to exercise their powers of observation whilst enabling them to create a poetic text by drawing upon their existing linguistic knowledge. The strategy has been used with a wide range of learners and appears to be effective, no matter what the age group. This is partly because the outcome is open-ended and involves the teacher eliciting language within the group's lexical range. As well as drawing upon existing language, the teacher uses the strategy to scaffold the construction of a text and then its redrafting, beginning with whole class writing, leading to group and, finally, individual work. It is important from the outset that the group is not aware they will be writing poetry. This reduces the chances of them bringing to the work preconceived notions of what a poem looks like, or negative feelings about poetry.

I usually begin by bringing the class together in a horseshoe formation around an object. I deliberately choose a large, colourful object, first, so everyone can see it and, second, because we tend to be more conscious of colour than other attributes of the world around us. Pupils are invited to spend a brief period just looking at the object and then I ask for individual words to describe it. I usually begin with colours because, as just stated, this is the object's most obvious attribute. Then I elicit words in lexical sets, including shapes in the object, names of parts of the object and words to describe its texture. I then get pupils to think of it as an animate rather than inanimate object and to consider how it might move. Eliciting words in these lexical sets generates: three types of word groups: adjectives, nouns and adverbs. In order to extend pupils' thinking and to generate further language resources, I ask them to tell me how it might feel if it had human emotions. This potentially leads us into personification and metaphor. Finally, I may ask them to compare the object with something that may look similar. This final request is often answered with a phrase rather than a word. During the whole of this stage of the activity words are written on individual cards and are placed where the pupils are able to see them. Scribing may be done by a teaching assistant or more able spellers among pupils.

The teacher needs to judge when it is appropriate to stop eliciting words in order to maintain children's interest, but it is important that a range of different types of words are collected. Before commencing the drafting process, I explain the words are going to be used to create a piece of writing and then invite one pupil to select the first word to start the first draft. The writing is developed by inviting other pupils, one by one, to select a word that seems to 'go with' the previous word or group of words already selected. At appropriate points I inform pupils they can choose to start a new line, if they wish. When all the words have been used, or at a point that seems appropriate, the first draft is complete.

The whole group reads the first draft aloud and I ask if it sounds right. Although aspects of most drafts flow well, other parts remain awkward and require further work. At this point I invite pupils to suggest what changes are needed, by telling them they can move words around, within a line, or between lines. They are also able to change the order of lines. The objective is to improve the draft and make it sound better. The emphasis is always on how it sounds because I am drawing upon pupils' implicit knowledge and 'ear' for language. The reworked draft is read several times until there is a consensus that it is complete. At this point, there is usually a great sense of collective ownership of the piece of writing because it is derived from the language of the group with the teacher performing, largely as a facilitator, guiding the construction of the piece. This shared process culminates in a class poem, which can be the first in the class anthology.

I follow the completion of the draft with a discussion of what type of writing pupils have produced. So far, they have never failed to identify it as poetry. This can lead to a discussion of the difference between a poem and prose, which further elicits pupils' knowledge of language and can help to sharpen their understanding of poetry and how it operates. By getting them to identify parts of the poem they particularly like, I foreshadow the process of evaluation they will need at the end of the lesson when listening to other poems, written by their peers. Although some groups may not be able to use specific metalinguistic terms such as simile, metaphor and alliteration, they express appreciation of these devices in their own ways. This signals the beginning of their appreciation of the power of poetry to communicate feelings and images by means of the interplay of words, *their* words, drawn from *their* common vocabulary.

Having modelled the process with the whole class, I then distribute objects on tables around the class and ask pupils to work in groups or pairs, drafting a new text, using the same technique. At the end of the process, pupils rehearse the reading of their poem and share it with the rest of the class. At the end of each reading, I invite pupils to give positive feedback and there is invariably something good to say about each poem. This final stage of the lesson, serves several purposes. It encourages critical evaluation and reinforces pupils, appreciation of poetic devices. Once pupils have the concept and can identify it in their own and their peers' writing, the exact term can then be applied. This is likely to be a much more meaningful way of learning metalinguistic terms and is likely to be better remembered than by means of decontextualised exercises in which pupils are required to identify simile and metaphor.

This activity generates learning on a number of levels simultaneously. First, pupils are learning a process for writing poetic language, one that will enable them to write independently at a later stage; second, they are drawing upon their implicit knowledge of language at word and text level; third, they are beginning to engage with poetry as critical readers and are, therefore, analysing text in order to do so; fourth, they are beginning to see that objects have a deeper significance; to see them not just as still life forms, but to explore their relationship to human experience.

I use this strategy with students, just as I used it with my pupils and the learning is much the same. With students I am modelling a process they can use themselves in their own classrooms. At the end of the session they usually express surprise and pleasure at their achievement because they did not think they could write poetry.

For me, the process discussed above reinforces the fact that teaching and learning are immensely social activities, requiring purposeful interaction between the teacher and learners. The strength of the activity resides in its empowerment of the learner. The teacher is largely a facilitator who elicits language from pupils and then enables them to use their own language in fresh and creative ways. But it is not just the process that is social; the end product, the poem, is the culmination of the collaborative process and is, therefore, a socially constructed artefact. The poem belongs to everyone and is, therefore, a symbol of collective effort and of group identity. The final lesson to be learned, albeit implicitly, is that language serves a deeply social function. As well as being a symbolic system by which human beings communicate meaning, in the act of doing so they use language to build collective identities.

At the end of the lesson, not only do pupils have a range of poems they can collect and share in a class anthology, they have a strategy for continuing to write poetry as individuals. In one school, where the class teacher and I turned the one-off writing session into an extended poetry writing project, we produced printed booklets of the collected poems and, after a poetry reading in the last session, handed each pupil their own copy of the anthology as they left the room for break-time. This was considered to be a school in a poor socio-economic area with challenging social conditions. Perhaps the fact that boys from this class of eleven-year-olds could be seen walking around the playground reading their poetry, rather than playing football and sharing it with friends from other classes, combined with the pupils' backgrounds, makes this image an enduring one for me. It was one of those supremely gratifying moments in teaching when you know you have made a difference.

Giving respect to pupils as writers

The importance of according pupils respect as writers is exemplified in the next example taken from a project undertaken by twelve PGCE students; their school placement teachers and the poet, Ann Sansom. The project fits closely the model I proposed in Chapter two. Pupils used jotters in which they recorded their poems. They were given complete freedom to write what they wanted and could decorate the jotters in whatever way they chose, a freedom that did not extend to other 'exercise' books. This 'act of freedom' signalled the very personal nature of the jotter to each pupil, which was reinforced by the rule that no one could read any part of the jotter without prior permission. All lessons began with a pupil reading to the class a poem of their choice, followed by questions about why they liked it. These readings were followed by a free writing activity. The first line for a poem was given by the teacher, which pupils responded to. In their evaluations of the project, pupils were particularly positive about these free writing 'starters'. Pupils not only had ownership of what they wrote and who was able to see their work, they also had control of the poems they presented for assessment. The requirement for them was to present one poem each week in a 'neat form' of their choice. They were encouraged to use dictionaries and thesauruses to widen their lexical choices. A strong feature of the project was peer evaluation. As with the project described above, a class poetry anthology was produced with each pupil having at least one poem entered (Sapiano 2008).

Both the above examples might be described as inclusive and personalised approaches to writing. In their different ways, they seek to empower pupils by not only allowing them ownership of their poetry but also of their critical voice, through the evaluation of the poetry of their peers. It might be suggested that such approaches lead to psychologically secure classrooms where pupils feel safe to explore language and to take risks without fear of ridicule. Maslow (1987) asserts that psychological 'safety' is an essential component of the learner's journey towards independent learning. We might speculate that children who develop as writers by means of a careful balance between collective understanding and individual exploration of thought, feeling and language will have a lifelong joy for written forms and will continue to write poetry.

Some practical strategies for writing poetry

Wilson and Hughes (1998: 14–15) offer a catalogue of strategies for initiating and developing poetry with primary age pupils. Among their suggestions are the following:

Walkabout poems begin with words collected during a walk around the school grounds or local community.

Sound maps involve the collection of sounds heard whilst a pupil is blindfolded. The child calls out what (s)he can hear and other pupils write the words down. Sound maps are likely to generate onomatopoeic words, which enables pupils to understand the concept of a word representing its physical sound before the term onomatopoeia is introduced to them.

Collections of the names of objects with strong visual or aural attributes.

Eavesdropping poems are ones in which a collection of snippets of different conversations are collected and then mixed up, sometimes to create humorous effect.

Dialect and accent poems are similar to eavesdropping poems in that they capture the way things are said. This type of poetry would be a useful way of developing linguistic awareness. In classrooms where more than one language is spoken, snippets of the different languages could be woven between different English dialects. This provides another means of showing value to the linguistic repertoires of the whole class. It is often small measures like this that make for the best form of inclusion.

Poetry microscopes involve the use of a small tube through which objects and people are viewed. The small aperture of the tube forces the viewer to focus on what is seen in a different way, causing unique observations to be made. Each 'snapshot' is succinctly described and then combined to form a poem of seemingly unrelated images.

The following suggestions of Wilson and Hughes lend themselves to the investigation of words and their semantic connections.

Word root poems draw attention to the spelling and morphology of words. For example:

Man
Woman
Man-made
Manly
Manual
Manuel

When certain types of words are chosen, as this example of the gendered nature of parts of the English language demonstrates, it is possible to explore how power relations are embedded in language. If done successfully such knowledge is likely to give pupils an understanding of how language influences our view of the world. An interesting comparison would be two poems developed around words and phrases based on the words, 'white' and 'black'.

Collective noun poems draw attention to the semantic connections of words. Examples include:

A city of rooves
A street of passers-by
A metro of commuters
A map of landscapes

In addition to these ideas, aspects of popular culture provide further initiatives for poetry writing. Poetry involves the creation of vivid visual and aural images in unique and unusual ways. From an early age children are inundated with visual images through watching television programmes, films, advertisements, pop-videos and computer games. As with everyday objects in the environment, poetry can be a means by which pupils can be encouraged to be more observant of the visual material presented to them. Any televisual material that tells a story or conveys a purposeful message by means of a succinct juxtaposition of images, provides a rich resource for poetry. Advertisements such as the atmospheric Stella Artois ones screened during the early twenty-first century are indicative of the type of material to which I am referring. In one, the passing of a hat gives the advertisement its textual coherence of different camera shots and, therefore, different views of the same scene. The short film can be shown to pupils and then replayed, shot by shot, giving pupils the chance to record their detailed observations. The juxtaposition of images in the film provides a structure for the juxtaposition of images in the poems. In addition, because the film evokes a sense of time, place and mood, without using dialogue, these features are likely to be reflected in pupils' poetry, giving their resultant work similar emotional depth. If it is deemed unethical to use a film that promotes alcohol, there are likely to be several less contentious examples available. An alternative is a short film without dialogue. *The Piano* (www.standards.dfes.gov.uk) or *El Caminante* (BFI 2001b) are excellent examples of the types of film I have in mind.

Poetic forms

Poetry offers a wide range of forms in which to write. In addition to the poetic forms already introduced, outlined below are further examples of types of poems that could be used in the primary classroom.

Alliterative poems

Alliterative poems play on the rhythms of language when consonants are repeated in consecutive words and syllables. The following is an example of an alliterative poem based on days of the week and children's names:

On Monday morning Mandy and Mandeep made a magical metal mouse;
On Tuesday Tariq and Tim taught it to dance;
On Wednesday Wendy and Waheed went to watch the wonderful mouse;
On Thursday Theo and Thelma threw the thing away;
On Friday Firdous and Fred found it and fetched it back again;
On Saturday Satpal and Susan slowly stroked its smooth soft skin;

On Sunday Sam and Sameena stepped suddenly on its slender tail – SNAP!

So …

On Monday morning Mandy and Mandeep mended the magical metal mouse.

By using the names of children in the class, as this example shows, the multicultural nature of many of Britain's classrooms is implicitly acknowledged. Other alliterative poems might begin with the months of the year, products in a shop or the pupils' favourite football teams. Follow-up work might include the investigation of environmental print and other media to identify where and why alliteration is used in general language use. Not surprisingly, this use of figurative language is commonly found in advertising and, as part of their investigation, pupils could be asked why this is the case. Another source of alliteration in everyday usage is newspaper headlines, particularly those of the tabloid press. Several possibilities for writing poetry might emerge from such an investigation. For example:

- Pupils write alliterative headlines based on events in their own lives. It might then be possible to combine headlines to create a longer poem.

- Read a news article and transform it into a poem (this need not be alliterative).

- Combine poetry and the marketing of a product made in Design Technology. Use alliteration to advertise the product.

Syllable poetry

Possibly the most widely known form of syllabic poetry is haiku, which originated in Japan. Using a strict pattern of three lines and seventeen syllables, the syllabic pattern is divided into five syllables in the first and third lines with the remaining seven in the second line. The haiku captures a single feeling or idea by describing an image in a 'snapshot' (Abbs and Richardson 1990: 157).

A violin moans,
The woman dances alone,
The moon smiles wanly.

The haiku appears deceptively simple to write but the very best examples of this form are rich in subtextual possibilities and are, therefore, open to wide interpretation. This emphasis on the sharpness of the image is closest to a Western approach to poetry called 'Imagism', of which Ezra Pound and T.S. Eliot are probably the best known advocates. Like haiku, most imagist poems are short and atmospheric. Abbs and Richardson (ibid: 149) show that imagist poetry develops imagery in a precise pattern as follows:

Object – image – development of image.

A typical imagist poem might read:

Object –	A breeze enters the courtyard;
Image –	Trotting on delicate feet
Development –	It snorts softly and is gone.

I should add that imagist poetry is not syllabic but that I have included an example here because of its similarity to the haiku.

Derived from the French for 'five', the cinquain is five lines long and follows a 2 – 4 – 6 – 8 – 2 syllabic pattern.

> The door
> Creaking open,
> Slither of light enters
> A blade of murderous intent
> I scream.

This form of poetry builds suspense in a crescendo of syllables in the fourth line and concludes with a short sharp image.

The third type of syllabic poetry identified by Abbs and Richardson is the englyn, which originates in Welsh verse (ibid: 159). An englyn is four lines long and has thirty syllables. The syllabic pattern is 10 – 6 – 7 – 7.

Syllabic poetry is useful for at least two reasons: first, it forces pupils to focus on the phonological pattern in words and their sonorous quality, a matter they may take for granted in everyday usage of those words; and second, it encourages a precise use of language in order to construct a tightly framed expression.

Other forms and sources of poetry

The kenning was widely used by the Norsemen in their Sagas; epic stories of voyages across the seas to distant lands. It comprises two word clusters in place of a noun. So, a wave might be a 'foaming monster'. Apart from the sagas, another useful introduction to kennings is through Philip Pullman's highly descriptive and humorous story, *The Firework Maker's Daughter* (2004). Early in the novel the fireworks that Lalchand and his daughter, Layla, make are given splendid names such as, 'java fountains'.

I have used this with pupils by giving them a noun and asking them to create a kenning in pairs. Pairs then combine kennings to form a two-line kenning on the same subject. Further combinations can be made until the whole class has a kenning poem. It may be necessary to redraft the poem with the whole class by rearranging lines to create something that sounds effective.

When introducing particular poetic forms to children, with the intention of encouraging them to imitate those forms, a degree of flexibility needs to be applied. The real purpose of a poetry lesson or project is to engage pupils' imagination and creativity. For some pupils the poetic voice may emerge in a form other than the one the teacher intended. When this happens we should respond to the quality of the poem, not whether it adheres to the intended form. This view is not in keeping with the structured content of the Literacy Framework but, given that standard Q8 requires teachers to exercise 'creative and critical judgements of innovation' it is very much in step with what being a professional educationist, and certainly what being a teacher of English, entails.

Reading poetry

Poetry is all around us, if we care to look. It is in the persuasive language of politicians who often resort to the repetitive power of three to make their point. Who will forget the simple exaltation to 'Education, Education, Education' of Tony Blair. It is in the names of shops. The name 'Top Shop' uses the assonance of the vowel sound to create a strong sonic quality. The language of advertising is seeped in poetic devices. Even a simple message on a shuttle bus between Luton Parkway station and the airport caught my eye because of its poetic voice – 'train2plane and back again'. This example demonstrates how the inclusion of numerals in our language has become common place as a result of text messaging and emails.

In the past, poetry reading in class has often been accompanied by comprehension-type exercises that require pupils to identify what the poem is about, what the poet is telling us. However, this may not be the most appropriate way to approach poetry. Indeed, evidence from those closest to the poetic form suggest otherwise. Returning to his craft guild theme, Dylan Thomas (1966) states that 'The best craftsman always leaves holes and gaps in the work of a poem so that something that is not in the poem can creep, crawl, flash or thunder in.'

We are familiar with the idea that novels and short stories have untold elements that make it possible for the reader to contemplate subtextual possibilities, but because of its succinct, economic form, there is a tendency to consider a poem as a complete, finished entity. By viewing a poem as a partially complete and dynamic artefact, we alter completely the role of the reader. Instead of being an interpreter of what the poet is telling us, the reader becomes a participant in developing the meaning of the poem. Indeed, Hamburger (1972) suggests that when reading a poem the reader 'is invited to participate in a process of exploration' and Gamble and Yates (2008: 166) state that because poetic language is so compressed 'many poems offer themselves up for different interpretations'. Eliot (cited in Holt undated) observed that 'genuine poetry can communicate before it is understood'. Viewing poetry in this way, as an art form in search of its own meaning, can be empowering for both teachers and pupils because it takes away the fear of not properly understanding what a poem is about and creates the possibility for a more creative pedagogy. Taking this point on board, whilst also reflecting the above discussion, The Poetry Society makes the following observation:

> By stressing that readers work alongside the poet to discover the poem teachers will be challenging the belief that experiencing art is an act of consumption rather than one of creation. This approach also invites students to see the poem as provisional, still growing, thereby encouraging re-reading.
>
> (Poetry Society 2008)

As a writer of poetry, I am well aware of the validity of this discussion. On a number of occasions when my role has changed from that of the writer to that of the reader, I have seen in my own work, meanings I had not been aware of when writing. The fact I had not intended such meanings does not invalidate their value; it merely adds to the enjoyment of the poetic mode of expression.

How does this repositioning of the pupil from an interrogator of what the poet meant to an active participant in the creative process translate into actual teaching and learning in the classroom? If comprehension activities are indicative of arid practice, what constitutes more enlivened approaches to poetry reading? There is nothing wrong with asking questions of a poem; it is more a matter of how questions are framed and who is asking them. When introducing a particular poem to students or pupils, I offer no preamble or commentary, just a request that they read the poem in small groups; that the poem be read several times and that they try to hear the 'voice' driving the poem. I then invite them to ask several questions about the poem they would like answered. Each question is written at the centre of a sheet of paper. The group then attempt to deal with their own questions in turn by going back into the poem to find possible answers. Given the above discussion, answers are often transacted interpretations arrived at through the interaction of the poet's language and imagery and the reader's own personal and worldly experience. Pupils and students justify their responses by drawing upon evidence situated either inside the poem, or their own lives and experience.

A kinaesthetic approach to poetry

As suggested earlier in the chapter some of the best ways into the meanings of specific poems is through dance, drama, music and art. Some sources suggest exploiting poetry's reliance on imagery by inviting pupils to create a collage of a poem or by making a collection of objects referred to in the text (poetryarchive 2008).

In addition, turning a poem into a short film provides a further opportunity for pupils to investigate a poem's use of imagery. As is discussed in the chapter on film in the classroom, film making gives pupils a purpose for collaborating to reach common understandings of the subject under investigation. The poetryarchive suggests ways in which the class might be prepared prior to listening to a poem. The advice emphasises the need to reduce environmental distractions, use listening games to accentuate pupils hearing and read the poem several times, encouraging pupils to listen for something different each time, such as the rhyme pattern, sounds created by the word and pictures created in the minds of pupils by aspects of the poem. Other prompts might include, the way the poem makes the reader feel; the identification of unfamiliar words and their possible meaning; whose voice is speaking in the poem and whether the poem is set in the past, present or future. Teachers are also recommended to seize opportunities to read poetry to their class for pleasure, without requests to them to respond. However, pupils who have developed a secure appreciation of poetry are likely to volunteer their views without prompting. This would be one indicator of what Michael Rosen might refer to as 'a poetry friendly classroom' (cited in Saguisag 2007: 7).

Poetic voice and poetic observation

Earlier in the chapter a distinction was made between poetry and prose. However, there is never a complete dichotomy. Some writers of prose write with a poetic voice and pupils seeped in poetry will recognise occasions when this occurs. It would be hard to conceive of a novel by Ted Hughes lacking flashes of poetic expression and sure enough even a partial reading of the *Iron Woman* (1993: 3) reveals delights of poetic description. Early in the story the protagonist, Lucy is looking over the parapet of a bridge watching an eel in the river. The movement of the eel is described as 'corkscrewing' in the water, and 'The black water moved silently, crumpling and twirling little whorls of light'.

Pupils who have themselves revelled in the play with words to create vivid images will deeply appreciate Hughes' metaphorical constructions. They will not need to be asked what is Hughes doing here, they will come to the text with the inner voice of themselves as writers and will tune to Hughes' voice speaking to them. They will acknowledge how the image has been created because they have done it, or attempted it, themselves, and will know what Hughes is doing because their teacher will have revealed to them that they did it in their own work. When pupils are viewed as real writers and perceive themselves as real writers they read texts with an 'insider' point of view. This is what Barrs (2000) means by the 'writer in the reader'. The development of reading and writing is symbiotic; the one influences the other. The best language use in the classroom should be seen as an holistic and integral process combining all four language modes: speaking, listening, reading and writing.

Poetry writing is critical to pupils' language development because as Wyse and Jones (2008) observe: 'Children are capable of extraordinary observations and often make startling conceptual links between what they see, hear, feel, know and imagine. ... Poetry writing should most of all be about searching for things that genuinely matter to the writer.'

Through poetry the cognitive and affective aspects of the individual combine with sensory experience in a fusion of learning about oneself and the world. If we can develop pupils' powers of observation, their joy for 'painting with words' and their appreciation of the words of others, then we launch them into a lifelong engagement with the power and joy of language. Such an achievement in the classroom will both enrich the lives of those we teach and enliven the language they will use throughout their lives.

Although I advise above that teachers should encourage pupils to develop a creative use of language through poetry before introducing them to the meta-language of poetic diction, it is important that we have, as part of our subject knowledge, a good command of the language used to describe poetry. Once pupils have experience of a particular poetic concept, the appropriate term to describe that concept can then be applied. The glossary below includes a range of terms that could be part of a teacher's subject knowledge in English.

Poetic language: some key terms

In addition to the terms defined here, others can be found in the references and web dictionaries listed at the end of this glossary.

Alliteration

The repetition of the same initial phoneme in consecutive words, e.g. funny phonemes; slithery, slimy snakes; autumn's auburn tint. The device is used for aural effect and its musical quality, as well as a means to emphasise a subject.

Ambiguity

Deliberate ambiguity, which means being able to read more than meaning into something, is used to create uncertainty. There are three types of ambiguity: lexical, grammatical and literary. Lexical ambiguity occurs in words that have several meanings or are polysemic. Usually the exact meaning of a word is clear from the context in which it is used but sometimes writers' reduce the context to make meaning operate on different levels. Grammatical ambiguity involves multiple meanings at sentence levels, e.g. 'They are cooking apples'. The meaning is determined here by knowledge of which word class the word 'cooking' falls into. As a verb, the sentence means apples are being cooked, but as a noun the apples in question are cooking apples. Literary ambiguity (for an explanation see p. 33, McArthur, T. (1992) *The Oxford Companion to the English Language*).

Assonance
The repetition of the same or similar sounds within consecutive words to create a rhyme or half-rhyme. Originally, assonance referred to vowel sounds but it is also now taken to apply to consonants too.

Ballad
Traditionally, a ballad was an oral narrative poem set to music. A ballad tells the story of a community. From the sixteenth century ballads were printed on broadside sheets and told of sensational events. They are usually written in four-lined stanza's (quatrains) and have a regular beat with an abba rhyme scheme. In popular culture the term ballad refers to a slow, romantic song.

Couplet
Two consecutive rhyming lines.

Elegy
A poem in which a dead person's life is mourned, often ending in calm consolation of loss.

Empathy
The ability to 'stand in someone else's shoes' and imagine how they feel.

Enjambment
Occurs when one line runs into the next so that the reader must read on in order to get the sense of what is written.

Epic
A long story or poem telling the story of heroic adventure. The *Illiad* or The *Odyssy* are classic examples.

Figurative language
Language that deviates from the norm by means of the use of alliteration, hyperbole, simile, metaphor etc. thereby making it more symbolic than literal language.

Free verse

Poetry without a rhyme scheme but possessing rhythm and figurative devices. Lines may be of variable length unlike the rhyme of other forms and are more usually demarcated by meaning.

Haiku

A traditional Japanese poetic form of three lines and 17 syllables with the first and third lines each with five syllables with line two having seven. In a haiku, a moment in time is captured in a clear visual image with an economy of words.

Idiom

Figurative language in everyday speech.

Image/imagery

The use of language to create a strong mental image.

Internal rhyme

Rhyme within a line.

Kenning

The description of something using compound words. A form used in Norse and Old English poetry.

Metaphor

A form of figurative language, and therefore, a non-literal expression, in which something is presented as though it is something else e.g. *the fire spat a spray of fiery sparks high into the night sky*. In this example the fire is given human or animalistic qualities denoted in the word *'spat'*.

Narrative poem

A poem that tells a story.

Onomatopoeia

Words that when spoken make the sound they describe, e.g. *crash, hiss, whisper.*

Oxymoron

The juxtaposition of words that appear contradictory in order to accentuate an image, e.g. *'parting is such sweet sorrow' 'a cold sun rose that morning'.*

Personification

A form of metaphor in which an inanimate thing or quality is given human attributes, e.g. *the wind rose up and hurled itself against the building, lashing it and howling in pain.*

Quatrain

A four line stanza.

Refrain

The repetition of a line or series of lines to accentuate an effect, feeling or mood as well as a cohesive device.

Simile

A figure of speech in which one thing is compared to another. The comparison is usually conjoined by the words *like* or *as.*

Stanza

In poetry, the equivalent of a verse in a song.

Voice

In literature the voice is the person who tells the story. This may be the author or the poet who speaks directly to the reader. Alternatively, it may be the perspective of a particular character who is not the author. Sometimes more than one voice is heard in a poem or story and can be conveyed through such devices as dialogue, indirect speech and first person accounts. In the case of the latter the same event is often narrated from the point of view of different characters in the story or poem.

Additional terms and definitions can be found at the following websites:

http://www.lovelandia.com/archive/008752.html
http://www.poetry-online.org/poetry-terms.htm
http://sun-design.com/poetry/index.html

CHAPTER

9

Reading for meaning

Exploring non-fiction

THIS CHAPTER EXPLORES the following:

- the form and structure of different non-fiction texts;

- practical ways of approaching non-fiction;

- directed activities related to texts (DARTs);

- collaborative learning.

Although language across the curriculum had been advocated for some time (DES 1975), the National Curriculum (1988) formally introduced into the Primary English curriculum a range and breadth of text types that had previously been overlooked. The first Literacy Strategy (DfEE 1998) and its successor, the Primary National Strategy Literacy Framework (DfES 2006), strengthened the teaching of non-fiction texts. That is not to say that non-fiction had been neglected before 1988, but that the various curriculum reforms formalised its place in the primary classroom. Pupils were presented with opportunities that required of them a different command of language and its comprehension than much spoken language and narrative writing. Teachers were presented with the challenge of helping pupils to bridge the linguistic gap between fiction and non-fiction.

The size of the linguistic gap was highlighted by Perera (1984) in her study of school texts. She identified three broad areas in which non-fiction differed from fiction, making it harder for pupils to process. The first of these differences was at word level. The vocabulary of non-fiction differed significantly from that found in most children's fiction. The former tends to have more nouns than fiction. The frequency of nouns increases the amount of information the reader has to process. In addition, there is a high incidence of pronouns in fiction, which provide relational cohesion whereas these are less frequent in non-fiction. A further difference at word level is in the types of verbs found in non-fiction, which makes use of the passive, rather than the active form that is more typical of fiction. The second major difference is at sentence level. Not only does non-fiction tend to have longer, more complex sentences, the syntactic features of non-fiction differ significantly from those of much children's fiction. In non-fiction, noun phrases tend to be longer; there is greater use of subordinate clauses and the gap between the subject of the sentence and its agent tends to be longer. The third difference is in the discourse features of fiction and non-fiction. Whereas most children's fiction is chronologically organised, the same is not true of non-fiction. In addition, the discourse connectors used in non-fiction are not usually found in fiction. In this respect, as well as other linguistic features, Perera notes that fiction shares more similarities with spoken everyday language than does non-fiction. Table 9.1 provides a more detailed account of the differences Perera found in her comparative analysis of the linguistic features of fiction and non-fiction.

Literacy and power

In addition to the features noted by Perera, Bakhtin (1988) draws attention to the way in which genres are imbued with 'specific points of view, approaches, forms of thinking, nuances and accents' that characterise the genre. Hence, the language of persuasion, of argument, of the recount; not only adhere as texts in different ways, using different types of textual cohesion, but they each have a 'voice' that is specific to their genre. In a further discussion, Bakhtin (1988) suggests that genre is stratified with social power and Martin (1984 cited in Czerniewska 1992: 133) asserts that undue emphasis on narrative forms in the primary years denies pupils sufficient access to the kind of expository texts that are 'needed to take control over their lives.' This discussion draws our attention to the fact that language is a social phenomenon and that its various forms, in different social contexts, convey socially significant, as well as linguistic, meanings. Not only do children need to be able to read and write well, they need to be able to make accurate judgements about the kind of language that is appropriate for particular purposes.

The ability to use language appropriately is broader than the correct use of standard English, although this, in itself, conveys social significance, as it is the language of academic success and social prestige. We might view standard English as the raw material of genre, a material that is then manipulated to construct further levels of power. The language of law, of medicine and even of education, is highly specialised. The ability to understand it and use it accurately, denotes, through occupational status, the social identity and contextual power of the user. It also demarcates those who can from those who cannot. Those who cannot use a specific form of language are disempowered because they are reliant upon those who have

TABLE 9.1 Features of fiction and non-fiction

Linguistic and textual features	Fiction	Non-fiction
Direct speech	Occurred in 48.7 per cent of sentences	None found
Non-sentence structures	Numerous examples, including commands, questions, exclamations etc.	Two examples
Pronouns	230	63
Personal pronouns	193	32
Subject as agent for action	Applies in most cases	Infrequent use
Chronologically sequenced	Normally the case in children's fiction	Rarely the case
Discourse connectors	Closer to everyday speech, e.g. next, then, so etc.	Unlike everyday speech, e.g. therefore, however, nevertheless etc.
Linguistic foreshadowing	Occasional	Frequent
Information processing, i.e. frequency of nouns introducing new information	Nouns are usually followed by pronouns, which link information	A greater number of information bearing nouns – rarely followed by pronouns
Syntactic distance between the subject and verb in a sentence	Close connection because sentences tend to be short and relatively simple	Sentences tend to be longer and more complex. The subject and verb tend to be separated by more words than in fiction
Use of verbs	Extensive use of active verbs. 75 per cent of verbs tend to be of this form	More infrequent use of active verbs. However, there is greater use of passive verbs and copulas
Use of noun-phrases	Tend to be short. Approximately two to three words. In a sample of 1500 words, 25 per cent were complex noun phrases	Tend to be complex, sharing similarities with adult non-fiction. In a sample of 1500 words, 43 per cent were complex noun phrases. Some including up to 17 words
Use of subordinate clause	Tend to be similar to those used in speech, e.g. familiar adverbial and nominal clauses	Greater use of relative clauses and adverbials not commonly found in speech

Source: Adapted from Perera (1984).

an in-depth knowledge of that form for help. This can sometimes require a considerable financial transaction and we might say that certain forms of language have an economic as well as social significance. This is particularly so in the case of law where often archaic lexis and convoluted discourse pervades legal documents. Even at the level of ordinary social interaction the ability to use a specific type of lexis in particular syntactic constructs implies power. For example, a formal letter of complaint to an organisation, written in a concise manner, using appropriate vocabulary and having an authoritative tone is likely to receive greater attention than one that is rambling, verbose and lacking succinct vocabulary. Justification for acting on each complaint might be equal but the first letter is more likely to receive a positive response as it conveys a higher degree of personal power because of the writer's use of language. The reader might conclude the first writer to be better educated and more likely to take the complaint further than the second writer. Just as some organisations use a person's postcode to discern their social position, an appropriate, authoritative command of language can have a similar effect.

The importance of acquainting pupils with a variety of genre and helping them to develop the ability to control and manipulate language in different contexts is an essential feature of education in a democratic society. In this sense, a varied language curriculum, one that not only equips pupils with a broad command of literate forms, but which also helps them to understand the way in which language is used, as a rhetorical device, is both empowering and creative. It is empowering because it gives pupils the potential to take personal control of their lives as adults, rather than passively accept what they are offered; and it is creative because, armed with linguistic expertise, they can use language to explore possible answers to problems they will encounter throughout their lives. Such an approach to texts might be located within what is termed 'critical literacy', which begins from the premise that texts are 'ideologically situated' and can culminate in opportunities to critique and transform dominant discourses, making them more egalitarian (Larson and Marsh 2005: 45).

Working in different genre

Elsewhere, Perera (1990) concludes that pupils need to have a range of non-fiction texts read to them from an early age so they are able to 'absorb' sentence structures and discourse features before they are asked to encounter them in their independent reading and writing. Listening to the language of a particular genre is important also if pupils are to be able to 'tune into the voice' of that genre. Creating opportunities for pupils to, first, develop 'an ear' for language and then to develop their own 'voice', is a central theme of this book. Having extensive exposure to different text types in order to encourage an ear for the variations in language that occur across a range of written discourses accords with a central thesis here.

Perera adds that the use of language in non-fiction can lead to different ways of thinking that flow back into spoken language.

Some publishers, recognising the linguistic and textual differences between fiction, who weave documentary material into their stories, creating a kind of 'faction' and non-fiction, have attempted to close the gap for younger readers, imparting factual information by means of narrative discourse, thereby blurring the edges between fiction and non-fiction. The practice has also been adopted by some writers. Michael Foreman's *War Boy* (1991) is a good example of this type of writing. Parallel to the story of a child's experience of German bombing raids over Suffolk are labelled diagrams of an incendiary bomb, an Anderson shelter and advice about what to do in the event of fire. The fact the illustrations are facsimiles of the period adds to the authenticity of the story within its historic setting.

While some writers have ventured into a genre that merges fiction and non-fiction, and some publishers have exploited a market niche by producing the 'narrative non-fiction' book, there is no avoiding the fact that pupils need to be able to work with the 'real McCoy', that is, the range of non-fiction texts that are part of the curriculum. These text types, or genres, include, recounts, reports, explanations, instructions, persuasive and discursive texts, biographical and autobiographical writing, formal and informal letters, as well as texts that deal generally with information giving. Each text type has its distinguishing features represented in different types of layout, voice, vocabulary, textual structure and discourse connectors. Some of these characteristic features are shown in Table 9.2.

TABLE 9.2 Characteristic features of non-fiction texts

Text type	Textual structure	Connectives	Voice	Tense
Recount	Chronological retelling of a sequence of events	Temporal – then, afterwards, next, following that …	Personal – I, we	Past time – I went; I saw
Report	Non-chronological – descriptive	Headings and subheadings classifying elements of subject. Lead sentences identifying focus of description.	Impersonal/ objective description of phenomena	Present time
Instructions	Chronological – informing of a sequence of actions/procedures	Numbered sequence – or chronological terms, first, second, third …	Impersonal – imperative – glue part a) to part b)	Present time – pour boiling water into a pan
Explanation	Logical sequence explaining some phenomenon	Temporal or causal – next, following that … As a result, because, therefore	Impersonal – objective explanation of phenomena	Present time – the inverted image on the retina is passed to the brain via the optic nerve …
Persuasive text	Logical sequence stating a case and then elaborating by means of additional supporting statements	Logical – this demonstrates that, therefore, because …	Impersonal – quasi-objective	Present time – this is because

However, unlike most fiction texts that are not specifically picture books or graphic novels, non-fiction often integrates pictures, diagrams and charts as complementary elements to the written texts. Indeed, one might say that with some non-fiction texts, full understanding necessitates the reading of a symbiotic relationship of visual imagery and written text. This is particularly the case with advertisements in newspapers, magazines and on billboards where the advertiser has to communicate a message in a matter of seconds, before the reader turns the page or the driver passes the large roadside hoarding. As mentioned elsewhere in the book, the use of what Bearne and Wolstencroft (2007) refer to as multimodal texts, is an increasingly common feature of non-verbal communication, causing educational linguists to reconceptualise the nature of literacy in the twenty-first century. Although there is recognition of writing being screen-based as well as on paper, the application of multimodal literacy only appears in the Primary Literacy Framework (DfES 2006) as a summative unit of work (Formal/ Impersonal Writing) at the end of Year 6. However, Educationalists such as Bearne and Wolstencroft (2007), Kress (2003) and Marsh and Hallet (2008) note how children's early literacy development is influenced by the increasingly multimodal nature of texts in the environment, including the internet, and how children use these texts in their own writing, from an early age. These educationalists also comment on how literacy is an embedded social practice. It would seem to follow, therefore, that the multimodal nature of literacy ought to feature more as a key element in literacy practices in the classroom throughout Key Stages 1 and 2. Creative teachers, who recognise that children's popular culture is an important aspect of the general knowledge that pupils bring to the classroom, will not be bound by the strictures of official programmes of work and will want to utilise children's knowledge irrespective of their age.

Ways into non-fiction

In addition to exposing children to a range of text types by reading non-fiction to them from an early age and then providing them with texts they can engage with for themselves, strategies are needed to help pupils develop their understanding of different genre. The emphasis on talk for learning is an essential pre-requisite, as suggested elsewhere in this book. The more pupils talk about the kind of subject matter they will encounter in non-fiction texts, the greater will be their capacity to understand the lexis and concepts they will encounter in the texts themselves. Prior to reading a non-fiction text on a specific subject, some teachers ask pupils to begin to map their existing knowledge of the subject. This can be done in various ways, including knowledge or concept maps. In the former, the subject to be studied is written at the centre of a blank sheet of paper and facts already known about the subject are added. Concept maps require lines to be drawn between these additions to show which items relate to other items. Other forms of mapping knowledge involve the use of mind maps (Buzan 2000, 2005; Harris and Caviglioli 2003). Although there is some variation in how mind maps are generated, they involve themed branches that radiate from the central subject under investigation. Mind maps are being increasingly used as a means of helping pupils to organise and record their thinking. Their application is most evident in Science teaching and topic planning in the primary classroom but as knowledge of their usefulness increases, they are being used across the curriculum for a range of purposes, including as a framework for note-taking and as an organiser for writing (Gardner and Jefferies 2008).

By mapping existing knowledge on a subject, pupils are bringing to the level of consciousness a set of schema. This refers not only to discrete fragments of knowledge but also the relationships that connect that knowledge. The schemata is likely to be different for different pupils and can be used by the teacher as a means of assessing individual and class knowledge, on a specific subject. Prior to reading the text, pupils can be invited to ask questions in the form of what additional knowledge on the subject they would like to acquire. For example, the subject might be an aspect of History, let us say, the Ancient Egyptians. A pupil might know that the root word of Egyptian is Egypt; that the Egyptians built pyramids and had Pharaohs. The questions they may ask in relation to this knowledge could be: Where is Egypt in the world? Why did the Egyptians build pyramids? Who were the Pharaohs? These questions give the pupils a purpose for reading that is self-initiated rather than imposed by the teacher in the way that traditional comprehension questions are. This discrete knowledge represents the landmarks around which they can construct new knowledge as they read the text. New knowledge is then added to the knowledge or mind map begun before reading. If new knowledge is written in a different colour pen to prior knowledge then both the teacher and the pupil can track progress and achievement.

Directed activities related to texts

A further set of strategies designed to enable pupils to engage with texts, particularly non-fiction texts, in order to deepen their comprehension of the text's content, were first introduced by Lunzer and Gardner (1979). Directed activities related to texts (DARTs) involves the completion of an ancillary activity using information gleaned from a written text. DARTs may be undertaken by individual pupils working independently but, given sufficient challenge, they are particularly effective in small group situations where members of the group must collaborate to complete the task. An example of this kind of collaborative text related activity can be found in Figures 9.1 a–d.

This activity is designed for a group of four to five pupils. The group is given a diagram of the eye which they must label correctly. A set of information cards is distributed among the group. Pupils who are confident readers will have more than one card. Each pupil reads the information they have been given and then puts the cards face down so the information cannot be seen. The group then shares the knowledge they have acquired from their reading of the cards and collaborate to identify the location of different parts of the eye. Once they have done this, they

(a)

The Lens	The Pupil
The lens is located in the middle of the eye, at the front. It rests mostly behind the pupil. The purpose of the lens is to help focus light from objects before it reaches the retina at the back of the eye.	The pupil is the dark circle in the middle of the eye at the front. It is surrounded by the iris. Its purpose is to let light pass from outside onto the back of the eye. Sometimes the pupil is larger than at other times. Why do you think this might be?

The Retina	The Cornea
The retina is the curved surface at the back of the eye. It is made up of many cells that are sensitive to light. When light reflects from an object into the eye, the image appears inverted (upside down) on the retina. The inverted image is passed to the optic nerve.	The cornea is a transparent film, located in front of the iris and the lens. Its purpose is to protect the eye but it also assists the lens to focus light as it enters the eye.

(b)

The Brain	The Optic Nerve
Reflected light from objects passing into the eye are passed to the brain by the optic nerve. The brain receives inverted (upside down) images of objects. Its purpose is to turn them the right way up.	The optic nerve connects the retina at the back of the eye to the brain. It acts like a visual messenger, taking images from the retina to the brain.

The Iris	Explanation Card
The iris is the coloured ring that surrounds the pupil. It is actually a muscle. Its purpose is to control the amount of light passing into the eye. It does this by controlling the size of the pupil. In dim light it makes the pupil bigger and in bright light it makes it smaller.	Use this card to explain the whole process of how we see something.

FIGURE 9.1 Sight and vision

(c) Instructions

There are seven information cards and one 'explanation' card. At the end of the activity use the explanation card to explain to someone who has not seen the other cards how the eye works to enable us to see images.

Before that, though, share the information cards in your group. Depending on the size of the group you may have one or more cards to read. Each person reads their card and then turns it over, without showing it to the others in the group. As a group, you must correctly label the diagram of the eye and then add the statements below to the appropriate labels. You may reread your card to yourself if you forget information but you must not show it to anyone else in the group.

(d) Statements

is a muscle that controls how much light passes into the eye.	allows light to pass into the eye.

receives messages and converts them so we see objects the right way up.	helps to focus light.

receives light and converts it into an image which is then sent to the optic nerve.

Protects the eye and helps to focus light.	takes messages to the brain.

FIGURE 9.1 (cont.)

then attach to the diagram statements that explain the functions of each part. Finally, on a blank card, the group pools their knowledge to write an explanation of how light from an object passes through the eye and is carried, via the optic nerve, to the brain, where the image is recognised. An alternative to the final stage could involve a group presentation to the whole class, explaining how we see.

Developing reading with learners for whom English is an Additional Language (EAL)

Cummins (1980) has drawn our attention to the dangers of assuming that verbal communicative competence in an additional language is the same as being able to use that language fully for cognitive and academic purposes. In his early work he made the distinction between what he called Basic Interpersonal Communication Skills (BICS) and Cognitive Academic Language Proficiency (CALP). Based on empirical research, he concluded that within two years of being immersed in a new language environment, a migrant child would be able to speak the target language to almost the same level as those who spoke the indigenous language, as their first language (BICS). However, the child's ability to communicate and comprehend curriculum-related or academic language (CALP) could take a further five years. This finding was used to support the proposition that EAL pupils required curriculum-related scaffolding beyond the initial stages of verbal EAL acquisition. Cummins and Swain later acknowledged that spoken language can also be cognitively challenging and modified their thinking by referring to learning that is either 'context embedded' or 'context reduced' and is 'cognitively demanding' or 'cognitively undemanding' (1986). This revised model is presented in Figure 9.2.

The model provides a useful means for locating the position of EAL learners in relation to their needs and the demands of the curriculum. For example, a child who is in the early stages of acquiring a second language might find listening to a story in English cognitively demanding because the act of listening and comprehending takes concentration and conscious mental processing. However, listening to a simple story in English becomes cognitively undemanding once familiarity with the vocabulary, syntax and textual genre has been acquired. If we combine Cummins' model with Vygotsky's concept of the Zone of Proximal Development (ZPD) (1962) we begin to see how learning is dependent upon the teacher's ability to identify for pupils: the next level of cognitive challenge (ZPD) and provide appropriate support structures until that level also becomes cognitively undemanding for the pupil. Wells (1897) noted that the best linguistic environment for young children, acquiring their first language, was one in which talk with an adult was located in the 'here and now'. Being able to talk about things that could be seen, heard and touched enabled children to make strong connections between the real world and the language used to represent items, actions and ideas in the real world.

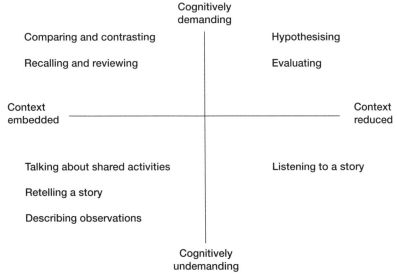

FIGURE 9.2 Second language acquisition: theory and practice

Source: Cummins (1980).

The application of Cummins' work to the classroom replicates Wells' findings by suggesting that the learning of new concepts in English for EAL pupils needs to be supported in equally context-embedded situations. We can also see in the model resonances of Bloom *et al.*'s taxonomy (1956). In addition to the retelling of a story, describing observations or talking about things a group share in common, locating factual information in a simple text is cognitively undemanding and context-embedded and requires a relatively low-level thinking skill such as comprehension. However, cognitively demanding, context-reduced learning involves higher order thinking such as textual analysis, synthesis and evaluation. Irrespective of whether English is their additional language or not, all pupils need to be supported through the various levels of Bloom *et al.*'s taxonomy but EAL learners may require longer support or particular strategies to assist their reading and writing in English. Hutchinson *et al.* (2003) make a strong case for this proposition. Noting that the literacy skills of many EAL pupils seemed not to be as developed as their English monoglot peers, Hutchinson used Miscue Analysis and then the Neale Analysis of Reading Ability (1997) to conclude that although EAL pupils were often very good in terms of reading accuracy, their levels of textual comprehension were not as advanced as their English counterparts. Furthermore, the gap between EAL pupils and monoglot English speaking pupils remained constant from Year 2 to Year 5. This finding concurs with that of Cummins' and leads us to the question of what can be done to support EAL pupils in their acquisition of the necessary skills to understand written texts in English.

This question was taken up by one of my B.Ed dissertation students, Krystle Fenn (2005) who undertook a small-scale intervention study whilst on placement in a vertically grouped Year 3/4 class in a multi-ethnic school. The majority of pupils in the class were EAL learners. Fenn noted all the pupils were able to converse confidently in English with both peers and adults. At the beginning of her placement she wanted to see if Hutchinson's findings could be replicated, using the Neal Analysis of Reading Ability (NARA). The NARA, which is administered individually, involves the pupil reading a series of short narratives of increasing complexity. The design of the test enables both reading accuracy and reading comprehension to be measured and reported as separate reading ages. This makes it possible to identify pupils who have good reading accuracy but relatively weaker comprehension, and vice versa. Although there is some evidence to suggest decoding scores and comprehension scores, using the test, cannot be separated (Spooner *et al.* 2004), findings did not relate to pupils with good decoding skills.

Fenn identified a mixed gender sample of six pupils and conducted the NARA before implementing any strategies designed to improve reading attainment. She then used a combination of predesigned DARTs activities (Gardner 2002) and collaborative learning strategies. The activities were based on a variety of non-fiction texts. Figures 9.1 a–d, referred to earlier are typical of the materials used by Fenn, although this particular activity was not used in her study. The sample group was taught in the mainstream classroom and all pupils benefited from the intervention strategies. In total 21 lessons involving DARTs and collaborative learning were taught over a seven-week period. At the end of this period, the six pupils were tested a second time using a different NARA test. The results showed that five of the six pupils improved their reading accuracy score by three months or more, and that four pupils had improved by a minimum of nine months. Three pupils had reading accuracy scores of over a year. Even better results were found to have occurred in relation to comprehension levels in four out of the six cases. One pupil had improved by seven months, whilst three had increased their comprehension scores by 18 months or more. While these findings need to be validated by further research on larger samples of pupils, the findings lend themselves to the view that both DARTs and collaborative learning enhances the reading comprehension and reading accuracy of EAL pupils. Given that these intervention strategies involved pupils reading non-fiction texts, which Perera suggests are more complex than narrative forms, the results are even more exciting.

Kinaesthetic approaches

Activities that involve pupils moving around rather reading or writing in the customary sedentary manner, are likely to appeal to individuals who learn best by 'doing things'. I recently heard of how a teacher had integrated instruction writing in her Physical Education lesson. The class was divided into groups each with the brief of devising a sequence of dance movements. Groups were hidden from view by means of a series of strategically placed screens. Once the sequence had been devised, each group set about writing a set of instructions so that another group would be able to replicate the sequence in exactly the same way as its originators. A third group then evaluated the instructions whilst watching the second group perform the sequence. Based on the feedback from the evaluators the first group revised their instructions. The structure of this activity unites the different modes of language and makes the writing of the instructions purposeful because the group must communicate effectively by means of written language. It also purposeful because there is an identifiable audience for the instructions. In order to devise the instructions the originators not only collaborate to create the dance, they also discuss how to construct a set of accurate instructions, paying careful attention to lexical choices and meaning. When they receive the instructions the second group must collaborate to decode and comprehend the instructions.

Through talk they clarify meaning and judge the accuracy of their movements against the instructions. This necessitates constant reference back to the text.

Another route into non-fiction and the development of language across the curriculum is through role play and talk. The discussion of moral issues is usually considered to be the domain of Personal, Social and Health Education (PSHE), but all subjects lend themselves to the consideration of human problems. Human geography and environmental issues, whether they are local or global, can include the raw material for information texts, argument and debate. Larson and Marsh (2005) provide several case studies of teachers using the local environment to provide such material. In one case a teacher took her class to the local park and, over several months, pupils recorded observations of the changes that took place in the park. Some of these observations were entered into a writer's journal; others were by means of digital photographs. The pupils, under their teacher's guidance, produced an information booklet and flyers about the park's fauna, which were made available to visitors (Larson and Marsh 2005: 31). A second case reveals how a teacher used the school barbecue as the impetus for writing in her class. During a discussion after the barbecue, it transpired that one boy, who was a vegetarian, had nothing to eat because vegetarians had not been catered for. The other pupils were concerned about this and began to ask questions about who had made the decision to have only meat-based meals at the barbecue. The pupils took the initiative by reading the flyer advertising the event. The first line had implied the barbecue was for everyone, which the pupils discerned not to be the case as one of them had been excluded. There followed a critical deconstruction of the text by pupils, taking account of word and sentence level analysis, which was followed by a letter to the chair of the organising committee. This initiated several more letters as the pupils delved deeper into the bigger issues surrounding their concerns about the marginalisation of vegetarians (Larson and Marsh 2005: 55).

Like Geography, History also contains rich data for discussion. I once worked with a teacher who wanted to inject something different into a study unit on the Tudors. After reading Peter Fryers, *Staying Power* (1984), I was aware that Queen Elizabeth I had declared that Black people in London should be repatriated. Since one of the requirements of the National Curriculum (DfEE 1999a) was to include study of the multi-ethnic nature of society at different periods, I suggested we investigate with pupils the lives of some of Britain's Black population in Tudor times. We discovered how Black people came to Britain in the 1600s, the jobs they did and the nature of their lives. The unit concluded with a debate around the figure of Sir Francis Drake. The class was divided evenly. One half of the class was given information about Drake that could be found in conventional history textbooks. This view portrayed Drake as a hero of the age. The other half of the class was given information about him as a slave owner and pirate. Earlier in the unit we had studied the appalling conditions of the slave ships and how millions of Black people had been brutally treated and how many had perished during the numerous voyages. After reading the two sets of information the teacher and I organised the classroom into a debating chamber with the two halves of the class seated opposite one another.

Pupils were asked to adopt roles as members of the local council. They had been assembled at an extraordinary meeting to consider a unique proposal. At this point I entered the chamber as a commissioner of the Heritage Fund. The fund managers had decided there were not enough statues of historic figures in British towns and I was touring the country offering money to councils for the erection of statues of key people from the past. This town had been selected to have a statue of Sir Francis Drake. However, before I could release the money, the council had to vote in favour of the proposition that a statue to Sir Francis Drake be erected in their town. The debate began with those in favour voicing their views. These views came invariably from those pupils who had been in receipt of the traditional view of Drake. Then the dissenting voices began from the other side; the side that had read of the alternative view of Drake. This side of the chamber drew on the texts they had been given to construct a passionate and persuasive argument for rejecting the proposition. They used rhetorical devices to win the vote by persuading the majority of the other side of the chamber to their view.

The cases cited by Larson and Marsh show how creative teachers situate literacy in social contexts that are meaningful to pupils. The context not only provided the stimulus for literacy and discussion of issues but it also provided the purpose for writing, combined with authentic audiences. Along the way, pupils undertook research, using information books, noting the details that were relevant to their concerns. In considering their audiences they made choices about their use of language at both word and sentence level and made decisions about how their texts should be structured and presented. The example cited from my own practice demonstrates that historical information can be used to generate discursive language by means of simulating social situations in the classroom. It is also indicative of the way non-fiction texts can be read and used to create opportunities for speaking and listening. Returning to the earlier discussion of Bernstein (1974, 1977, 2000 cited in Larson and Marsh 2005: 6) and Barnes (1976), these literacy practices are only possible in classrooms where the curriculum is not overly prescriptive and where teachers and pupils have strong control over the means by which learning operates. They are classrooms where pupils' learning outside the classroom is valued as bona fide material for further learning and where teachers negotiate talk rather dominate it.

As more and more schools move to thematic modes of curriculum delivery the opportunities to integrate the four modes of English across what were once subject demarcations should abound. However, this model of curriculum necessitates creative thought and the flexibility to respond to pupils' interests.

The Primary National Strategy framework for literacy (DfES 2006) still tethers teachers to particular genres at specific points of each Key Stage. However, it should be noted that the teachers in the cases cited above were able to find ways of manoeuvring within just such a curriculum. Creative approaches apply equally as much to working with non-fiction as they do to working with fiction texts. However, alongside more flexible ways of organising the curriculum, there are equally innovative approaches to the way knowledge is negotiated. The use of DARTs and collaborative activities moves learning away from traditional forms of comprehension in which the teacher dominates the navigation of the text by means of set questions that need to be answered in formulaic ways. Through collaborative work and DARTs, pupils construct meaning by means of discussion in relation to texts. These approaches are inclusive because they enable pupils with limited literacy skills to demonstrate understanding and language skills that are not reliant upon extensive writing.

References

Abbs, P. and Richardson, J. (1990) *The Forms of Poetry: A Practical Study Guide for English.* Cambridge: Cambridge University Press.

Ahlberg, J. and Ahlberg, A. (1978) *Each Peach Pear Plum.* London: Kestrel Books.

Alexander, R. (2008) *Towards Dialogic Teaching: Rethinking Classroom Talk*, 4th edn. York: Dialogos.

Almond, D. (1998) *Skellig.* London: Hodder Children's Books.

Almond, D. (1999) *Kit's Wilderness.* London: Hodder Children's Books.

Almond, D. (2003) *The Fire Eaters.* London: Hodder Children's Books.

Auden, W.H. (1954) *Secondary Worlds, 1.* London: Faber and Faber.

Baird Shuman, R. (ed.) (1978) *Educational Drama for Schools Today.* London: The Scarecrow Press.

Bakhtin, M.M. (1988) Discourse in the Novel, in N. Mercer (ed.) *Language and Literacy, Volume 1.* Milton Keynes: Open University Press.

Barnes, D. (1976) *From Communication to Curriculum.* Harmondsworth: Penguin Books.

Barrs, M. (2001) *The Reader in the Writer.* Oxford: Blackwell Publishers.

Bassi, L.K. (1999) How Storytelling Affects the Stories Children Write, in E.A. Brock (ed.) *The Enchanted Forest: Language, Drama and Science in Primary Schools.* Stoke-on-Trent: Trentham Books.

Bawden, N. (1987) *The Finding.* Harmondsworth: Puffin, Penguin Books.

BBC (2008) *Holby City.* London: BBC.

Bearne, E. and Wolstencroft, H. (2007) *Visual Approaches to Teaching Writing: Multimodal Literacy 5–11.* London: Paul Chapman Publishing.

Bernstein, B. (1974) *Class, Codes and Control. Vol. 1*, 2nd edn. London: Routledge and Kegan Paul.

Bernstein, B. (1977) Class and pedagogies: visible and invisible, in J. Karabel and A.H. Halsey (eds), *Power and Ideology in Education.* New York: Oxford University Press.

Bernstein, B. (2000) *Pedagogy, Symbolic Control and Identity: Theory, Research, Critique.* Revd edn. London: Taylor & Francis.

Blatchford, P., Kutnick, P., Baines, E. and Galton, M. (2003) Towards a social pedagogy of classroom group work. *International Journal of Educational Research* 39(1): 153–72.

Bloom, B., Engelhart, M., Furst, E., Hill, W. and Krathwohl, D. (1956) *Taxonomy of Educational Objectives: The Classification of Educational Goals, Handbook 1: Cognitive Domains.* New York: Longmans Green.

Board of Education (1921) *The Teaching of English in England.* (The Newbolt Report) London: HMSO.

Board of Education (1933) *Infants and Nursery Schools.* (The Third Hadow Report) London: HMSO.

Bolton, G. (1984) *Drama as Education: An Argument for Placing Drama at the Centre of the Curriculum.* Harlow: Longman.

Bourdieu, P. and Passeron, J.C. (1977) *Reproduction in Education, Society and Culture.* London: Sage.

British Film Institute (2001a) *Story Shorts: A Resource for Key Stage 2 Literacy.* London: BFI.

British Film Institute (2001b) *Story Shorts.* London: BFI.

British Film Institute (2003) *Look Again: A teaching guide to using film and television with three to eleven year olds*. London: BFI.

Britton, J. (1970) *Language and Learning*. Harmondsworth: Penguin Books.

Browne, A. (1992) *Gorilla*. London: Walker Books.

Browne, A. (1994) *Zoo*. London: Red Fox, Random House.

Browne, A. (1997) *Changes*. London: Walker Books.

Browne, A. (1999) *Voices in the Park*. London: Walker Books.

Bruner, J. (1986) *Actual Minds, Possible Worlds*. Cambridge, MA: Harvard University Press.

Bruner, J. (1990) *Acts of Meaning*. London: Harvard University Press.

Buckingham, D. (1990) Making it explicit: towards a theory of media learning, in D. Buckingham (ed.) *Watching Media Learning*. London: Falmer Press.

Bunting, R. (2000) *Teaching About Language in the Primary Years*. London: David Fulton Publishers.

Burnard, P., Craft, A., Cremin, T., Duffy, B., Hanson, R., Keene, R., Haynes, L. and Burns, D. (2006) Documenting Possibility: a thinking journey of collaborative inquiry. *International Journal of Early Years Education* 14(3): 243–62.

Butts, D. (ed.) (1992) *Stories and Society: Children's Literature in its Social Context*. Basingstoke: Macmillan.

Buzan, T. (2000) *The Mind Map Book*. London: BBC.

Buzan, T (2005) *The Ultimate Book of Mind Maps*. London: Thorsons.

Carter, D. (1998) *Teaching Poetry in the Primary School: Perspectives for a New Generation*. London: David Fulton Publishers.

Carter, D. (2000) *Teaching Fiction in the Primary School*. London: David Fulton Publishers.

Carter, R. (ed.) (1990) *Knowledge about Language and the Curriculum*. London: Hodder and Stoughton.

Central Advisory Council in Education in England (1967) *Children and their Primary Schools, Report of the Central Advisory Council for Education in England (The Plowden Report)*. London: HMSO.

Clark, L. (2001) Foundations for talk: Speaking and listening in the early years classroom, in P. Goodwin (ed.) *The Articulate Classroom: Talking and Learning in the Primary Classroom*. London: David Fulton Publishers.

Clipson-Boyles, S. (1997) Drama, in K. Ashcroft and D. Palacio (eds) *Implementing the Primary Curriculum: A Teacher's Guide*. London: Falmer Press.

Clipson-Boyles, S. (1999) The role of drama in the literate classroom, in P. Goodwin (ed.) *The Literate Classroom*. London: David Fulton Publishers.

Close, R. (2004) Television and Language Development in the Early Years: A Review of the Literature. http://www.literacytrust.org.uk/research/TV.html (accessed 5/12/08).

Cooper, P. and McIntyre, D. (1992) *Teachers' and Pupils' Perceptions of Effective Classroom Learning: conflicts and commonalities*. Paper presented at the Annual General Conference of the British Educational Research Association, Stirling University, Scotland, August 1992.

Corden, R. (2000) *Literacy and Learning Through Talk: Strategies for the Primary Classroom*. Milton Keynes: Open University Press.

Cox, B. (1989) English for Ages 5–16. (The Cox Report), London: Department for Education and Science.

Craft, A. (2000) *Creativity Across the Primary Curriculum*. Abingdon: Routledge.

Craft, A. (2005) Changes in the landscape for creativity in education, in A. Wilson (ed.) *Creativity in Primary Education*. Exeter: Learning Matters.

Cremin, T. (2007) Revisiting reading for pleasure: diversity, delight and desire, in K. Gouchre and A. Lambirth (eds) *Teaching Reading, Teaching Phonics: Critical Perspectives*. Milton Keynes: Open University Press.

Cremin, T., Bearne, E., Goodwin, P. and Mottram, M. (2008) Primary Teachers as Readers, *English in Education* 42(1): 8–23.

Cremin, T. and Powell, S. (2008) *Reading Teachers and Children: Stories from TARS II*. Paper presented at the British Educational Research Association Conference: Herriot-Watt University, September 2008.

Crossley-Holland, K. (2001) *Arthur: The Seeing Stone*. London: Orion Books.

Crossley-Holland, K. (2002) *Arthur: At the Crossing Places*. London: Orion Books.

Crossley-Holland, K. (2003) *Arthur: King of the Middle March*. London: Orion Books.

Crossley-Holland, K. (2006) *Gatty's Tale*. London: Orion Children's Books.

Cummins, J. (1980) The cross-lingual dimension of language proficiency: implications for bilingual education and the optimal age issue. *TESOL Quarterly*, 14: 175–87.

Cummins, J. and Swain, M. (1986) *Bilingualism in Education*. London: Longman.

Czerniewska, P. (1992) *Learning about Writing*. Oxford: Basil Blackwell.

D'Adamo, F. (2004) *Iqbal*. London: Simon and Schuster.

Dahl, R. (2001) Little Red Riding Hood, in *Revolting Rhymes*. Harmondsworth: Puffin, Penguin Books.

Dean, J. (1995) *Teaching History at Key Stage 2*. Cambridge: Chris Kington Publishing.

Department for Education and Skills (DfES) (2003) *Excellence and Enjoyment: a strategy for Primary Schools*. London: Department for Education and Skills.

Department for Education and Skills (DfES) (2006) *Primary National Strategy: Primary Framework for Literacy and Mathematics*. Norwich: OPSI.

Department for Education and Skills (DfES) (2007) *Practice Guidance for the Early Years Foundation Stage: Setting the Standards for Learning, Development and Care for Children from Birth to Five*. Department for Education and Skills. Nottingham: DfES Publications.

Department of Education and Science (DES) (1967) *Children and Their Primary Schools (The Plowden Report)*. London: HMSO.

Department of Education and Science (DES) (1975) *A Language for Life: Report of the Committee of Inquiry appointed by the Secretary of State for Education and Science under the Chairmanship of Sir Allan Bullock*. London: Her Majesty's Stationery Office.

Department of Education and Science (DES) (1988) *National Curriculum*. London: Department of Education and Science.

Department of Education and Science (DES) (1989) *National Curriculum: From Policy to Practice*. London: Department of Education and Science.

Department of Education and Science (DES) (1995) *National Curriculum*. London: Department of Education and Science.

DeSouza, M. (2003) *An Investigation into Mixed Age Circle Time and the Contribution This Makes to Young Children's Speaking and Listening Skills (unpublished)*. B.Ed Dissertation. Bedford: De Montfort University.

DfEE (1998) *The National Literacy Strategy: Framework for Teaching*. London: Department for Education and Employment.

DfEE/QCA (1999a) *The National Curriculum: Handbook for Primary Teachers in England: Key Stages 1 and 2*. London: Department for Education and Employment/Qualification and Curriculum Authority.

DfEE/QCA (1999b) *The National Curriculum: Handbook for Secondary Teachers in England, Key Stages 3 and 4*. London: QCA.

DfEE (2000a) *Curriculum Guidance for the Foundation Stage*. London: QCA.

DfEE (2000b) *The National Literacy Strategy: Grammar for Writing*. London: Department for Education and Employment.

Domaille, K. and Edwards, J. (2006) Partnerships for learning: extending knowledge and understanding of creative writing processes in the ITT year. *English in Education* 40(2). Sheffield: NATE.

Edwards, D. and Mercer, N. (1987) *Common Knowledge: The Development of Common Understanding in the Classroom*. London: Routledge.

Egan, K. (1988) *Teaching As Storytelling: An Alternative Approach to Teaching and the Curriculum*. London: Routledge.

Eliot, T.S. (1966) Tradition and the Individual Talent, in J. Scully (ed.) *Modern Poets on Modern Poetry*: London: Collins.

Esslin, M. (1987) *The Fields of Drama: How The Signs of Drama Create Meaning on Stage and Screen*. London: Methuen.

Ewart, F.G. (1998) *Let the Shadows Speak: Developing Children's Language Through Puppetry*. Stoke-on-Trent: Trentham Books.

Fenn, K. (2005) Does the use of DARTs improve the higher order reading skills of EAL pupils in KS2? (unpublished) B.Ed dissertation. Bedford: De Montfort University.

Film Education (2008) *Creative Rights: Digital Responsibilities*. London: Film Education.

Fleming, M. (1997) *The Art of Drama Teaching*. London: David Fulton Publishers.

Fogg, D. and Taylor, M. (1992) *Looking at the Language of Poetry*. Huntingdon: Language in the National Curriculum.

Foreman, M. (1991) *War Boy: A Country Childhood*. Harmondsworth: Puffin, Penguin Books.

Fryer, P. (1984) *Staying Power: The History of Black People in Britain*. London: Pluto Press.

Gaine, C. and George, R. (1999) *Gender, 'Race' and Class in Schooling; A New Introduction*. London: Falmer Press.

Gamble, N. and Yates, S. (2008) *Exploring Children's Literature*, 2nd edn. London: Sage.

Gardner, P. (2002) *Strategies and Resources for Teaching and Learning in Inclusive Classrooms*. London: David Fulton Publishers.

Gardner, P. (2007) Living and learning in different communities: cross-cultural comparisons, in P. Zwozdiak-Myers (ed.) *Childhood and Youth Studies*. Exeter: Learning Matters.

Gardner, P. and Jefferies, P. (2008) *Mind Mapping with Reluctant Writers*. Paper presented at the British Educational Research Association, Annual Conference, Heriott-Watt University, Edinburgh, September 2008.

Geekie, P., Cambourne, B. and Fitzsimmons, P. (1999) *Understanding Literacy Development*. Stoke-on-Trent: Trentham Books.

Genette, G. (1988) *Narrative Discourse Revisited* (translated by J.E. Lewin). Ithaca, NY: Cornell University Press.

Goldoni, C. (1970) *A Servant to Two Masters* (English version by E.J. Dent). New York: Samuel French.

Goodwin, P. (2004) *Literacy Through Creativity*. London: David Fulton Publishers.

Goodwyn, A. (2009) Research With a Secondary Focus: The Subject of English, in English: Readings for Discussion. www.ite.org.uk/ite_research/research_secondary_focus/003.html (accessed 11/1/2009).

Grainger, T. (2005) Teachers as writers: learning together, in *English in Education* 39: 1. Sheffield: NATE.

Grugeon, E. (2005) Listening to Learning Outside the Classroom: Student Teachers Study Playground Literacies. *Literacy* 39(1), April 2005.

Grugeon, E. and Gardner, P. (2000) *The Art of Storytelling for Teachers and Pupils*. London: David Fulton Publishers.

Halliday, M.K. (1985) *Spoken and Written Language*. Oxford: Oxford University Press.

Hamburger, M. (1972) *The Truth of Poetry: Tensions in Modern Poetry from Baudelaire to the 1960s*. Harmondsworth: Penguin Books.

Hardy, B. (1977) 'Towards a poetics of fiction: an approach through narrative', in M. Meek, A. Warlow and G. Barton (eds) *The Cool Web*. London: Bodley Head.

Harris, I. and Caviglioli, O. (2003) *Think it – Map it!: How Schools use Mapping to Transform Teaching and Learning*. Stafford: Network Educational Press.

Haworth, A. (1999) Bakhtin in the Classroom: What constitutes a dialogic text? Some lessons from small group interaction. *Language and Education* 13(2): 99–117.

Heath, S.B. (1983) *Ways with Words: Language, Life and Work in Communities and Classrooms*. Cambridge: Cambridge University Press.

Heath, S.B. and Wolf, S. (2005) *A Way of Working: Teachers in Drama Education*. London: Creative Partnerships.

Heathcote, D. (1978) Of these seeds becoming: drama in education, in Baird-Shuman (ed.) *Educational Drama for Today's Schools*. London: The Scarecrow Press.

Hillocks, G. Jr. (1995) *Teaching Writing as Reflective Practice*. New York: Teachers College Press.

Hilton, M. (2001) Writing process and progress: where do we go from here? *English in Education* 35(1), 2001.

Her Majesty's Inspectorate (HMI) (1984) *English from 5–16, HMI Series Curriculum Matters, No. 1*. London: Her Majesty's Stationery Office.

Hoffman, M. (2002) *The Colour of Home*. London: Frances Lincoln.

Holt, N. (undated) *The Wit and Wisdom of Great Writers*. Kings Sutton: House of Raven Books.

Houlton, D. (1985) *All Our Languages: A Handbook for the Multilingual Classroom*. London: Edward Arnold.

Howe, M.J.A. (1999) *A Teacher's Guide to the Psychology of Learning*, 2nd edn. Oxford: Blackwell.

Huckle, J. (1997) Towards a critical school geography, in D. Tilbury and M. Williams (eds) *Teaching and Learning Geography*. London: Routledge.

Hughes, T. (1993) *The Iron Woman*. London: Faber and Faber.

Hutchins, P. (1992) *Rosie's Walk*. London: Random Century.

Hutchinson, J., Whiteley, H., Smith, C. and Connors, L. (2003) The developmental progression of comprehension-related skills in children learning EAL, *Journal of Research in Reading* 26(1), 2003.

Iser, W. (1980) *The Act of Reading: A Theory of Aesthetic Response*. Baltimore: The John Hopkins University Press.

Jennings, C. (1991) *Children as Storytellers: Developing Language Skills in the Classroom*. Oxford: Oxford University Press.

Johnson, C. (2000) 'What did I say?': Speaking, listening and drama, in R. Fisher and M. Williams (eds) *Unlocking Literacy*. London: David Fulton Publishers.

Johnston, R. and Watson, J. (1998) *Accelerated Reading and Spelling with Synthetic Phonics: A Five Year Follow Up*. Edinburgh: Scottish Education Department.

Johnston, R. and Watson, J. (2008) *Teaching Synthetic Phonics*. Exeter: Learning Matters.

Kay, J. (2008) www.poetryarchive.org/poetryarchive/singleinterview.do?interviewsId=6580# (accessed 13/6/2008).

King, C. and Briggs, J. (2005) *Literature Circles: Better Talking, More Ideas*. Royston: United Kingdom Literacy Association.

Kingman, J. (1988) *Report of the Committee of Inquiry into the Teaching of English Language*. London: HMSO.

King-Smith, D. (1997) *The Merman*. London: Viking.

Kress, G. (1994) *Learning to Write*, 2nd edn. London: Routledge.

Kress, G. (2003) *Literacy in the New Media Age*. London: Routledge.

Labov, W. (1988) The logic of non-standard English, in N. Mercer (ed.) *Language and Literacy, Vol 1*. Milton Keynes: Open University Press.

Laird, E. (2003) *The Garbage King*. London: Macmillan Children's Book.

Larkin, P. (1956) *BBC Third Programme*, 13 April 1956.

Larson, J. and Marsh, J. (2005) *Making Literacy Real: theories and practices for learning and teaching*. London: Sage.

Lee, H. (1966) *To Kill a Mockingbird*. London: Heinemann.

Lloyd, D. (1991) Exploring Puppet Potential, *Language and Learning*, 5 May 1991.

Lunzer, E. and Gardner, K. (eds) (1979) *The Effective Uses of Reading*. London: Heinemann.

McArthur, T. (1992) *The Oxford Companion to the English Language*. Oxford: Oxford University Press.

McIntyre, J. (2008) *NATE Reviews – Theory and Practice: Language*. www.nate.org.uk/site/reviews/ReadReview (accessed 6/6/2008).

Many, J.E. (2002) An exhibition and analysis of verbal tapestries: Understanding how scaffolding is woven into the fabric of instructional conversations. *Reading Research Quarterly* 37(4): 376–407.

Marsh, J. and Hallet, E. (2008) Introduction, in J. Marsh and E. Hallet (eds) *Desirable Literacies: Approaches to Language and Literacy in the Early Years*. London: Sage.

Marshall, B. (2002) *English Teachers – The Unofficial Guide*. London: Routledge Falmer.

Marshall, J.D., Smagorinsky, P. and Smith M.W. (1995) *The Language of Interpretation: Patterns of Discourse in Discussions of Literature*. (NCTE Research Report no. 27) Urbana, IL: National Council of Teachers.

Martin, J.R. (1984) Types of writing in infants and primary school. *Proceedings of the Macarthur Institute of higher Education, Reading Language Symposium 5: Reading, Writing and Spelling*.

Martin, T. (2003) Minimum and maximum entitlements: literature at Key Stage 2, *Reading Literacy and Language*, Vol. 37(1).

Martin, T., Lovat, C. and Purnell, G. (2007) *The Really Useful Literacy Book: Being Creative with Literacy in the Primary Classroom*, 2nd edn. Abingdon: Routledge.

Maslow, A.H. (1987) *Motivation and Personality*, 3rd edn. New York: Harper Collins.

Medwell, J., Wray, D., Poulson, L. and Fox, R. (1998) *Effective Teachers of Literacy: A Report of the Research Project Commissioned by the Teacher Training Agency*. Exeter: University of Exeter.

Meek, M. (1998) Important Reading Lessons in B. Cox (ed.) *Literacy is not Enough: Essays on the Importance of Reading*. Manchester: Manchester University Press.

Mercer, N. (2000) *Words and Minds: How We Use Language to Think Together*. London: Routledge.

Moseley, J. (1996) *Quality Circle Time in the Primary Classroom: Your Essential Guide to Enhancing Self-esteem, Self Discipline and Positive Relationships*. Wisbech: LDA.

Moyles, J., Hargreaves, L. and Merry, R. (2001) *The Development of Primary Teachers' Understanding and Use of Interactive Teaching. End of Award Report (R000 238200)* Swindon: Economic and Social Research Council.

Mroz, M., Hardman, F. and Smith, F. (2000) The discourse of the literacy hour. *Cambridge Journal of Education* 30(3): 379–90.

Myhill, D. (2002) Bad boys and good girls? Patterns of interaction and response in whole class teaching. *British Educational Research Journal* 28(3): 339–52.

Myhill, D. and Fisher, R. (2005) *Informing Practice in English: A Review of Recent Research in Literacy and the Teaching of English*. www.ofsted.gov.uk (accessed 24/7/2008).

Neale, M.D. (1997) *Neale Analysis of Reading Ability – Revised*. Windsor: National Foundation for Educational Research.

Naidoo, B. (1985) *Journey to Jo'burg*. London: Collins.

Naidoo, B. (1989) *Chain of Fire*. London: Collins.

Naidoo, B. (1995) *No Turning Back*. Harmondsworth: Puffin, Penguin Books.

Naidoo, B. (2000) *The Other Side of Truth*. Harmondsworth: Puffin, Penguin Books.

Naidoo, B. (2001) *Out of Bounds*. Harmondsworth: Puffin, Penguin Books.

Naidoo, B. (2007) *Burn my Heart*. Harmondsworth: Puffin, Penguin Books.

National Advisory Committee on Creative and Cultural Education Report (1999) *All Our Futures: Creativity, Culture and Education (The Robinson Report)*. London: Department for Education and Employment.

Nicholls, G. (1988) in M. Styles and H. Cook (eds) *There's a Poet Behind You*. London: A and C Black.

Office for Standards in Education (2007) *Poetry in Schools: A Survey of Practice 2006/7*. London: Ofsted.

O'Rourke, P. and O'Rourke, M. (1990) English Teachers and the History of English in R. Carter (ed.) *Knowledge About Language and the Curriculum*. London: Hodder and Stoughton.

Parker, D. (2002) Show us a story: an overview of recent research and resource development work at the British Film Institute', *English in Education*, 36(1): 38–45.

Perera, K. (1984) *Children's Writing and Reading: Analysing Classroom Language*. Oxford: Blackwell in association with Deutsch.

Perera, K. (1990) Grammatical differentiation between speech and writing in children aged 8 to 12 in R. Carter (ed.) *Knowledge About Language and the Curriculum*. London: Hodder and Stoughton.

PIRLS (2001) PIRLS 2001 International Report: IEA's study of reading literacy achievement in primary schools in 35 countries. Chestnut Hill, MA: International Study Center.

poetryarchive (2008) www.poetryarchive.org (accessed 7/7/2008).

Poetry Society (2008) Teaching the Reading of Poetry. www.poetrysociety.org.uk/content/education/reading (accessed 7/7/2008).

Pound, E. (1966) A Retrospective, in J. Scully (ed.) *Modern Poets on Modern Poetry*. London: Collins.

Protherough, R. and Atkinson, J. (1994) Shaping the image of an English teacher, in S. Brindley (ed.) *Teaching English*. London: Routledge.

Pullman, P. (1996) *Clockwork*. London: Random House Books.

Pullman, P. (2000) *I Was a Rat*. London: Corgi Books.

Pullman, P. (2002) *His Dark Materials*. London: Scholastic.

Pullman, P. (2004) *The Firework Maker's Daughter*. London: Corgi Yearling.

Qualifications and Curriculum Authority (QCA) (1998) *Maintaining Breadth and Balance at Key Stages 1 and 2*. London: QCA.

Qualifications and Curriculum Authority (QCA) (2005) *Creativity: Find It! Promote It! – Promoting Pupils' Creative Thinking and Behaviour Across the Curriculum at Key Stages 1,2 and 3 – Practical materials for Schools*. London: QCA.

Richmond, J (1990) What Do We Mean By Knowledge About Language? In R. Carter (ed.) *Knowledge About Language and the Curriculum*. London: Hodder and Stoughton.

Rose, D.L. (1990) *The People Who Hugged Trees*. Scull, West Cork: Roberts Rinehart International.

Rose, J. (2006) *Independent Review of the Teaching of Early Reading*. London: Department for Education and Skills.

Rosen, H. (1993) *Open University, M.A. Summer School*: Nottingham University, July 1993.

Rosen, M. (1989) *Going on a Bear Hunt*. London: Walker Books.

Rosenblatt, L.M. (1994) *The Reader, the Text, the Poem: The Transactional Theory of the Literary Work*. Carbondale, IL: Southern Illinois University Press.

Rosenblatt, L. (1995) *Literature as Exploration*, 5th edn. New York: Modern Language Association of America.

Rosenblatt, L. (2005) *Making Meaning with Texts: Selected Essays*. Portsmouth, NH: Heinemann.

Rosenthal, R. and Jacobson, L. (1968) *Pygmalion in the Classroom*. New York: Holt, Rinehart and Winston.

Rothery, J. (1984) The development of genres – primary to junior secondary school, in *Deakin University Course study Guide: Children Writing*. Victoria: Deakin University.

Saguisag, L. (2007) Performance, politics and poetry for children: Interviews with Michael Rosen and Benjamin Zephaniah in *Children's Literature Association Quarterly*. Spring 2007, 32(1).

Sapiano, C. (2008) Poetry Class: Exeter Model. http://www.poetrysociety.org.uk/lib/tmp/cmsfiles/File/Poetryclass%20Exeter%20Model.pdf (accessed 3/7/2008).

SCAA (1995) *Planning the Curriculum at Key Stages 1 and 2*. London: School Curriculum and Assessment Authority.

Schmidt, M. (ed.) (undated) *The Great Modern Poets: An Anthology of the Best Poets and Poetry Since 1900*. London: Quercus.

Skidmore, D. (2003) From pedagogical dialogue to dialogic pedagogy. *Language and Education* 14(4): 283–96.

Searle, C. (1975) *Classrooms of Resistance*. London: Writers and Readers Publishing Co-operative.

Smith, F. (1982) *Writing and the Writer*. London: Heinemann.

Smith, V. (2005) *Making Reading Mean*. Royston: United Kingdom Literacy Association.

Soyinka, W. (1991) Telephone Conversation in S. Fuller (ed.) *The Poetry of Protest*. London: BBC Longman.

Spooner A.L.R., Baddeley, A.D. and Gathercole, S.E. (2004) Can reading accuracy and comprehension be separated in the Neale Analysis of Reading Ability? *British Journal of Educational Research* 74: 187–204.

Stannard, R. (1989) *The Time and Space of Uncle Albert*. London: Faber and Faber

Stannard, R. (1991) *Black Holes and Uncle Albert*. London: Faber and Faber.

Stead, C.K. (1967) *The New Poetic: Yeats to Eliot*. Harmondsworth: Penguin Books.

Stephens, J. and McCallum, R. (1998) *Retelling Stories, Framing Culture: Traditional Stories and Meta-narratives in Children's Literature*. London: Garland Publishing.

Strube, P. (1990) Narrative in science education, *English in Education*, 24(1), 56–60. Sheffield: The National Association for the Teaching of English.

Sutcliff, R. (1973) *The Capricorn Bracelet*. London: Red Fox.

Thomas, D. (1966) Notes on the art of poetry, in J. Scully (ed.) *Modern Poets on Modern Poetry*. London: Collins.

Thorne, J. (1980) *The Voyage of Prince Fuji*. London: Macmillan Children's Books.

Tizard, B. and Hughes, M. (1984) *Young Children Learning: Talking and Thinking at Home and at School*. London: Fontana.

Tolkien, J.R. (2001) *Lord of the Rings* London: Harper Collins.

Training and Development Agency (2007) *Professional Standards for Teachers*. London: Training and Development Agency.

Trudgill, P. (1975) *Accent, Dialect and the School*. London: Edward Arnold.

Twist, L., Schagen, I. and Hodgsen, C. (2006) *Readers and Reading: The National Report for England 2006 (Progress in International Reading Literacy Study)*. Slough: National Foundation for Education Research.

United Kingdom Literacy Association/Primary National Strategy. *Raising Boys' Achievement in Writing*. Royston: UKLA.

Vygotksy, L.S. (1962) *Thought and Language*. Cambridge, MA: Massachusetts Institute of Technology.

Washtell, A. (2008) Getting to Grips with Phonics, in J. Graham and A. Kelly (eds) *Reading Under Control: Teaching Reading in the Primary School*, 3rd edn. London: Routledge.

Wegerif, R., Mercer, N. and Dawes, L. (1999) From social interaction to individual reasoning: an empirical investigation of a possible sociocultural model of cognitive development. *Learning and Instruction* 9(6): 493–516.

Wells, G. (1987) *The Meaning Makers*. London: Hodder and Stoughton.

Wilson, A. and Hughes, S. (eds) (1998) *The Poetry Book for Primary Schools*. London: Poetry Society.

Wilson, J. (2006) *The Suitcase Kid*. London: Yearling, Random House Books.

Woodruff, E. and Brett, C. (1999) Collaborative knowledge building: pre-service teachers and elementary students talking to learn. *Language and Education* 13(4): 280–302.

Woods, P. and Jeffrey, B. (1997) Creative teaching in the Primary Curriculum, in G. Helsby and G. McCulloch (eds) *Teachers and the National Curriculum*. London: Cassell.

Worton, M. and Still, J. (eds) (1990) *Intertextuality: Theories and Practices*. Manchester: Manchester University Press.

Wyse, D. and Jones, R. (2008) *Teaching English, Language and Literacy*, 2nd edn. London: Routledge.

Yeats, W.B. (1966) A general introduction to my work in J. Scully (ed.) *Modern Poets on Modern Poetry*. London: Collins.

Index

DATE DUE

GAYLORD			PRINTED IN U.S.A.